Lawyers as Leaders

WHY IT MATTERS AND WHAT IT TAKES

DONALD J. POLDEN AND
BARRY Z. POSNER

AMERICAN BAR ASSOCIATION
Law Practice Division

Cover design by Sara Wadford/ABA Design

Printed in the United States of America.

28 27 26 25 24 5 4 3 2 1

Library of Congress Cataloging-in-Publication Data

Names: Polden, Donald J., author. | Posner, Barry Z., author.
Title: Lawyers as leaders : why it matters and what it takes / Donald J. Polden and Barry Z. Posner.
Description: 1st edition. | Chicago : American Bar Association, 2024. | Includes index. | Summary: "This book has two parts. The first part begins by addressing why leadership development and training are essential in preparing lawyers for the roles and responsibilities they will have in their careers. The following six chapters describe The Five Practices of Exemplary Leadership®, providing qualitative and quantitative evidence of how these leadership practices improve personal and organizational productivity and stature. This operational system for leadership forms an accessible and practical basis for learning to lead and becoming the best leader you can be. The five chapters in the second part address the context in which lawyers exercise leadership. For example, thinking about leading in client relationships, in internal relationships (such as within the law firm or corporate legal office), and public roles. Examined are vital issues regarding client development ethics, effective decision-making, building emotional intelligence, diversity, equity and inclusion, and handling conflicts and adversity. In the Afterword, we focus on developing and adopting a leadership development mindset necessary for leading in challenging times. We also offer perspectives on how to be a lawyer leader who positively impacts the legal profession and the world"– Provided by publisher.
Identifiers: LCCN 2024015758 | ISBN 9781639055074 (paperback) | ISBN 9781639055081 (epub)
Subjects: LCSH: Lawyers–United States. | Lawyers–United States–Psychology. | Leadership–Study and teaching–United States. | Practice of law–Study and teaching–United States.
Classification: LCC KF298 .P65 2024 | DDC 658.4/09208834–dc23/eng/20240409
LC record available at https://lccn.loc.gov/2024015758

Discounts are available for books ordered in bulk. Special consideration is given to state bars, CLE programs, and other bar-related organizations. Inquire at Book Publishing, ABA Publishing, American Bar Association, 321 N. Clark Street, Chicago, Illinois 60654-7598.

www.shopABA.org

Contents

Dedication

We dedicate this book with appreciation to the many lawyers over the years who have shared their experiences and, through their challenges, sharpened our thinking about what is required to exercise leadership within the context of the legal profession. We also gratefully acknowledge the support and encouragement of our colleagues—in law firms' professional development experts, skilled professional coaches, and corporate legal departments—in believing that leadership matters in the many capacities in which lawyers work and make a difference. We have benefitted greatly from our educational collaborations with business and law students. We have learned from their zeal to develop leadership skills and become more effective lawyer-leaders.

As with our previous books, we continue to recognize the love and support of our spouses, Susie and Jackie. They have been our friends, partners, advisors, and loving critics for decades, with more to look forward to.

Introduction

"The value-added competency for lawyers and legal organizations is leadership."

—Barry Z. Posner

"Developing leadership in lawyers should be an important part of every law firm's professional development efforts, because leadership skills are what young lawyers need to distinguish themselves in today's complex legal profession."

—Donald J. Polden

There is no doubt that developing leadership in those involved in the legal profession is critically important. This book targets lawyers in settings of all sizes, especially associates in law firms, junior lawyers in government law offices, and those in corporate counsel offices. However, managing partners, general counsels, law firm professional development experts, and other lawyers in firm management positions will benefit from a lawyer-focused treatment of leadership. We also believe that a comprehensive treatment of leadership in the legal world will inspire lawyers who are asked to lead or aspire to lead to become more capable and skilled at doing so.

Of course, lawyers as leaders are essential to social, economic, and political systems; after all, leadership matters in nearly all areas of life. There is no shortage of opportunities for leadership to be exercised. However, this book's specific focus is on learning to be a leader within the legal profession and the roles and responsibilities of lawyers as leaders in the ways that they serve others in their profession.

In addition to preparing lawyers to be leaders—regardless of their titles, roles, positions, or settings—through the exercise of those behaviors associated with leading (leadership), this book also addresses the need for law firms and professional services organizations, irrespective of their purpose or size, to develop their ability to lead themselves and others (both internally and externally) effectively and ethically. A central lesson of this book is our belief that leadership development makes better organizations, especially those that serve clients and communities—essentially, civic engagement. As we point out in later sections of the book, the research on law (and other) organizations' performance confirms this premise.

Traditionally, law schools have been expected to develop and train their students for the demands of a profession that is ethically based, complex, and often volatile, and one in which mastery of a broad array of skills, behaviors, and attitudes is necessary to be successful. Increasingly, law schools are turning to leadership development courses and programs to strengthen the formation of attitudes and abilities that are needed for success in today's legal profession. Similarly, many law organizations, including law firms we have advised, are progressively realizing the importance of leadership skills to the success of their organizations and to the legal profession. Lawyers and their law firms and organizations, even sole practitioners, can advance their leadership capabilities and become stronger, better counselors and advocates for their clients.

Our book fills an important niche, for while there are tens of thousands of books on leadership and about leaders, only a handful focus on the legal profession and lawyers.[1] There is a dearth of books that provide a method and approach for developing leadership skills, attitudes, and behaviors in lawyers, judges, and other legal professionals. Providing a method and approach to developing leadership skills, attitudes, and behaviors is the "secret sauce" this book brings to leadership education and development.

CONTENTS AND ORGANIZATION

Our answer to the public need for lawyer-leaders (and law-educated experts who are called on to lead) is through sound instruction in leadership. In this book, we provide a framework for educating lawyers to lead in today's rapidly changing environment. Producing lawyers prepared to be effective leaders in the legal profession will yield more competent representation in law firms, public defender and legal aid offices, and other legal service delivery environments if those organizations are effectively run by people who are well versed and skilled in leadership. Effective leadership in these organizations produces better outcomes, including, but not limited to, significantly improved case management, greater justice, and hardier and healthier lawyers.

We identify and describe the critical aspects of effective leadership by lawyers—not only for lawyers connected with a firm or legal office but also for lawyers as public servants, in nonprofit organizations, and in many other "callings" where lawyers function. The book addresses leadership challenges and opportunities in several types of law organizations, including small, medium, and large law firms as well as other organizations in which lawyers are expected to provide leadership. We build on a foundation of research and information gathered from surveys, interviews, and empirical information to provide an opportunity both to reflect on the challenges that lawyers face in the practice of law and to practice approaches for advancing the ability to assume leadership roles in dealings with clients and within lawyer-leaders' organizations.

Since the publication of our first leadership book for law school students, *Leading in Law*, we have received many helpful suggestions from lawyers and professional development experts about enhancing the treatment of leadership development for lawyers—hence, the preparation of this book for lawyers about how to do just that. We are encouraged by the importance being placed on emphasizing and developing leadership skills to make better lawyers and enhance the legal profession.

The Five Practices of Exemplary Leadership® and Lawyer Leadership Education

Barry Posner, coauthor of this book, and his coauthor, Jim Kouzes, created The Five Practices of Exemplary Leadership model, described in detail in Part I. This framework emanated from qualitative and quantitative research conducted over more than four decades and which still continues. Their book, *The Leadership Challenge*, details the methodology and provides rich examples of and evidence supporting The Five Practices. The book (now in its seventh edition) has received numerous awards (it has been named one of the ten best books on leadership of all time, it has been translated into twenty-two different languages, and to date it has sold over three million copies).

Donald Polden, the other coauthor of this book, and Barry (then dean of the Leavey School of Business) first met in 2003 when Don arrived at Santa Clara University to serve as dean of the School of Law. After discussing the prevalence of leadership education in business schools and why law schools were not teaching leadership, Barry gave Don a copy of *The Leadership Challenge*. Don immediately saw the importance and relevance of teaching leadership to lawyers.

In the mid-2000s, Santa Clara University's School of Law offered what Don believes is the first leadership course taught in a Juris Doctor (JD) program at an American law school. Shortly thereafter, he began regularly teaching the leadership course himself. Because of his duties as dean, he didn't have much time to spend in the classroom, but he taught the course because of the importance he placed on the subject matter. He led Santa Clara Law in becoming a leader among American law schools in creating a leadership development program, including some inspiring lawyer-leaders and curious law students in the process. One of the most significant challenges was finding materials on leadership in the field of law, so he began developing his own materials using the central lessons of *The Leadership Challenge* and materials from business, politics, government, and medicine.

Parts and Chapters

This book has two parts. Part I begins by addressing why leadership development and training are essential in preparing lawyers for the roles and responsibilities they will have in their careers. Then Chapters 2 through 7 describe The Five Practices of Exemplary Leadership®, providing qualitative and quantitative evidence of how these leadership practices improve personal and organizational productivity and stature. This operational system for leadership forms an accessible and practical basis for learning to lead and becoming the best leader you can be.

The five chapters in Part II address the context in which lawyers exercise leadership—for example, thinking about leading in client relationships, in internal relationships (such as within the law firm or corporate legal department), and public roles. Examined are vital issues regarding client development ethics, effective decision making, building emotional intelligence, diversity, equity and inclusion, and handling conflicts and adversity.

In the Afterword, we focus on developing and adopting a leadership development mindset necessary for leading in challenging times. We also offer perspectives on how to be a lawyer-leader who positively impacts the legal profession and the world.

OUR MANTRA: LAWYERS GO FORTH, INSPIRED TO LEAD, TO BE A LAWYER-LEADER

Those outside the legal profession often jokingly ask, "Lawyers say they 'practice law'; why don't they 'do' law?" The fact is that lawyers practice to become better lawyers and to do the work of lawyers. Similarly, lawyer-leaders practice to become better lawyers and leaders and to do the work of lawyers *and* leaders—and this book endeavors to assist them in this undertaking.

Donald J. Polden, San Jose, California
Barry Z. Posner, Berkely, California

Part I

THE PRACTICES OF LAWYER LEADERSHIP

CHAPTER 1

Foundations of Educating Lawyers for Leadership: Why Leadership Development Is Essential for Lawyers

"Developing the leadership abilities and potential of law students, lawyers, and people leading legal institutions is essential to their careers and the legal profession."

With more than 1.3 million lawyers in the United States[1] (or approximately 1 lawyer for every 255 people, and just behind Israel as the country with the most lawyers per capita in the world),[2] many people would contend that the legal profession hasn't done much to educate lawyers about being leaders and providing leadership. Leadership development for most is left for them to learn "on the job" and generally doesn't happen until quite late in their careers. Law schools have made a fairly lackadaisical effort toward leadership education, and all too many students have the viewpoint (reinforced by their instructors) that "if it isn't on the bar exam, why bother with it?" Similarly, most law firms haven't invested in developing leadership skills in their lawyers. However, most lawyers know that their firms and clients face challenges that would be more successfully addressed by better leadership. This shortsighted perspective has damaged the reputation of what was once the most respected of all professions, and it shortchanges the success of individual lawyers, their clients and firms, and society in general because of the critical value-added role that leadership provides. Taking for granted your competence in understanding the statutes, policies, precedents, and rules of law, leadership is the variable that differentiates high performance from average and mediocre productivity and profitability. Furthermore, lawyer leadership is relevant to all law organizations, whether small practice groups or national law firms, the Navy JAG Corps, or corporate counsel offices. Effective and inspired leadership is a common trait of successful lawyers and law organizations.

LEADERSHIP: A LEARNED SKILL

Some people believe that leaders are born, not made. This couldn't be farther from the truth. Leadership is not a position in an organization or a status that one inherits, and it is not necessarily a case of "either you have it or you don't." Instead, it is the product of a process by which a person employing specific skills, behaviors, and attitudes influences others to achieve positive and ethical change. Exemplary leadership can be learned, developed, and honed.

Developing the leadership abilities and leadership potential of lawyers and people leading legal institutions is essential. In a country of laws and a society devoted to the rule of law, the roles that lawyers play are critical to the success of the nation's political and economic regimes. Performing those roles well demands exceptional leadership, and those leadership abilities must be taught to and developed in lawyers, beginning with their law school experience and continuing throughout their professional careers.[3]

LAWYERS IN LEADERSHIP POSITIONS

The need to develop the leadership competence of lawyers is due, in no small part, to the critical roles they play in communities, government institutions, and significant commercial, business, and interpersonal transactions.[4]

Lawyers act and serve in many leadership roles and capacities. They lead in their firms and government law offices, in political and public-sector roles, in their community work for nonprofit organizations, and in private practice. They guide and counsel their clients to resolve disputes, seek justice, and craft collaborative and durable transactions.

We asked lawyers about the importance of their ability to lead others. We learned that most of them perceive leadership abilities as essential to their work as lawyers and as anchors in their communities. One new partner told us that "leadership skills have real meaning to lawyers in relationships with their clients." Others viewed it as essential to their work within the law firm: "My leadership means bringing people up and blossoming into great attorneys." Another explicitly linked strong leadership skills to business development because, as she put it, her leadership abilities "were observable and valued by clients and people in the community." Surveys and research on the perceived importance of leadership skills confirm these conclusions. In one survey of more than a thousand practicing lawyers and law faculty, 33 percent of the respondents stated they wished they had learned leadership skills before beginning law practice.[5]

While lawyers make up an extremely small percentage of the population—less than four-tenths of 1 percent of the U.S. population[6]—they are overrepresented in leadership positions, including elected officials, judicial officers, members of numerous civic and community task forces and teams, in senior positions in private and public organizations, on boards of directors of corporations and nonprofits, and in small businesses and private practices. Consider that twenty-seven of the forty-six presidents of the United States were lawyers, and in the most recent Congress (118th Congress), one hundred thirty-two members of the House (30.5 percent) and fifty-one senators (51 percent) hold law degrees.[7] Furthermore, 34 percent of state governors have law degrees,[8] and 14 percent of all state legislators indicate "attorney" as their occupation.[9]

The fact that lawyers serve in many important leadership positions is actually not a recent revelation. As early as the nineteenth century, British commentator Alexis de Tocqueville observed that, in America, "lawyers consequently form the highest political class"[10] and are essentially the keepers of the rule of law.[11] Perhaps this explains why only about 6 percent of Americans have ever thought about running for political office, yet 58 percent of lawyers have considered the idea.[12]

INSUFFICIENCY OF LAW SCHOOL EDUCATION: THE NEED FOR PROFESSIONAL DEVELOPMENT

Learning how an automobile engine works doesn't necessarily result in being able to drive a car, to drive one safely, or to race competitively with maximum efficiency and speed. Similarly, while knowledge about the law and thinking like a lawyer are necessary, they are actually insufficient for the effective practice of the law (and they won't be the chief factors in building your reputation as a lawyer). The information and knowledge provided in law school do not fully prepare lawyers to perform professionally and ethically in the complex world they will encounter. What lawyers are being asked to do and the skills they need to be effective in doing those things go far beyond information—and, often, even the law as currently constituted. The skills required are simply not addressed in law school curricula, and we have found that they are too often missing in law firm professional development programs and even much of the continuing legal education world. What skills *are* necessary for the twenty-first-century lawyer, functioning in highly volatile and unpredictable environments as a lawyer and public servant? They can be captured in a single word: *leadership.*

Lack of Leadership Development in the Legal Profession

Leadership development has been a core tenet in many professions and is viewed as essential for those in business, education, medicine and health care, the military, and even the clergy. Leadership education courses, programs, and academic scholarship are abundantly evident in business education curricula and in schools for public policy, management, and political science, and in military training. What has been missing for too long, though, is a similar commitment by the law profession, although we are seeing greater interest in developing strong leadership capacity in many law organizations. Fewer than one in four American Bar Association–approved schools offer leadership education, training, and development courses and programs,[13] although the number of such programs is growing through the work of the Section on Leadership of the Association of American Law Schools. Similarly, although most employers believe that leadership development opportunities should be a part of every student's educational experience,[14] legal firms rarely offer such opportunities. Fortunately, much of this myopic view of what law students and young lawyers need to do to be successful is changing, and there is increasing emphasis on developing leadership abilities and opportunities. Indeed, in this book, we describe what leadership development has done to strengthen legal firms—including some we have advised—and their lawyers. We also hope this book will provide a blueprint for law organizations that want to strengthen their lawyer leadership capacity and skills.

The fact that lawyers are an outsized presence in leadership positions makes it all the more remarkable that legal education has long neglected formal training in leadership. Considering the long-standing prominence of people with legal education and training in national, state, and local government leadership roles, it is both surprising and disappointing that the introduction of leadership into law school curricula has been only a recent phenomenon and, at that, is not particularly widespread.

However, the same might be said about the legal profession in general, with the idea of leadership development for lawyers failing to gain traction. Far too many general counsels and managing partners view leadership as a "soft" skill, with the misguided view that either it can be learned on the job (via "osmosis") or "you either have it or you don't." We make the case that leadership is essential for sustaining both individual and organizational excellence, and the behaviors associated with leadership are accessible to everyone and highly relevant to the effective practice of law.

Ethics and the Need for Leadership Development

Lawyers are asked to answer or advise others on many critical questions, and many of the answers can't be found in textbooks or legal precedents alone but are questions that require judgment when forming a response. They are less about "Can we get away with doing this?" and more about "What should we do?" They are less about "What is correct?" and more about "What is right?"

Understanding more about leadership, and about yourself in the process, will address and rectify the perception of the vast majority of the public that most attorneys are more interested in "winning than in seeing that justice is served" or in "making money than in serving their clients."[15] An online poll found that lawyers are perceived as having high levels of competence but low levels of warmth (friendliness and trustworthiness), which is problematic because this combination erodes the public's perception of lawyers' credibility.[16] Studies have found that even law students, whether in the United States or elsewhere (England, Scotland, Germany, Australia, and Argentina), *on their first day of class*, rate lawyers as not altogether honorable (i.e., trustworthy and ethical), ratings that are even lower than those from the general public.[17]

Recent National Discussion

The current national discussion in the legal profession focuses on two essential questions:

- "What do lawyers do in their law or legal organizations and in their communities?"
- "What are the skills and competencies they need to do that work?"[18]

The impact of the 2008 financial recession and, later, the COVID-19 pandemic created great urgency for meaningful responses to these questions. Then, law firms were challenged to address the issues of remote or return-to-office work schedules, which present significant leadership challenges. Throughout this time, law organizations faced critical decisions concerning their efforts to enhance diversity and inclusion in their workforces. They were not just "another day at the office" trials and issues; they were fundamental to the existence and success of the firm and the ethical treatment of their workforces. Are law schools, legal employers, and professional education programs (such as the ABA or state or local bar associations) training and educating legal professionals, especially newer entrants, with the skills and attitudes they need to be effective?

This ongoing discussion is important because it attempts to contemporaneously pinpoint the roles that lawyers play in society and then draw definitive conclusions about what skills, behaviors, and attitudes lawyers need to effectively perform those roles. We hear from experts in law and legal education that lawyers need a complex set of skills and abilities and that they should be able to perform them in a fast-changing society and economy.[19] What they are *not* saying is that lawyers need to know more about tort law or how to draft better motions for summary judgments. Rather, they are indicating that lawyers need to be more flexible and adaptive in terms of demonstrating new abilities and behaviors in the many roles they will perform as lawyers.

The essential qualities, abilities, and behaviors required for today's lawyers can be summed up as the same qualities, abilities, and behaviors that today's leaders require. Becoming an exceptionally skilled and respected lawyer rests on learning about and practicing essential leadership behaviors. It is necessary to enhance leadership capabilities as applied to building and leading teams, creatively thinking and problem solving, influencing others through highly effective communication abilities, demonstrating entrepreneurial abilities, and exercising first-rate decision making and professional judgment.[20] The discussion among thoughtful commentators and experts has concluded that without enhancing leadership capabilities, the legal profession will become increasingly narrow in its focus and irrelevant in the broader societal sense.[21]

Linking with Individual Leadership Development

Law schools and law firms have yet to fully offer the kinds of personal and professional development that emerging lawyer-social and lawyer-community activists need to develop critical leadership skills, behaviors, and attitudes and entirely change the legal and economic landscapes. In short, leadership has not been an essential part of the legal curriculum, and law schools have been deficient in providing a systematic approach to lawyers' leadership development.[22] Equally concerning is that only recently have law firms, usually larger national ones but also, increasingly, medium- and small-sized firms, been adding leadership skills and attributes to the reach of their professional development programs. Yet, surveys of lawyers suggest that leadership training was something they wish they had had in law school, and an overwhelming reason that lawyers, especially younger lawyers, are calling for more development opportunities to advance their personal and professional skills, such as leadership. They have seen what the future of law practice looks like and what lawyers will need if they are to make a difference. That future requires their mastery of those skills and abilities; leadership education is a pathway to that mastery.

Thinking more about developing your leadership abilities, and preparing yourself to do the same, is actually the chance to remind yourself why you came to study and practice law and what you aspired to accomplish as a lawyer. Reading this book gives you the opportunity to focus on who you are, what you care about, and why the law and a legal career can help you find meaning and purpose in your life.

CHAPTER HIGHLIGHTS

- Leadership is not something that you either have or you don't. It is a learned skill—and you, too, can learn it. And since you can learn it, you can build your proficiency, getting better at it.
- Lawyers comprise an outsized role in leading the country, so educating them in leadership skills, behaviors, and attitudes is essential.
- Traditional law school curricula, which focus on "thinking like a lawyer," are necessary but not sufficient for educating people to be the most effective in the practice of law.
- Leadership development programs are necessary to fill the gap in educating lawyers to be leaders, to be able to exhibit the full set of skills necessary in today's complex legal environment, and to recommit themselves to the ideals of the law.

Chapter 2

Leadership: What It Means and Why It's Important to Lawyers

"Leadership is a relationship between those who aspire to lead and those who choose to follow."

Do those in positions of authority always exhibit leadership, and are those who exhibit leadership always leaders? The word *leader* typically conjures up an image of someone with a title or an upper-level position in a firm or company, such as managing partner, CEO, chief legal counsel, director, or senior associate. More often than not, the title carries some authority (position of power) and generally assumes that lower-level people report to that individual. The dictionary definition of *leader* conveys this same notion: "a person who manages or controls other people. . . ."[1]

Yet, it is readily apparent that while an organization can give someone a title, that doesn't necessarily make that person a leader in the sense of exercising leadership. When you look up the word *leadership* in a dictionary, you won't find it capitalized or referring to a position or place in an organization.

So, if *leadership* is not synonymous with *leader* in the sense of a person with a title, what is it exactly? Leadership is a set of qualities, abilities, and behaviors—and these are available to and accessible by anyone regardless of title, role, or authority. In fact, in the most high-performing organizations, every individual feels like they are a leader and can make a difference no matter where they are in the organization. In law firms, the firm's "leaders" are not only managing partners or practice group chairs, but the designation is for anyone—associates, junior partners, and the like—who is in a position to help others in the firm (including staff and interns) to be more successful in the firm's work. In other words, there is no shortage of opportunities for everyone to provide leadership.

DEFINITIONS OF *LEADERSHIP*

Pinning down a specific definition of *leadership* is an excellent place to start understanding the concept of leadership. Academic literature on the matter has more than forty distinctive theories of leadership and over two hundred definitions of *leadership*; generally, they are more similar than different in their emphases.[2]

One of the more robust and nuanced definitions is this: "Leadership is the art of mobilizing others to want to struggle for shared aspirations."[3] Another definition that is particularly apt in the context of lawyer leadership is that it is "a process by which an individual or a group influences others to achieve positive and ethical change."[4] Consider these important *distinctive* characteristics in understanding leadership:

- Leadership is an *art*. Contrast art with science, and you get an appreciation for the artistry of being a leader. It is the difference between understanding the science of colors and their combinations and being able to use color to paint across multiple mediums. Artists, like leaders, have their own unique style, meaning that leaders can employ the science of leadership according to their own personality, preferences, and circumstances (i.e., they each paint the canvas differently and uniquely while using the same brushes and palettes).
- Leadership involves *mobilizing others*. Leadership involves action—getting people up and moving from the status quo to where they have never been before. Moreover, let's acknowledge that leadership involves motivating others to take action because leadership is not a solo enterprise.
- Leadership means getting *others to want to*. This phrase signals that people will act because of their intrinsic or internal motivation rather than based on a command-and-control hierarchy. Leadership involves influencing others to action through reason and persuasion.
- Leadership necessarily involves *change*. Change may be necessitated because of a crisis, threats to the organization, or the group having lost focus and ambition. Change may be required as well to take advantage of new circumstances and opportunities. In all instances, responding to the need for change requires leadership. For lawyers, change is directed at achieving positive and ethical outcomes.
- Leadership necessitates *struggle*. If you ask people to do something they have never done before, you have to admit that, realistically, it will require more effort than is currently being expended. Often, people will have to make some sacrifice by giving up something on

which they are currently spending time and effort in order to take on this new challenge.

- Leadership encompasses *shared aspirations.* For leaders, the goals are always beyond the horizon, in the future, and something they hope to achieve (without any guarantees). Moreover, this dream must be not only in the mind of the leader, but also in the minds of those who would want to struggle to achieve that desired state—in other words, all must embrace the vision.
- Leadership is *a process.* It is neither a static nor a one-and-done effort. A series of behaviors and actions is necessary to achieve a desired end, and the path forward seldom resembles a straight line. Moreover, this process can be learned, demonstrated, taught, and improved through deliberate practice, like any other skill. This reinforces the notion that anyone can exercise leadership regardless, as we reiterated, of their title, position, rank, or authority.

Still another essential understanding of leadership is found in the answer to the question "How would you know if someone is a leader?" While there are undoubtedly many ideas and actions that would apply, the most straightforward and most all-encompassing response to this question would be "because they have *followers.*" The point is that it is hard to imagine that someone can be a leader without followers. If you accept this premise, then what most defines leaders, or what makes someone a leader, is that they have followers. The relationship between leaders and their followers is often complex and intricate, but nonetheless both parties need each other, and when the relationship works well, everyone benefits.[5]

It is also helpful to compare and distinguish managers from leaders because it is a common error made by many to treat them as synonymous, and they are not.[6] Leaders inspire action by others through a vision for change or innovation. Managers take the status quo and attempt to maintain it for the organization's good. Consider Dr. Martin Luther King Jr., who inspired his followers toward outstanding achievements in civil rights. But he had staff who managed, controlled, and administered the day-to-day operations of his organization. Surely, the two "titles" or concepts are not mutually exclusive, and the very best managers are generally effective leaders, and often the best leaders are not particularly adept at management.

Leaders and Followers: Relationships Matter

What naturally follows from the "requirement" that leaders have followers is that there is a relationship between the two. Specifically, leadership is a relationship between those who aspire to lead and those who choose to follow.[7] This is true regardless of whether the relationship is one-to-one or one-to-many. And this is true across various disciplines, occupations, and settings—including law, lawyers, and law practice. When clients seek out a lawyer, they are looking not only for a person with legal abilities to help them deal with their legal, business, and personal difficulties but also a relationship with someone who cares about them.[8] If you are going to be a leader whose guidance others want to follow willingly, there needs to be a human connection—something that binds you and others together. Law firm leaders (partners managing project or litigation teams, or those heading up practice groups) repeatedly told us about the importance of leadership in growing good associates into excellent practicing lawyers.

Many movies have recognized the importance of this kind of relationship. In *Jerry Maguire*, for example, a sports agent, disillusioned by dishonesty in his industry, starts his own company, focusing on personal relationships—and it is personal relationships that lead to his success as a leader. Lawyer movies, too, portray relationships as a critical element of good leadership (lawyering). For example, in *The Client*, lawyer Reggie Love takes a personal interest in her eleven-year-old client.

Regardless of the setting, the quality of the relationship will determine over the long term whether others will follow your lead. A relationship between people characterized by fear and distrust will seldom produce anything of lasting value. A relationship characterized by mutual respect and confidence will overcome the greatest adversities and leave a legacy of significance.

BASIC INSIGHTS INTO LAWYER LEADERSHIP

There are three distinct categories of critically important skills, behaviors, and attitudes of successful lawyers that emerged from the recent survey of "Law Firm Competency Expectations for Associate Development":[9]

- *Traditional Legal and Communication Skills*: Legal analysis, written advocacy, clear communications, legal knowledge/expertise, judgment/common sense, and oral advocacy
- *Character Traits and Relationship Skills*: Responsibility/reliability, teamwork/collaboration, initiative, and attention to detail
- *Client-Focused Orientation*: Responsiveness to the client and understanding client's business/circumstances

While the first competency reflects the bread and butter of traditional legal education and of what young lawyers are all expected to be able to perform, the survey authors noted that the "competencies related to Character Traits/Relationship Skills and Client-Focused Orientation—not traditionally focused on in legal education—were emphasized by firms in the study and that might be surprising to some."[10] It's not surprising at all to us, and their conclusions underscore the need for leadership development as a necessary component of legal acumen. In fact, 88 percent of the survey firms singled out "leadership" specifically as one of the desired competencies. But, as we discuss in later chapters, merely "desiring" the skills and attitudes doesn't mean new lawyers will have developed and can demonstrate them. Most often, more is needed to possess these skills and abilities fully.

Effective leadership in law firms is often a function of the challenges presented to the firm and the capacity for leadership by members of the firm, irrespective of the size of the firm. Smaller firms face different problems than larger firms, such as cash flow, undue revenue stress on a few clients, or major cases or transactions. From a leadership perspective, firms of all shapes and sizes confront (or are confronted by) the periodic need for change, sometimes seismic changes, such as when a small- or medium-sized firm loses a key rainmaker or a client moves a major case to another firm. Correspondently, large firms often face similar internal challenges and must be nimble and decisive to effect change.

The Ethics of Lawyer Leadership

Definitions clearly show that leadership is a positive attribute. But can it be problematic from an ethical perspective? The ABA's *Model Rules of Professional Conduct* provides lawyers with guidance on the lawyer–client relationship, which implicates leadership issues. Thus, before embarking on a path to leadership, it is worthwhile to consider whether there is any ethical reason not to do so. We assert that the answer is no, but it is important to explore potential ethical issues as with every other aspect of being a lawyer.

Do lawyers lead their clients? Are clients' "followers" of their lawyers, whether the client is a corporation or a person facing criminal charges? These are frequent questions in leadership classes and academic discussions about lawyer leadership, and they deserve serious consideration. While law students as well as lawyers on occasion dream of a world without hypothetical questions, they both learn quickly that hypothetical questions train them to deal with real-life ambiguity and paradoxes, and this is one of the most persistently paradoxical areas in law practice.

The *Model Rules of Professional Conduct* articulate the relationship between attorney and client. Rule 1.2 provides in part the following:

> (a) Subject to paragraphs (c) and (d), a lawyer shall abide by a client's decisions concerning the objectives of representation and, as required by Rule 1.4, shall consult with the client as to the means by which they are to be pursued. A lawyer may take such action on behalf of the client as is impliedly authorized to carry out the representation. A lawyer shall abide by a client's decision whether to settle a matter. In a criminal case, the lawyer shall abide by the client's decision, after consultation with the lawyer, as to a plea to be entered, whether to waive jury trial and whether the client will testify.[11]

Note that the rules state that lawyers must abide by the decisions made by the client, especially in terms of settling or entering a plea and other forms of final outcome of the proceeding or legal matter. Moreover, the lawyer shall "reasonably consult with the client about the means by which the client's objectives are to be accomplished."[12]

However, this does not mean that the client is the leader and the lawyer is the follower. A thorough look at the *Model Rules of Professional Conduct* shows that although lawyers must allow their clients to have autonomy, lawyers would be derelict in their duties if they didn't make every effort to guide clients toward the best decisions by giving them clear direction on how the clients should exercise their authority to make the final decisions. For example, according to Rule 1.1, lawyers must be competent in the advice they provide to permit the client to make an informed decision—leaving the final decision to the client.[13] Rule 2.1 states that lawyers must provide independent, professional, and candid advice. In giving this advice, lawyers "may refer not only to law but to other [relevant] considerations such as moral, economic, social and political factors."[14]

Clients hire lawyers because they do not possess or cannot learn the information needed to make decisions in their best interests. We live in a highly complex world with many sources of sometimes conflicting responsibilities and rules that require careful study and understanding so they can be acted on. Legal systems have complex rules of procedural and jurisdictional requirements and complicated access points to have a case heard and resolved. The modern growth of myriad regulatory agencies adds a layer of forums for adjudicating rights and duties. Many people believe that we live in a highly litigious society where having access to legal counsel is almost as important as access to competent medical care and advice.

In short, clients need attorneys to work through these complicated situations and, as a result, rely heavily on the advice and assistance provided by their lawyers.

Lawyers serve in multiple ways other than by direct representation in legal proceedings: they serve as mediators, advocates in litigation or other proceedings, policy advisors, governmental officials, and, of course, legal advisors for clients. Accordingly, there are many avenues through which lawyers inspire their followers toward a shared goal or vision—often toward resolution of a difficult challenge or need for change. In nearly all these situations, lawyer-leaders move others toward shared goals through persuasion or influence; they guide others toward these goals; and that guidance is willingly accepted and followed. Lawyers lead their clients through shared objectives (e.g., a favorable outcome in a trial, a successful negotiation of a real estate transaction, or approval by the Securities and Exchange Commission of a major transaction) by candid discussions, their zealous commitment to the client's best interests, and exercise of their best professional judgment and advice.

Thus, the concept of the lawyer as the "leader" in the relationship with the client is not contradictory to the ethical rules or the perceived "model" of the attorney–client relationship under the *Model Rules,* or the description of lawyers' duties to the client, or the fiduciary nature of the relationship between attorney and client.

Thinking Like a Lawyer versus Thinking Like a Leader

Is "thinking like a lawyer" the same as "thinking like a leader"? The two concepts overlap in some respects but in other respects are, in fact, diametrically opposed.

At the start of your legal career, in the first year of law school, most likely you were introduced to the notion that you had to learn how to "think like a lawyer." For many students, this notion conjured up a perception of a secret recipe or acumen-imbued insight that enlightened only some students, who, by reason of education or intelligence, were especially adept at it. To this day, rumors persist that the law school entrance examination tests for this ability and that "you either have it or you don't."

The reality is that intelligence or cognitive thinking skills are important to success as a lawyer, but much of the "thinking like a lawyer" is actually a deductive reasoning ability that is useful in the U.S. (and English) common law system, where a judge deduces the correct (or best) outcome in a case from the precedent established in prior cases with similar factual predicates. Many lawyers still marvel at the time devoted in their first-year contracts law class to study a case involving a lengthy definition of what constitutes a "chicken."[15]

However, there is more to the notion of thinking like a lawyer than the ability to reason from prior cases. An essential part of how a lawyer presents to clients, other lawyers, and judges is their character and essential personality traits. Portrayals of lawyers in media often present an inaccurate depiction of their personalities and personal attributes, such as the notion that all trial lawyers are extroverted, glad-handing schmoozers, or that all tax or transactional lawyers are bookish, dull, and numbers driven. The more than one million lawyers in the United States are a much more diverse and nuanced group in terms of their personalities and traits.

However, empirical studies of lawyers' personality traits tend, with some uniformity, to describe them as particularly strong in certain traits or attributes and less so in others.[16] For example, some of the comparisons between the personality characteristics of lawyers versus the general population reveal that lawyers are:[17]

- *Introverted.* Fifty-seven percent of lawyers are introverts compared with 43 percent who are extroverts. Introverts generally prefer to work alone and tend to be somewhat quiet and reserved, taking questions into consideration and processing them internally rather than discussing them with others.
- *Analytic.* Seventy-eight percent of lawyers score as "thinkers" versus 47 percent of the general population. Lawyers tend to use logic and rely on expertise, rather than their feelings, to reach decisions.
- *Skeptical.* Lawyers score considerably above the average in skepticism compared with the population at large. They tend to view the glass as half empty (versus abundant and half full), questioning and expressing skepticism about people's comments and motives.
- *Autonomous.* Lawyers strongly prefer being in control and consequently push back when someone is telling them what to do and how to do it.
- *Inflexible.* Lawyers score considerably below the general population on resilience or the ability to handle criticism and setbacks. In this regard, they are often viewed as dogmatic or stubborn.
- *Unempathetic.* Lawyers generally don't score very high on their ability to be empathetic; they often fail to pay attention to or consider others' viewpoints and feelings. As the old joke goes, "Lawyers have feelings too . . . allegedly."

Some of these traits are helpful in law practice; others, not so much. For example, skepticism and autonomy are helpful propensities for creative problem solving, independent thinking, and finding flaws or potential problems in a client's case. Analytical thinking and dexterity in considering opposing arguments are also helpful attributes for practicing law. On the flip side, low levels of resilience make it more difficult to trust others, make it more prone to overthink actions, and exaggerate negative consequences. Low levels of empathy can adversely affect the ability of lawyers to understand their client's needs and concerns. Some of these traits are reflected in the joke about a lawyer summarizing their client's criminal case to a jury this way: "Could my client be innocent? Probably not, but it is interesting to think about."

However, remember that these traits are just generalizations—not every lawyer exhibits them to the same degree or even at all. Furthermore, as psychologists will point out, these traits are not immutable. You can address, enhance, or ameliorate them in various ways—for instance, through training and a conscious commitment to other, more desirable approaches to your legal work.

The ability to shape these traits is important because these same traits of lawyers can also present challenges for lawyer-leaders—those who lead their firms and organizations, for example. Leadership requires a particular skill set, which is not necessarily the same skill set needed to be an effective lawyer.

Effective leaders tend to be collaborative and inclusive. Leaders generally, in contrast to lawyers, for example, often score above the median on empathy and their ability to connect with others through persuasive influence and shared values. Leaders tend to be out and about—"walking the halls" and talking with their constituents, inspiring them in ways that shape and communicate shared goals and aspirations. In sum, leadership is primarily about interpersonal behaviors and building authentic relationships with followers.

Thinking like a lawyer is an essential skill in the practice of law, and some of the attributes of those who think like a lawyer are also important for leaders. Building a toolbox that includes more than thinking like a lawyer is necessary for lawyers aspiring to be leaders.

THE FOUNDATION OF LEADERSHIP: CREDIBILITY

What sort of person would you listen to, take advice from, find influential, and *willingly* follow? In other words, for people to want to follow an individual over the course of a project or a career, what do they most want to see in that person's behavior?

Following the lead of other researchers,[18] we surveyed hundreds of law school students about the personal values, traits, and characteristics they feel are most important to them in an individual they would willingly follow. The key word is *willingly*: it is one thing to follow someone because you believe you have to, "or else"—and yet another to follow someone because you want to.

The results not only were strikingly similar across different law schools and demographics *but also consistently correlated with normative data from over 150,000 people from around the world.*[19] Essentially, the top characteristics law school students look for in someone they would willingly follow are no different from what other people across industries, functions, fields, nationalities, ages, and genders desire.[20] People, especially clients, law firm associates and interns, bar association members, and others, follow lawyers because of their credibility—an attribute that encompasses character and competence.

Our survey of law school students showed that the number-one trait they wanted from an individual they would willingly follow is *honesty* (being truthful, having integrity, demonstrating trustworthiness), selected by nearly four out of five respondents. Other traits selected by law school student respondents included *competent* (capable, proficient, effective, gets the job done, professional), *inspiring* (uplifting, enthusiastic, energetic, cheerful, optimistic, positive about the future), and *forward looking* (visionary, foresighted, concerned about the future, has a sense of direction). You earn the designation of leader when others *perceive* you as having these essential characteristics. You may believe you exhibit these characteristics, but leadership, like art, is in the eye of the beholder and may be dependent on contextual factors as well as both implicit and explicit biases.[21] Still, lawyers who are seen as lacking integrity, having less than exceptional competence in their work, being tired and dull, or lacking a big-picture perspective will not be followed with the strongest commitment and internal drive.

These survey findings have a solid conceptual foundation in what social psychologists and communications experts call "source credibility."[22] In assessing the believability of sources of information—whether lawyers, newscasters, salespeople, physicians, priests, business executives, military officers, politicians, or civic leaders—researchers typically evaluate them on three criteria: their perceived trustworthiness, expertise, and dynamism. People considered to be credible sources of information rate highly in these areas. This is particularly true for lawyers because of their personal and professional obligations toward others.

Credibility elevates leaders because of the ideals of both clients and other lawyers and contemporaries: character and competence. Client demands drive law organizations (across the spectrum of law firms, district attorneys' offices, etc.), and clients are motivated by attorney track records and their counsel and perspectives, or, as is often remarked, based on their sound legal and business judgment. Clients want successful outcomes and sound professional advice and, consequently, seek to retain highly skilled advisors and representatives. Moreover, lawyers in firms select their outstanding colleagues to lead the organization because of their trustworthiness, commitment to the common good, and capabilities, in addition to any rainmaking propensities. Law firm colleagues want their leaders to tell the hard truth and to put the truth out there on the line. People follow individuals with skills that those people value, and lawyers only follow leaders who are themselves good lawyers. "Good" is, of course, a subjective belief, but colleagues' selections of leaders always reflect their judgment about character, competence, inspiration, and vision.

Clearly, the characteristics that lawyers and clients generally want from those they would willingly follow are the same as what scholars have conceptualized as constituting credibility. To follow willingly, people must believe that leaders' words can be trusted, they are personally passionate and enthusiastic about their work, and they have the knowledge and skill to make a difference. Credibility is the foundation of leadership and the bedrock of any lawyer's success.

THE FIVE PRACTICES OF EXEMPLARY LEADERSHIP®

What do people do to build and sustain credibility? What do they do that makes others see them as capable and trustworthy leaders? What behaviors do people exhibit that motivate others to want to follow? What are people actually *doing* when leading and making extraordinary things happen?

To answer these questions, Jim Kouzes and Barry Posner collected thousands of case studies over many decades from people about what they were doing at their personal best as leaders. These were times when individuals excelled at leading and getting others to operate at peak performance—and the examples cut across a wide variety of settings, nationalities, organizations, levels, ages, genders, educational backgrounds, and the like.[23]

Two prevailing lessons emerged from these cases. The first was that *everyone had a story to tell.* Regardless of who was asked, people could identify a time when they did their best as a leader. The second was that despite differences in settings, circumstances, and individual or organizational demographics, the actions and behaviors of people when they were at their best were *much more similar than different*. People demonstrated a common set of behaviors when they functioned at their personal best as leaders.

Kouzes and Posner grouped these behaviors into a *leadership operating system* called The Five Practices of Exemplary Leadership® (The Five Practices). When making extraordinary things happen, leaders Model the Way, Inspire a Shared Vision, Challenge the Process, Enable Others to Act, and Encourage the Heart. More than a thousand studies have validated this framework, documenting how The Five Practices make a significant difference in people's levels of well-being, commitment and motivation, work performance, and the success of their organizations.[24]

Those people who most frequently use the behaviors associated with The Five Practices are viewed as considerably more effective across a variety of outcomes than their counterparts who use them less often.[25] The same relationship is found even for those who indicate they are "individual contributors" (as opposed to people in hierarchical positions).[26] Net Promoter Scores are a widely used market research metric employed by companies worldwide to assess customer and employee loyalty and predict business growth,[27] and they can be applied to leadership. Instead of asking, "How likely would you recommend this product (or company) to a friend?" consider what happens when you ask an individual's managers, peers, coworkers, and direct reports, "How likely would you recommend this person to your colleagues as a good leader?" Figure 1 shows that the percentages of those strongly agreeing with this statement *dramatically* increase with greater frequency of The Five Practices of Exemplary Leadership.

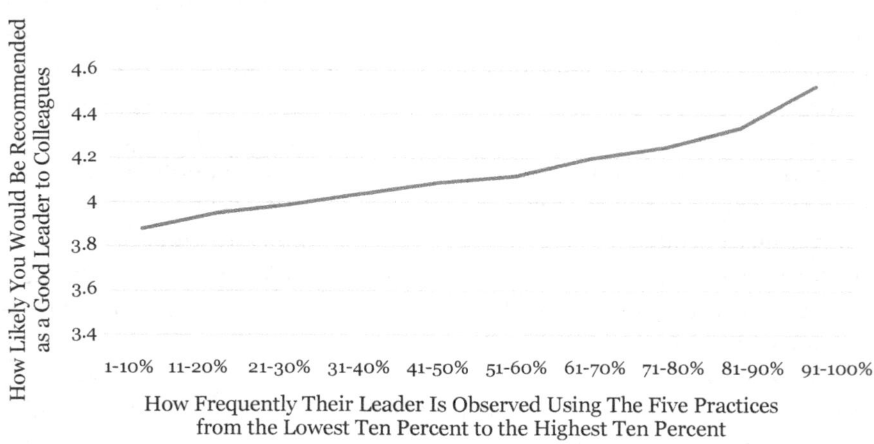

Figure 1 The Likelihood of Being Recommended as a Good Leader Increases with Greater Frequency of The Five Practices

Regarding the legal profession, the viewpoints of the hundreds of law school students we surveyed affirmed the viewpoints of the general population. These law office students, interns, and clerks reported on their perceptions of leadership by attorneys, staff, and other supervisors in those settings. The students' analyses and insights documented that where a managing partner, law firm lawyer, corporate counsel, or district attorney demonstrated The Five Practices, these junior "lawyers-in-training" had more positive professional experiences and perceived the organization as more successful in meeting its responsibilities. Equally important, law school students reported a much higher propensity for replicating these same positive behaviors in their own careers. Kouzes and Posner have also found that The Five Practices make a difference in how peers evaluate their colleagues' leadership effectiveness and their desire to collaborate with them.[28]

The bottom line is that, regardless of whether or not you are in a leadership position, the more you utilize The Five Practices, the more likely you'll positively influence other people and the organization. To have a significant impact on the people around you and the organizations with which you are involved, you must invest in learning the leadership practices and behaviors that will enable you to become the very best leader you can be. This is precisely the aim of the following five chapters in Part II.

CHAPTER HIGHLIGHTS

- Being a leader involves more than having a lofty title or high-level position.
- There are many definitions of *leadership*. A simple, all-encompassing definition is that leadership is a relationship between those who aspire to lead and those who choose to follow.
- The ABA's *Model Rules of Professional Conduct* governs the lawyer–client relationship, and lawyers can be leaders with respect to their clients without violating ethical boundaries.
- A strong sense of professional ethics will strengthen a leader's reputation as credible and competent.
- Thinking like a leader entails more than thinking like a lawyer because leaders demonstrate characteristics that lawyers may not necessarily exhibit.
- Credibility, which encompasses both character and competence, is the foundation on which leadership rests.
- The behaviors that build and sustain credibility are encapsulated in The Five Practices of Exemplary Leadership® operating system.

CHAPTER 3

Lawyer-Leaders Model the Way

"Unable to find your voice, you will end up mouthing other people's words and thoughts, using a vocabulary and adopting a perspective that doesn't represent you at all."

Young lawyers, when asked what they perceive to be the critical attributes of the most effective leaders they have worked with, frequently identify those lawyers who model the way for others. For example, they note that if the firm's leaders punctually submit time reports, others, including associates and firm professionals, are likely to do so. We commonly recognize that the proper actions flow from the examples demonstrated by those in charge. They are key role models. Associates and young lawyers in legal organizations arrive at the same conclusions about the firm's leaders, department chiefs, and mentors. When figuring out what it takes to be successful in the firm and as a lawyer, emulate the good lawyers and model their core strengths and attitudes.

Model the Way includes *clarifying your values, finding your voice,* and *setting an example for others.* Leaders set an example for others through their actions. In order for their actions to be authentic, however, leaders must first clarify their values and find their voice. Doing so will build a firm foundation of credibility for their actions because they will do what they say they would do: they will keep their promises. Empirical data shows that leadership effectiveness increases directly to how often other people observe leaders engaging in the Model the Way leadership practice.[1]

CLARIFYING YOUR VALUES AND FINDING YOUR VOICE

When you took a class in law school, were provided a partner in the firm as your mentor, or got assigned to a work group with a practice leader at a law firm, what is one of the first things you wanted to know? While you might have been unable to select the instructor, mentor, or team leader, didn't you want to know something about this person? It is the same for the partner or senior associate you are linked to on cases or transactions. You might be curious about their background and experience, their qualifications to lead the firm's mergers and acquisitions department or the Chicago office, or how they were selected. You might wonder how they treat the people around them at the office or what they value in a relationship. You might wonder about something even as simple as how they would prefer to be addressed.

Similarly, what is the first question people have of any individual who will be their supervisor or manager? Whether as the leader of a firm or as the lawyer in any new attorney–client relationship, the first question you can expect from your audience (be they one or many) is some variation of "Who are you?"

Before you can answer that question for another person, a group, a client, or even a jury, though, you have to be able to answer it for yourself. You have to be able to answer, "Who am I?" To do this, you have to be able to clarify your core values because only then can you give voice to those values, feeling comfortable and confident talking about and sharing your values with others.

Since leadership is a relationship, you can't expect to build a connection with someone else without being both able and willing to share information about who you are, what you care about, and why you do what you do. After all, people are unlikely to either respect or trust someone—much less *willingly* follow someone—they don't know. Would you hang around very long in a relationship with someone you can't figure out or make sense of? Indeed, isn't it true that much of the conversation you have in an initial meeting with a client comprises talking about and sharing information about who you are, your background and experience, and your standards, beliefs, and expectations for the relationship and case?

If you take a moment to think about people you most admire, whether in history or your own life experiences, it should be evident that one of their common characteristics is that they are individuals with strong beliefs about matters of principle. They are passionate about their cause, demonstrating an unwavering commitment to a clear set of values and being willing to speak out on matters of principle and conscience. This characteristic is especially prevalent among lawyers whose calling is to give voice to those without one and advocate on their behalf.

People expect this from their leaders. If you are going to speak out or step forward, like them, you need to know and be clear about what is important to you, what you care about deeply.

Clarify Your Values

We've asked hundreds of students in law leadership classes and lawyers in law firm professional development programs to clarify their values: "Take a moment to reflect on what you believe in and what you stand for. Then, after some reflection, write a series of 'I believe . . .' statements."

We have found that most students and lawyers had never been directly asked questions about their values. However, they find that this exercise, while challenging, is rewarding and helps them clarify and come face-to-face with their guiding principles. One of our clients even had his values subsequently printed on a coffee mug so he could keep them front and center on his desk, while a young lawyer framed and mounted her values on the wall in her home study. Why is it important to identify one's core values and then keep them front and center?

Values are your moral guides, your personal bottom line. They supply you with an internal moral compass by which to navigate the course of your daily life. Clarity of values is essential to discerning which way is north, south, east, and west. The clearer you are about your values, the easier it is to stay on your chosen path. Guidance like this is especially critical in difficult, complex, and uncertain times. When daily challenges throw you off course, you must have signposts that tell you where you are and move you to the right path. An added bonus is that researchers have consistently demonstrated a significant relationship between leaders' clarity and commitment to a set of core values and the strength of their credibility and effectiveness.[2]

For lawyers especially, having a moral compass is considered "a central constituent of all legal practice,"[3] requiring a clear-eyed understanding of their own values, personal and professional ethics, and sense of duty to others. In law schools, law firms, and many legal workplaces, attorneys demonstrate their values on multiple levels and across many constituencies.[4] Even though, at times, much of the practice of law is data driven and even mundane and routine, it is still very much a value-driven profession, involving questions about right and wrong actions, clear or questionable motives or intent, and "doing the right thing." Advising and representing others effectively and ethically can be extraordinarily difficult without a clear sense of your own values, beliefs, and moral compass. While law is a profession that is value driven, not all practitioners are value driven, but you can ensure that your highest values animate you in your work.

Values serve as guides to action. They inform your decisions about what to do and what not to do. They help you know when to say yes and when to say no, understand why you made this or that choice, and make decisions in a consistent manner. If, for instance, you believe that "heated debate" can stimulate thinking and creativity, such as in law firm committee meetings (e.g., litigation strategy), then you know that you need to speak out or do something when people with differing viewpoints challenge the conversation and are ignored. If you value collaboration, then you will make sure that your most experienced colleague doesn't write off meetings but instead comes to them and shares information with others. If you value independence and initiative over conformity and compliance, you will be more likely to speak up and challenge a policy when you think it is misguided.

You cannot effectively exercise leadership without being clear about your values. Clarity brings about an internal sense that something is grabbing hold of you and won't let go and requires taking initiative—that is, leadership. In essence, you care enough about an issue or situation to act. Many people find it easy enough to look around and find something to complain about or point to something that is not working correctly; it is only leaders, however, who are willing to grapple with such issues by getting out of their comfort zone and doing something about them. Leaders journey into their hearts and souls to discover their values. They must wrestle with what is inside themselves long enough to determine what's truly vital to them, what's underlying their choices, what boundaries and standards they need to set, and what motivates them to step up and speak out.

Find Your Voice

By exploring your inner territory, you will discover what you are about, both figuratively and literally, and you will find your voice. By finding your voice, you will express who you are and what you stand for, which is essential to becoming an authentic leader. Suppose you are unable to find your voice, which is extremely unfortunate for a lawyer. In that case, you will end up mouthing other people's words and thoughts, using a vocabulary and adopting a perspective that don't represent you at all, which significantly damages your credibility. There is the message you want to deliver, and then there is the expression of that message. You need to both *have* a voice and *give* a voice.

This can be difficult for lawyers because of their temperaments. For example, as noted in Chapter 2, lawyers are significantly above their professional peers in introversion and analytic thinking.[5] They tend to internalize their thought processes, taking questions under advisement rather than engaging in discussion with others. Indeed, these lawyers generally tend to be quiet and don't feel the need to be around people all the time, preferring to work alone in their offices. Their analysis of problems or situations is often abstract, unemotional, and sometimes devoid of much empathy.

These attributes are often helpful to much of the work that lawyers do, and alternatively, they may result in some people being left behind during fast-moving collaborative activities or in situations that call for sympathetic responses.

This doesn't mean that there is something wrong with the people who are lawyers. However, while some of these characteristics may be helpful in practicing law, many can hinder the exercise of leadership. The most successful lawyers and leaders strive to listen empathetically to what a client or colleague is saying, consider a broad range of feelings and emotions, and communicate thoughtfully and expressively.

To lead yourself and others, you have to understand, appreciate, and fully own the values that drive you. No matter what you are doing or where you are in an organization, you have to freely and candidly choose the principles you will use to guide your actions. But it is not enough to be clear about the message you want to deliver—you also have to clearly communicate that message in a variety of ways.

LEAD BY EXAMPLE

When you are sure you *mean* what you say, you are prepared to *do* what you say. While you must be able to forthrightly articulate the principles for which you stand, words themselves are insufficient. Leadership happens when you put your values into action. You enact the meaning of your personal philosophy (values, beliefs, assumptions, and principles) in how you behave, your decisions, and the steps you take to move toward the future you envision. You bring your values to life across various settings—in team meetings, one-to-one discussions, tweets, emails, social media, informal conversations over breaks and meals, and visits with clients, associates, partners, legislators, judges, and the like. In concluding what the essential traits or characteristics of effective law firm leaders are, experts state that they lead by example, giving others guidance and inspiration for the firm's direction.

Lawyer-leaders lead by their own example and model the way for change in various ways and for various types of law organizations. Corporate general counsel often has the force of the company's hierarchy and management behind its positions of responsibility and authority, while boutique and smaller firms have more decision making by consensus. However, success for both types of firms depends on firm leadership that can earn the support of other members of the firm.[6]

Leading-by-example illustrations abound regarding lawyers volunteering their time for pro bono work. There are many high-profile examples: Sid Wolinksy left his "second-choice" job as an entertainment industry lawyer to pursue public interest law opportunities focused on those with disabilities, veterans, and the disadvantaged because he "went to law school . . . to make a contribution."[7] Todd Belcore's public interest work was inspired by the struggles of growing up in a poor family with a single mother and paraplegic brother.[8] The WilmerHale law firm donated $17 million worth of hours to represent six Algerian terrorist suspects, resulting in a Supreme Court decision that granted habeas rights to Guantanamo Bay detainees.[9] Young associates often begin to lead by example by mentoring newer associates, summer interns, and other firm professionals; volunteering to take a leadership role in a nonprofit or bar organization; or canvassing a political district for a candidate for office. Many continue this inclination to serve others throughout their professional lives, enriching the legal profession and their communities.

When you lead by example—when your actions are consistent with your words and the values you espouse—people will consider you credible. Keep in mind that while people first listen to your words, they then observe your actions. They take note of the talk but pay great attention to how you "walk the talk." They listen to your promises and then seek evidence that you keep your commitments. When people do not see consistency, their verdict is that you are, at best, unreliable and, at worst, an outright hypocrite; the price is a loss of trust. When your words and deeds are congruent, the judgment handed down is credible.

There is not just one particular method of developing such leadership credibility. Several powerful methods of leading by example include how you allocate time, how you handle matters when things don't work out, the stories you tell, the words and language you choose, the questions you raise, how you listen, and your openness to feedback.

Lead by How You Allocate Time

Take a moment to think about how you spend your time. This is important because time is a finite commodity, and how you spend it is the most significant signal you can send about your priorities and what is important to you.

Time is a lawyer's most valuable resource. It is finite; an hour spent on one task necessarily means that hour cannot be spent on something else. You will often find yourself making trade-offs in how you allocate this precious resource and being challenged to find creative ways to juggle multiple tasks and relationships. What lawyers spend their time paying attention to and working on, and the people with whom they spend time, speaks volumes about their actual priorities, as compared with what they might say they care about.

Visibly spending time on what you have said matters because it shows that you are putting your "money where your mouth is." It's about being the first to do something you believe everyone else should value and do. Whether the value involves family, teamwork, hard work (arriving early, staying late), timeliness, or even camaraderie, the most valid measure of what leaders deeply believe is how they spend their time. People use this to measure whether a leader lives up to their espoused principles and standards.

Furthermore, if others are to believe that your values are important to you, those values have to show up on your calendar. Calendars never lie when it comes to broadcasting your priorities to others and demonstrating how your time allocation aligns with your values and priorities. You have to make sure that how you distribute your time is in sync with what you say is important and consistent with what you and your colleagues have agreed on as priorities.

During their first months, new associates tend to be highly receptive to leading-by-example signals from supervising and managing attorneys about what is essential. For example, are the firm's attorneys willing to put in the time and offer their expertise to the associates they were responsible for recruiting and mentoring? To what extent is the workload on the project or case equitably shared? Are interns or associates asked to do things the attorneys are unwilling to do? Leaders who are conscious and conscientious about allocating time to lead by example will gain willing followers. We heard over and over again from associates that "the concept of 'modeling the way' goes hand in hand with the importance of earning and sustaining credibility as a leader."

Lead by Teachable Moments

Spending time on core values is essential to convey the message that you are serious about them. Nevertheless, you cannot plan everything about your day. Even for the most disciplined people, things can happen beyond their control. However, just as with orchestrated events, unplanned and unexpected occurrences can create *teachable moments* about solving problems and resolving disputes in ways consistent with shared values.

Chance occurrences, particularly during times of stress and challenge, can become opportune moments to model and teach others valuable lessons about appropriate norms of behavior. You can't plan them, but you can think about how you will handle these critical moments and interruptions should they occur. As with any hypothetical, you can envision how to be direct and realistic without being blunt or mean-spirited and shape the event as a way, for example, to develop others. How you link your actions and decisions to your values conveys a great deal about what really matters to you. By stepping up and confronting an unplanned situation (e.g., a judge's ruling), you show what it looks like when actions and decisions are taken based on values. By standing up for guiding principles under adverse circumstances, you demonstrate that shared values require a mutual commitment to keep words and deeds in sync. The civil rights lawyers who risked personal harm by traveling to the Deep South in the 1960s to protect the rights of Black citizens to vote inspired a subsequent generation of young lawyers who sought to achieve an even greater set of social and economic goals for underrepresented communities.

During the 9/11 terrorist attacks, real-life heroes emerged. A group of passengers on United Flight 93 banded together to confront the terrorists and prevent the plane from hitting a major U.S. government building; the plane ended up landing in a Pennsylvania field, killing all aboard. At the Twin Towers, numerous people risked their own lives to save others from the burning buildings, such as an equities trader who helped over a dozen people escape.[10] Such heroism is not required to be a good lawyer, but it is essential to act with your best instincts, shaped by a desire to serve others.

Lead by Storytelling

Another powerful way to lead by example is by telling stories and, through those stories, calling attention to what's important and what is not, what works and what doesn't, what is and what could be.

Stories are important because they translate intangible ideas into tangible actions. You can't just order people to do something like "follow the rules," because most people don't actually read the rule book (assuming there is such a thing). However, people will listen to or read a story about an individual fired for breaking a rule (violating a company principle), or alternatively about someone who took actions consistent with the firm's values, even at some risk, and received a commendation or bonus, and they get the message.[11] Stories serve as mental maps that help people connect what is essential and how to put important ideas into practice in a particular context. When people hear a story about how people like themselves enacted a value, they are much more likely to envision themselves doing the same.

Lawyers are inveterate storytellers, most often about their prior cases, clients, successes, and, yes, failures in court or deals. Many exceptionally talented lawyers credit the stories they heard from mentors for "learning the ropes" and successfully developing their acuity and practice skills. Although "war stories" can get old, stories about how a complicated point was explained to a jury or how a unique reading of the *Federal Rules of Civil Procedure* gave a client an advantage in litigation—that is, stories with a learning point—seldom get old, are worth repeating, and are always invaluable to young and new attorneys, and even those who have been around for some time.

For example, an antitrust trial lawyer told a story about how he educated a federal court jury on a complicated issue regarding the definition of *competition* by using the local state university football team as an example of competition. His point was the importance of making complicated issues easier for jurors to understand, and this story endured in the minds of his audience for years and indeed for the duration of the trial.

Research shows that storytelling is not a "soft" way of getting the hard stuff done; instead, it is an effective way to make essential points.[12] If you are trying to communicate the values of your organization, what do you think would have more of an impact: a policy statement that reads "Thou shalt provide timely services to our clients" or a story about how an associate took it upon themselves to go directly to the client's site to nail down some crucial information? Similarly, what would be more persuasive: seeing statistics about how much stress criminal lawyers experience or hearing a story about a local prosecutor who, suffering from a severe stress disorder, committed suicide? Stories are generally more effective than policy statements or statistical charts alone. Information first presented in the form of an example or story is more accurately and quickly remembered than facts, figures, and formal policy pronouncements.[13] Storytelling is an effective leadership practice because stories are simple, straightforward, timeless, and appeal to almost everybody regardless of age, gender, or ethnicity.

Storytelling comes naturally to many lawyers, and they know that it is essential in a jury trial to weave a story to help the jury understand their party's case. They often present the beginning of the story in opening arguments and then conclude it during closing arguments, with the purpose of sending the jurors to the jury room to figure out what happened and which side had the story that most aligned with the facts presented in the trial.

Young lawyers often comment about experiencing "imposter syndrome"—the feeling of vulnerability after stepping into a complex, demanding, and uncertain workplace (or courtroom). Women, first-generation and LGBTQ associates, law students, and students of color often report that they have a heightened sense of "not belonging" in law school and the practice of law. The fear of making an error of great magnitude or appearing insufficient to the task of being a "perfect" lawyer can be paralyzing, especially for women and people of color.[14] One way of dealing with this is to hear stories from your mentors and other practicing lawyers describing their honest reflections about navigating through these fears. Time and experience will eradicate imposter syndrome; still, the process will be easier if leaders model the way for others through storytelling.

Lead by the Words You Choose

The words and language that leaders use also set a tone for action. The phrase "watch your language" takes on an entirely different meaning in the context of leading by example than in the context of being scolded by a teacher for using an inappropriate word in school. In terms of leadership, it is about setting an example for others in how your language frames the context for thinking and talking about events and ideas, as well as focusing attention on certain aspects of the subject.

Your choice of language affects others' perceptions of you as a leader. The words you choose give voice to your mindset and beliefs. They evoke images of what you aspire to create and how you expect others to behave. Just think about the impact of changing the expression "I have to do this" to "I choose to do this" or "They want me to do this" to "I think this is the best way to do this." It's evident that the latter expressions put you in the driver's seat, signaling a sense of personal responsibility and accountability—establishing credibility in the eyes of your followers for your actions.

Your choice of words also has a powerful effect on how others see themselves and those around them, as well as the events they experience. Consider, for example, experiments in which researchers told participants they were playing the Community Game or the Wall Street Game.[15] In both scenarios, people played the same game by the same rules, the only difference being that experimenters gave the game two different names. Of those playing the Community Game, 70 percent started playing cooperatively and continued to do so throughout. However, the reverse happened for those told they were playing the Wall Street Game: 70 percent did not cooperate. Of the 30 percent in this scenario who did cooperate, they quickly stopped after noticing that others were not cooperating. Again, the name of the game—not the game itself—changed! You can influence people's behavior simply by giving the task or the team a name that evokes the kind of behavior implied by the name. If you want people to act like a community, use language that evokes a feeling of community. If you want people to act like citizens of a village, you have to talk to them as if they were citizens of a village, not subordinates in a hierarchy.

Would you want to join a law firm that likens itself to a hospital, a factory, a plant, a hot air balloon, a carnival, a university, or a clinic? What words and images best resonate with you? Are you thoughtful about words that may trigger cultural sensitivities? Words matter to lawyers, and they matter to the people lawyers attempt to influence.

Lead by Focused Questioning

Similar to language, the questions you ask and the issues you raise force attention on the connections, or gaps, between espoused and enacted values. In the course of everyone's daily lives, many questions are raised. Most of these are to gather more information, get clarification, or reach a greater understanding. However, your questions should do more than this from a leadership perspective. The substance of your questions should reveal the values that warrant attention and the energy that needs to be devoted to them. Well-phrased questions present opportunities to teach and reinforce values—and thus constitute another measure of how serious you are about your espoused beliefs. Let's face it, some lawyers are not good listeners, but great lawyers are great listeners. They have honed that skill through thoughtful commitment and practice.

A key to asking good leadership questions is to think first about the *quest* in your questions. Where do you want to take this client (person, group, or organization) with your questions? What value or values are you trying to reinforce with your questions? To what extent do the questions you typically ask ensure commitment to collective values? What evidence do you want to ask about that will illustrate whether the decisions are consistent with values?

Challenge yourself to identify a routine set of questions that will get people to reflect on core values and what they have done and can do daily to act on those values. Such questions should be somewhat predictable because you want the people you are working with to think about them well before you ask them. As a leader, you should expect people to have your questions in their minds as they make decisions. In one way or another, the questions you ask should all be a variation of a single theme: what are we doing to live out our values and shared commitments? The point is not to ask rhetorical questions (ones that have obvious answers or responses) but to get people to think about how their own actions are consistent with shared values. Your questions should help keep people focused and paying attention to what really matters. Watch a skillful cross-examination of a witness by a very good lawyer, and you will understand the tremendous importance of listening as a prelude to thoughtful, effective questioning.

It is helpful to think about the quantity and quality of your questions. Studies suggest that the more questions you ask, the more your emotional intelligence improves, which in turn makes you a better questioner.[16]

Research generally shows that people who ask the most questions, relative to their peers, are perceived as both smarter and more interesting than those who do not ask questions or seek advice and input from others.[17] There are, however, definitely differences in how men and women communicate, who gets heard, and how.[18] Keep in mind that not all questions are equally important; rather, the ones that solicit more information have special power. Follow-up questions in a conversation, for example, signal that you are listening, care, and want to know more, making your conversation partners feel respected and heard.[19]

Of course, sincerity must underlie the asking of questions. In other words, you must honestly want to listen to their responses, rather than thinking about your own rejoinders. Listening to what others have to say implies that you give their opinions and feedback serious consideration in subsequent decisions.

Lead by Soliciting Feedback

How can you know whether you are doing what you say if you never receive feedback about your behavior? How can you be sure that your words and actions match if you do not get information about how much others see them aligned? Asking others for their input gives you a perspective about yourself that only others can see. With their insights, you have the opportunity to make improvements, as well as determine whether your actions are being perceived in ways that you intended. Most people are not used to providing feedback, even when solicited, so unless you ask, people are unlikely to tell you what they think. One way to start is by asking for advice about a specific way you could improve rather than a general "How am I doing?"

Initially, you might not like the feedback that you receive. Many lawyers who solicit postverdict jury surveys are disappointed in how their message didn't resonate with the jury or surprised at the outright hostility that jurors felt toward the lawyer or their client. However, the more that request for feedback becomes part of everyday conversations, the easier it will be to listen to the information and learn from it, especially when everyone involved shares similar values and aspirations.

The point is not to affix blame but to exercise curiosity about what happened and focus on what can be learned. In this way, any problems, mistakes, misunderstandings, and the like that may have occurred are not repeated. The firm's managing partner asked all the summer interns about their experiences, and this made quite an impression on several, who told us that "the partner showed a real interest in what the interns had to say, and actually took notes. He got back to us again before we returned to school and asked us how we felt about the changes being proposed that were based on our feedback. This made us realize that a good leader seeks feedback and then does something with the information received." Similarly, annual performance review sessions for associates, while sometimes nerve-wracking, provide an opportunity to measure how good the fit is between the firm and the young lawyer and to identify areas where improvement is necessary. Firms often use these occasions, for instance, to emphasize timekeeping practices as a critical factor in the associate's billable hours.

Obtaining feedback has many benefits, among which researchers have found that people who seek out disconfirming feedback (i.e., feedback contrary to their self-perceptions) perform better than those who listen only to people who see their positive qualities.[20] Self-reflection, the willingness to seek feedback, and the ability to engage in new behaviors based on this information have been found to predict future success in managerial jobs.[21]

Remember, though, that if you do nothing with the feedback you receive, people will stop giving it. They are liable to believe that you are arrogant, or worse, and you don't care about what anyone else has to say. But if you incorporate feedback from others, it is more likely that others will accept straightforward input and advice from you, which, in the end, benefits everyone.

CHAPTER HIGHLIGHTS

- The path to becoming an exemplary leader begins by discovering and owning your personal values and beliefs and then finding your voice by developing the capacity to express who you are in unique ways.
- Setting an example is demonstrating that you genuinely mean what you say. Walking the talk, doing what you say, and being consistent in word and deed build credibility.
- How you spend your time, how you deal with critical, unplanned incidents (teachable moments), the stories you tell, the language you use, the questions you ask, and your receptivity to feedback provide tangible evidence that you are the "real deal" and worthy of being listened to and followed by others.
- Leadership abilities are important in all types and sizes of law firms. While the demands on leadership may differ between a six hundred–lawyer firm and a five-person "Main Street" firm, the ability to lead others is critical to success.

Chapter 4

Lawyer-Leaders Inspire a Shared Vision

"Every endeavor begins in the mind's eye with the belief that what's now only an image can one day be made real."

Practicing attorneys, law firm professionals, and law students seek inspiration and guidance from many exceptional leaders. In the classroom and professional development discussions designed to help in understanding the roles that lawyers play in seeking justice and serving their clients' need for legal expertise and advice, young lawyers and law students often refer to public role models such as Martin Luther King Jr., Michelle Obama, Malala Yousafzai, Thurgood Marshall, and Ruth Bader Ginsburg, as well as local role models such as lawyers staffing legal clinics and those involved with social justice organizations and movements. What these leaders have in common is a dream of what might be, with an end in mind that serves more than themselves—and the ability to enlist people in that shared vision by appealing to their aspirations and together envisioning a future of exciting and ennobling possibilities.

Inspire a Shared Vision involves *envisioning the future* and *getting others on board*. From surveys of people around the world, including our own with lawyers and law school students, the findings clearly show that leaders are expected to be forward-looking—to describe what can be, not just what is. Like the role models recognized by lawyers and students, the challenge is how you take your vision to others so that they will be as inspired and determined as you are to make something extraordinary happen. To be compelling, visions have to be less about you and more about others; indeed, others (be they colleagues or clients) have to see themselves squarely within the vision and find common ground in order for them to enlist and commit, not merely comply. According to research involving both their managers and coworkers, leadership effectiveness assessments are strongly correlated to the frequency with which people are reported as engaging in the leadership practice of Inspire a Shared Vision.[1]

ENVISIONING THE FUTURE

In exercising leadership, you have to be able to visualize a positive future and to give the work that is being done a sense of meaning and purpose.[2] The ability to be forward-looking is one of the key expectations that people have of their leaders and those they would *willingly* follow. This trait is particularly important in legal organizations, regardless of their size, be able to communicate a clear vision for the firm's future.[3]

Before you can inspire others, though, you have to inspire yourself. Remember our discussion of values in Chapter 3? Before you can model values for others, you must clarify those values for yourself, and, similarly, before you can expect to enlist others in a shared vision, you must clarify for yourself your vision of the future. Your inner passion is a good indicator of what you feel most deeply about and find worthwhile in and of itself. It's a clue to what is *intrinsically* motivating. If you don't care deeply for and about something, then you cannot expect others to feel a similar sense of conviction. How can you expect others to endure the inevitable long hours and hard work if you're not similarly inclined?

Every endeavor begins in the mind's eye with the belief that what's now only an image can one day be made real. No matter what you call it—*vision, purpose, mission, legacy, dream, calling,* or *burning agenda*—the intent is the same. There is something greater than what is happening today that infuses life and work with meaning and importance—something that transcends the here and now and draws people forward.

Look Ahead

You can expand your ability to be forward-looking by spending more time thinking about the future. The future is the domain of leaders, and this means regularly carving out opportunities and time to peer into the distance and imagine what might be out there. You simply have to put in the time today to have perspective on tomorrow.

Just because you can't predict the future doesn't mean you should not, or cannot, imagine a better one. Otherwise, why would people invest money for their retirement, parents save for their children's education, youth activists speak up for racial and social justice, or lawyers even take on a difficult (not slam-dunk) case? The same reasoning could even apply to your decision to attend law school and pursue a legal career. Your belief that you could be a lawyer and that you would enjoy the practice of law is often what gets you through the hard work demanded while in law school and on the bar examination. These are all forward-looking actions that are undeterred by all the uncertainties of the present.

Representing forward-looking, visionary clients requires similar attributes in their lawyers. For example, lawyers representing young climate change policy activists were instrumental in getting their clients to turn ideas into action. The youth activists were puzzled as to why more people were not composting; the lawyers refocused their question into action and created a strategy to seek more systemic changes to the government's inaction on climate and environmental challenges.

Similarly, law firm leaders must provide leadership, inspiration, and direction to smart, successful, and highly motivated colleagues in the firm or organization, irrespective of its size or type. Those colleagues require a clear and exciting vision for the firm's future and measures to take on a challenge or crisis successfully.[4]

Knowing that a vision is essential doesn't make one magically pop out of your head like a bright light bulb, but it does shine some light on the need to be forward-looking. When people first begin to exercise leadership, they typically don't have a *clear* vision of the future. After all, there's no map, interstate highway, or case law book to serve as a guide to the future. Envisioning the future is a process that begins with inspiration, a feeling, or a sense that something is worth doing. Your vision of the future may initially be fuzzy—the feeling you might have experienced in law school as you first dealt with hypotheticals—but the important thing is that you're focused on forward momentum.

As you begin acting on your instincts, you will find that the vision gets a little clearer. You do something, take some action that moves you forward, and the vision gets a little clearer still. You pay attention to it, experience it, and immerse yourself in it. You start the process, and over time, you see more detail in your dream. It's an iterative process that eventually results in something that you and others can articulate and see as a possibility.

For example, the vision could involve thinking about expanding your practice group by reaching out to develop expertise in new or emerging practice areas. A relatively new partner in a New York financial services law firm department became curious about blockchain technologies and wondered whether there would be new opportunities for the law firm. This led him to contact more experienced lawyers in regulatory and corporate law practice groups for ideas and ultimately establish the firm's cryptocurrency practice group. Similarly, a new development announced by the state supreme court or the state legislature can create novel opportunities for plaintiffs and defense firms to change litigation strategies and secure new clients.

Leaders eventually realize that their vision is an elaboration, interpretation, and variation on a "common thread," or theme. Envisioning the future is much like composers finding a musical theme from all the notes that swirl in their minds. Think about the fundamental beliefs and assumptions that keep recurring in your life. Equality, justice irrespective of race or sexual orientation, fairness, and helping others are beliefs and aspirations shared by many lawyers and most law students before they go to law school. Consider the causes you contribute to and those to which you don't. What are the issues that keep popping up on your radar? What things keep you up at night or get you jumping out of bed in the morning? What are the "I wish . . ." statements that you find yourself echoing?

More than likely, these reflections will reveal that your central theme has been with you for a long time. For example, surveys have shown that people are motivated to go to law school for public-spirited reasons, including public or government service (44 percent), to be helpful to others or useful to society (35 percent), and to become an advocate for social change (32 percent).[5] Service to others is a compelling value, or theme, for law students and for lawyers.

Thus, although visions might be a bit fuzzy at first, what leaders clearly have (and what you have too) are concerns, desires, hypotheses, propositions, arguments, hopes, and dreams—core concepts around which you organize your actions and aspirations as you look ahead to the future.

Look Behind

Ironically enough, you also need to look back into your past to imagine the future. Looking backward enables you to see further than if you were only to stare straight ahead. Understanding your personal history can help you identify themes, patterns, and beliefs that underscore both why you care about particular issues or circumstances now and why making them better in the future is such a high priority. Recalling the richness of your past experiences deepens your sense of what might be. In recalling the past, you also appreciate how long it can take to fulfill aspirations and accept that the path to the future will not be a straight line. Like sailing upwind, because you can't control everything around you, you have to tack, zig-zagging back and forth as you progress. No doubt there will be ups and downs in any worthwhile pursuit, and you'll veer into territory that you haven't traversed before, which is all the more reason why you need to have a firm picture in your mind of where you were in order to get to where you are going and to remember why it is important to keep going in order to get there.

Lawyers can benefit as leaders by looking backward as inspiration for continually looking forward and creating new visions. Think about why people go to law school and what they hope to accomplish in their lives after they graduate and pass the bar exam. Studies of lawyers have found a relationship between their dreams and goals in deciding to go to law school and the worlds they experience in practicing law, representing clients, and solving problems.[6] Many of the primary motivations to attend law school—for example, interacting with smart people, working on complex issues, and helping others by solving problems—are among the major activities that lawyers enjoy in their law practices. Certainly, achieving a level of economic security is an important factor in going to law school in the first place; however, attaining personal satisfaction in the work is just as compelling, or more so, for many lawyers—and surveys show lawyers are generally satisfied with their decision to attend law school. In many cases, obtaining a legal education meets their dreams of being a lawyer.[7] Looking backward, lawyers should feel inspired by such successes to continue looking forward in envisioning the future, shaping the goals and aspirations of their constituents.

Incorporate the Present

None of this is to say that the past *is* your future. There is still the reality of the here and now, and visions are influenced by what's happening around you. For example, during the coronavirus pandemic, applications for new businesses went through the roof, at their fastest pace in more than a decade. By being present in the present, you can increase your ability to conceive of new and creative solutions to today's problems. Only when you understand the current challenges can you imagine a better tomorrow. Immersing yourself in the present, apart from the work that you are doing, however, means getting yourself off automatic pilot, not believing that you know everything you need to know, not viewing the world through pre-established categories, and paying attention to the subtle clues around you about what's happening in the world.

In other words, you have to stop, look, and listen. If you are like most people, and certainly if you are one of the vast majority of overscheduled attorneys, you need to start noticing more of what's going on around you right now. For example, ask yourself the following: What are people doing now that they didn't do a few years ago? What are the issues they are litigating now that differ from just a few years ago? How are people interacting? How do workplaces and communities look and feel now compared with how they once did? What trends are popular these days? Why? What are people talking about? What are their hot topics of conversation? What are they saying they need and want? What are they saying gets in the way of doing their best? What do they think should be changed?

Listen not only to these clues but also to the weak signals—that is, to what's not being said, such as what people are no longer talking about or paying attention to. Listen for things you've never heard before. What does all this tell you about where things are going? What's it telling you about what lies just around the corner or just beyond the horizon? How can all this inform your vision as a leader?

GETTING OTHERS ON BOARD

Leadership requires more than just having a vision. Of course, you need to imagine the end result, but you also must be able to sell your personal view of the world to others. In other words, you must be able to enlist others to sign on board.

When you envision the future that you want for yourself and others and feel passionate about it, you are much more likely to take that first step forward; the same is true for others. In global case studies of personal-best leadership experiences, leaders frequently mentioned the need for buy-in from others on the vision.[8] This was similar to what we learned from law school students and corporate attorneys. Nearly all of them explained that their personal-best leadership experience required persuading others to embrace a common goal or desirable outcome. They explained how they had to communicate the purpose and build support for a unified direction. They recognized that everyone had to commit to a common cause. They understood that to get everyone to take the same journey, they had to be able to communicate *why* others should want to join in, what it would mean to them, how they would benefit, and whom they would serve. That New York law firm junior partner who envisioned a new practice group for cryptocurrency and blockchain clients generated interest in the idea from other lawyers in the financial services group, and then they got other lawyers in the firm excited about this emerging practice area. That excitement laid the groundwork for the managing partners to approve the new practice group when few other firms were providing those services nationally.

Creating a common vision is about developing a *shared* sense of destiny. It's about enabling others to see how their own interests and aspirations are appreciated and aligned with—and will be incorporated into—the vision. It's about enabling others to see themselves in the future that you envision and to want to be included in the vision development process. A shared vision enables all the people connected with the work to see more clearly what's ahead of them and what the future will look like when they have added their piece—and, in this way, it motivates everyone to commit their individual energies to its realization.

Visions seen only by the leader are insufficient to generate organized movement. You must also motivate others to see a way forward, one that is filled with exciting possibilities that lie ahead. You must breathe life into visions by crafting a compelling mental image; listening to the hopes and dreams of others so that they clearly understand how their values and interests will be served; showing how they can make a difference; stressing the uniqueness of the vision; and being upbeat and expressive to attract followers through your energy, optimism, and sincerity.

Craft a Compelling Mental Image

To get other people on board with a vision, leaders must speak about the future long before the journey forward even begins. They must convey a mental picture of what things will be like when everyone arrives at the destination. For law firm leaders, this requires engaging others in the firm—from partners to associates and, often, staff—by explaining what that future looks like and what it means for those who support it.[9]

Visions are images in the mind: they are impressions and representations. A beacon of light cutting through the fog is an image that you can picture in your mind. You make this image real to others by expressing it in concrete and tangible terms. For example, think about the city of Paris, France. What things first come to mind? Probably the Eiffel Tower, the Arc de Triomphe, the Seine, Notre Dame, good food, wine, and romance—all of which are images of real places, experiences, and emotions. No one recalls Paris's kilometers, population, or gross domestic product. The same would be true for your colleagues, team, or organization. This is because human memory is stored in images and sensory impressions, not numbers. People recall images of reality, not abstractions from reality.

Images are windows looking out on the world of tomorrow. When leaders talk about going to places people have never been, they start by imagining what they would look like. This process is similar to planning a vacation. You think about the travel involved, the amenities associated with the place where you are staying, the weather and how that influences the clothes you will pack and the activities you hope to participate in and enjoy, the people who live in the place you are visiting, the people who may accompany you on the trip, and so on. Similarly, leaders paint a picture of the future and make manifest the purpose so that others can see it, hear it, taste it, touch it, and feel it.

Painting a picture of the future requires making full use of the power of language to communicate a shared objective and giving life to visions. Using stories, metaphors, and other figures of speech provides vividness and tangibility to abstract ideas.[10] Express your hopes for the future using descriptive language, examples, and anecdotes. In making concrete the intangible vision, you must ignite people's passion, developing a shared sense of destiny. What's key is getting others to imagine in their mind's eye the image of what could be, how it could be, and why it must be.

Listen Deeply

Listening is actually more important than talking to get people on board. No matter how grand the dream, if others don't see in it the possibility of realizing their own hopes and desires, they won't follow. That is where listening comes in. Leadership requires attentively listening to constituents—and understanding people at a much deeper level than you may normally find comfortable. It requires exploring their strongest yearnings and deepest fears and being profoundly aware of their joys and sorrows. By getting to know your constituents, listening to them, and soliciting their advice, you can better give voice to their feelings and aspirations—not just your own. The very best divorce lawyers, for example, are attentive to what both parties are saying to actually "hear" their feelings about what is punitive, what is essential, and what is negotiable.

Listening is part and parcel of your realization and understanding that leadership is a relationship. People want to be listened to and are genuinely motivated when they feel that you understand, appreciate, and plan to incorporate their hopes and dreams. Make the time to hear what people say by getting out of your cubicle, moving away from your desk or machine, and wandering into other people's workplaces. Share coffee, breakfast, lunch, an afternoon break, a virtual check-in, or some unstructured occasion with others, and find out what's going on with them, what's possibly frustrating them, and what they care about. The loftier your position in the hierarchy, the more important it is that you spend time on the ground because those voices and issues get filtered as they move up the chain of command.

Few people can easily articulate what they want or know what they need, which is even more reason for you to listen deeply to them. Listening is not just about words; it's about paying attention to what's unspoken, noticing what makes people smile or grimace, observing how they spend their time, reading between the lines. High-level listening skills are essential for lawyers. They reformulate and reposition their clients' claims and grievances, transforming those into strategies for success in a transaction or litigation.

Without close, thoughtful listening, you cannot effectively perform those key functions for your clients.

Listening for the purpose of building a relationship is different from listening with an intent to reply rather than reflect and understand. Many potential agreements are missed because someone focused more on making their point than understanding what the other party was trying to say. Listening also opens you up to learning, which again is too often a neglected characteristic of lawyers, thinking they have to know the answer to every question in advance and always be right.

Apprehensive about joining a large national law firm shortly after the coronavirus pandemic hit, a young lawyer told us how the partners made every effort to assure him that the firm would endure, that the lawyers and staff would be rewarded for their hard work, and that the firm's leaders remained strong and united in inspiring their team to continue doing great work for the firm's clients. "This is exactly what I needed to hear," he told us, "because while I'm not afraid of putting in the hours, I wanted to feel that the firm had a long-term perspective and had the best interests of people at heart." By listening and being sensitive to prospective hires' concerns, the partners got him on board with their shared vision of the future.

Show How Followers Can Make a Difference

Leaders can attract followers by showing how their vision can make a difference.

Everyone wants a better tomorrow, and while people do not all want the same thing, they all want an improvement. Leaders must discern what that improvement would look like for the people with whom they interact and work.

There is a deep yearning inside people to make a difference. They want to know that they're doing something meaningful on this planet—that their existence has a purpose. Work can provide that purpose: increasingly, in fact, the workplace is where people pursue meaning and identity. The best teams and workplaces can bring out and make use of this human longing by communicating the meaning and significance of what's being done so that people understand their own important role in creating it. When you can clearly communicate a shared vision of an organization, you ennoble those who work on its behalf. Studies involving respondents from forty different countries (encompassing sixteen different languages) found that connecting employees with purpose increased their engagement and productivity.[11] Stressing the "why" to people—as in "Why are we doing this, and why does it matter?"—activates the brain's reward system, increasing not only how favorably people feel about what they are doing but also how much effort they put into it.[12]

The job searches of law students and new lawyers confirm this desire for meaningful work. After graduation, law students look for a firm or company with values they share and can embrace, including a philosophy that newcomers to that organization are more than "cannon fodder," doing the grunt work that no one else wants to do. Associates want to feel they play a crucial role regardless of job title or specific task responsibilities.[13] One contributing factor for associate turnover in law firms is that they don't feel their work is valued, especially concerning working relationships with clients. Meaningful engagement with the firm's work and a sense that the firm's values mesh with associates' values increase their sense of being valued and appreciated.

While you can't impose your vision of the future on others, you can liberate the visions that are already stirring inside people. When you communicate a shared vision, you awaken and stir the belief that people can achieve something grand and unique. What truly pulls people forward, especially in more challenging and volatile times, is the exciting possibility that what they are doing can make a profound difference in the lives of their families, friends, colleagues, clients, patients, congregations, and communities.

Tout the Unique Aspects of the Vision

You are unlikely to successfully enlist others in a project, campaign, or cause by announcing, "I'd like you to join me in doing the ordinary." Most people have an innate desire to accomplish something that no one else has yet achieved, so touting the unique aspects of your vision will attract followers. There's no advantage in being on a team or working in a company or law firm that does precisely the same thing as the one across town. If you want people to sign up with you, they must understand how whatever you are proposing is distinctive.

Uniqueness fosters pride and boosts the self-respect and self-esteem of everyone associated with the organization—and the prouder people are of the work they are doing and the organization for which they work, the more engaged they're likely to be. The fairly recent explosion of startup companies bears out this desire for uniqueness: the business world is rife with companies that offer not only unique products but also unique visions—and young people, attracted by the nature of these businesses, have been flocking to them.[14]

Exhibit Energy and Positivity

In getting everyone on board, leaders need to heed the research, which shows that people want to follow those who are enthusiastic, exude energy, and have a positive attitude.[15] Upbeat people attract others and convey the feeling that the journey will be an invigorating adventure and that the leader is in it for the long haul. People want to follow those with a can-do attitude rather than those who are cynics and give ten reasons why something is impossible or those who make others feel bad about themselves. When negative remarks become the norm, people's brains lose mental efficiency,[16] which is why you need to focus on the bright side. A positive approach to life broadens people's ideas about future possibilities, and these exciting options build on each other.[17] In affirming environments, people are more open to seeing possibilities and more willing to experiment. Positivity increases the ability to cope with adversity and strengthens resiliency during times of high stress.

In explaining why they are magnetically attracted to particular leaders, people often describe those individuals as charismatic. But *charisma* has become such an overused and misused term that it's almost useless as a descriptor of leaders.[18] To better understand this elusive quality, social scientists observed the behavior of individuals deemed charismatic. What they determined was that these people are simply more animated than others. They smile more, speak faster, pronounce words more clearly, and move their heads and bodies more often.[19] The most successful talks on TED.com, for example, were attributed to presenters who used nearly twice as many hand gestures as their less frequently viewed peers.[20] This finding was even replicated in studies that used simple animated stick figures as the speakers. The speakers judged to be most energetic and enthusiastic employed many more hand movements overall, and their frequency of physical movements was predictive of those who received the most applause from their audience.[21] Much of the same has been shown to be true of courtroom attorneys.[22]

Accordingly, *charisma* can best be understood as a willingness to be expressive. The more expressive you are, the more likely your enthusiasm will infect those around you. Successful trial lawyers understand that being expressive and enthusiastic encourages jurors to feel positive about themselves and the lawyer's clients, which is important irrespective of the legal merits of the case or proceeding.

Think about how engaging people are when they start talking about their personal-best leadership experiences or their ideal futures, or even their upcoming holidays and vacations. When relating hopes, dreams, and successes, people are almost always emotionally expressive: they lean forward in their chairs, they move their arms about, their eyes light up, their voices ring with excitement, and they smile. Adding such expressivity and emotion to your words and behavior will increase the likelihood that people will remember what you say and act on it. Consider how you will share your enthusiasm with others rather than locking it away and assuming that expressiveness is somehow unprofessional or not lawyer-like.

Of course, none of these suggestions about being positive and more expressive will be of any value whatsoever if you don't believe in what you're saying. You can't just put on an act or performance for very long; your enthusiasm must be sincere and authentic. If the vision is someone else's and you don't own it, you will have difficulty enlisting others in it. If you have trouble imagining yourself being part of the future described in the vision, you certainly will be unable to convince others that they ought to sign up for making it a reality, and if you're not truly excited about the possibilities, you can't expect others to be. Most of the meaning of a lawyer's professional life is derived from their service to clients and causes.

CHAPTER HIGHLIGHTS

- Leaders inspire a shared vision by enlisting other people to achieve a dream of the future that serves more than themselves.
- Leaders need buy-in from followers to take a vision from a singular idea to a shared aspiration.
- Inspiring a shared vision includes envisioning the future and getting others to see in that future the realization of their own long-term interests.
- Leaders who envision the future are always forward-thinking, and the process to get to that end includes not only looking forward but also looking behind and incorporating the present.
- Leaders enlist others by crafting a compelling mental image, listening deeply, showing how followers can make a difference, touting the unique aspects of the vision, and exhibiting energy and positivity.

CHAPTER 5

Lawyer-Leaders Challenge the Process

"Developing learning only happens outside of your comfort zone, by doing things that you don't already know how to do."

Lawyers make their living by challenging processes, rules, and the actions of others. They advocate for clients, and often for themselves, by taking on the government, corporate interests, employers, and others in positions of power and influence. Lawyers frequently challenge the status quo for the benefit of their clients. Lawyers in leadership roles must, like leaders in other contexts, challenge the processes and influences that confront their law firms, nonprofit organizations, and government offices or agencies. Of course, leaders challenge not simply for the sake of stirring things up, making waves, or rocking the boat but for something better—for example, an improved legal rule or policy or a fairer outcome for the affected parties. Leaders, as well as lawyers, are at the front lines of seeking change and improvement and securing justice.

The recurring nature of change and challenges to the current way of doing things requires lawyers leading law organizations to be flexible, creative, and responsive. Recent technological advancements in law practice, from artificial intelligence (AI) to blockchain, have begun to transform how legal services are delivered. Lawyers' clients are facing similar transformational challenges in their fields.[1] Similarly, litigation finance is a fast-growing industry, allowing parties to fund their legal cases through external investors and funding sources, and it can expand access to justice, help spread risks associated with litigation, and incentivize resorting to alternative means of dispute resolution. These trends threaten the current way of practicing law but at the same time provide enormous potential benefits and opportunities for law firms prepared to master them.

Challenge the Process includes *seizing the opportunity to improve* and *experimenting and taking risks.* Leadership is about more than maintaining the existing conditions or doing what everyone else is doing. Leadership happens when you actively look outside job descriptions and venture beyond current limits, standards, and norms to find innovative ways to improve.

This demands a willingness to experiment and fosters taking risks, where the outcomes are focused as much on learning as they are on results. "Nothing ventured, nothing gained" is the leaders' mantra because the only people who don't make mistakes are those who don't attempt anything new, different, or better. When managers and coworkers are asked to designate their most effective leaders, their responses are closely related to how frequently these people engage in the leadership practice of Challenge the Process.[2]

SEIZING THE OPPORTUNITY TO IMPROVE

Nothing stifles creativity and innovation more than accepting the axiom "If it ain't broke, don't fix it." Something always needs fixing. Opportunities for improvement exist in every organization, law firm, community, school, and home.

Taking on a new job or assignment is an ideal opportunity to ask probing questions and challenge how things have always been done. Those are the times when you should ask, "*Why* do we do this?" But don't just ask this when you're new to a job or assignment; make this one of your everyday inquiries. Treat every day as if it were your first day. Routine is too often the enemy of great, leading to ruts and paralysis by analysis. Ask yourself, "If I were just starting, what would I do differently?"

These are tough questions that do not have easy answers. Ask the lawyers leading law firms, corporate counsel offices, and district attorneys' offices when the 2008 recession impacted the legal community (and many others) with depressed revenues, layoffs, downsizing, and strong new competition from non–law firm competitors. Clients pulled back legal business, and firms jettisoned recently hired lawyers. The period was defined by increased commodification of legal services, sweeping changes in technology, poor management decisions, and other disruptive forces at work in the legal services fields.[3] Those economic, social, and professional factors created a situation akin to a new job or assignment, requiring great leadership and management actions and initiatives by lawyers leading those impacted organizations. Some failed, but many found ways, as a result of their leadership, to seize the opportunity to adjust and improve, thus stabilizing their organizations and positioning themselves for success. Similar phenomena were experienced during the coronavirus pandemic and accompanying economic and societal turmoil.

Be Proactive

While external factors contribute to change—often in unanticipated ways—this does not mean that you should wait for something to happen that upsets the proverbial apple cart; you must proactively seek opportunities to improve. Proactivity consistently produces better results than reactivity or inactivity.[4] In shadowing senior executives, researchers discovered that the most successful were not waiting for information to come to them but rather were out and about gathering knowledge so that they could understand what to do next.[5] Furthermore, research indicates that people who rank high in proactivity are considered to be the most effective leaders. For example, in assessing their peers, high marks for proactivity were given to those who were most often engaged in extracurricular and civic activities targeted toward bringing about positive change—and they were rated as better leaders.[6]

Proactivity involves making something happen when you notice or find out about something that isn't working—creating a possible solution for the problem, gaining buy-in from constituents, and implementing the desired outcome. Ask your colleagues what really bugs them and what gets in the way of them doing the best job possible. Take time to periodically wander around your workplace or community and look for things that don't seem right. As they say in basketball, none of the shots you *don't* take ever go in the hoop. You must make something happen—to shoot the ball—to score some points.

The work of one junior associate with a national law firm exemplifies proactivity. She saw ways that the firm could improve when developing young talent. She drafted a seventy-some-page handbook for junior attorneys to follow in their early, often difficult, days at the firm. The practical guide bridged the gap between graduating from law school and assimilating into law firm practice; importantly, it became a model for communication between partners and the firm's newest attorneys on how to integrate their skills and perspectives into the law firm. Her initiative in creating the handbook also led to better work assignments for her on law firm deals as other lawyers realized how her resourcefulness helped the firm integrate new talent. Similarly, young lawyers have reported higher satisfaction with their legal employer if they have been permitted to take on additional (and often nonbillable) activities for the firm (such as management roles and tasks in representing the firm).

Although proactivity is a critical factor in finding challenges, it's not so important whether you find the challenges or they find you. What's important is whether you are proactive in dealing with challenges when they arise. When opportunity knocks, will you be willing to open the door?

Pinpoint Motivations

Part of the answer to opening that door or not is knowing what motivates *you* to do your best, day in and day out. Meaning and purpose motivate people not only to deal with life's challenges and uncertainties but also to actively seek change and overcome the general tendency toward homeostasis. The research evidence is well established that if people are going to do their best, the task or project they are engaged in must be intrinsically motivating.[7] When it comes to excellence, it's definitely *not* "what gets rewarded gets done"; it's "what *is* rewarding gets done."

Our experience with law firm junior associates is that they are, by and large, a highly motivated group. Surveys show that "solving complex problems," "making a difference in my community," and "helping others who don't understand the complexities of law" are frequent reasons why people decide to go to law school and become lawyers.[8] They like challenges and are willing to put in the work necessary to meet them, both for themselves and their clients. This desire to make a difference, within the firm or outside of it, is a common attribute of young lawyers in all different firm sizes and types.

The desire for challenges actually looms large in all groups of people. Researchers have conducted intensive studies to explore the nature of activities that contain rewards within themselves.[9] Findings show that people enjoy their chosen activity because of the pleasure they derive both from the experience and from using their skills; extrinsic rewards such as power, prestige, and glamour were ranked least important as motivators. Researchers have concluded that for a task to be rewarding in and of itself, "it seems that its most basic requirement is to provide a clear set of challenges."[10] People who justify their employment solely on economic grounds seldom contribute more than the minimum.

Routines are often the antithesis of challenge—and change. So are established procedures and demands—all those memoranda, telephone calls, reports, meetings, plans, documents, and emails. You can get so busy in the day-to-day details of your work that you become ensnared in an activity trap, where you are very busy but not making much progress toward anything meaningful. Also, given the process in litigation where cases, especially large cases, can take years to resolve, associates often do not get to experience the beginning-to-completion of a matter. They can lose out on feeling any sense of accomplishment and purpose.

Use Outsight to Achieve Innovation

If you are going to detect opportunities for challenge (and change!)—before those opportunities wither, become demands, or create huge problems—you must use your *outsight.* Outsight is the sibling of insight, and it means seeing beyond yourself and your individual perspective to perceive external realities more clearly. Without outsight, innovation cannot happen. Insight without outsight is like seeing clearly with blinders on—you just won't get a complete picture.

Studies into how the brain processes information suggest that to see things differently and more creatively, you have to bombard your brain with things it has never encountered. Neuroscientists explain that novelty is vital because the brain, which evolved for efficiency, routinely takes perceptual shortcuts to save energy. Only by forcing yourself to break free of habitual thinking patterns can you get your brain to recategorize information.[11] Consider the practice of "associating," which involves making connections across "seemingly unrelated questions, problems, or ideas."[12] Consider how you might stir imagination by starting a discussion with your law firm colleagues about how Disney would handle your client relationships or how your recruitment and onboarding programs would be developed by Southwest Airlines. While a serious lawyer may think this would be a whimsical approach in their firm, it is not so if done with the purpose of generating ideas about imagining what change could look like.

Relatedly, a key factor in finding meaningful solutions to challenges is the ability to look around and see your environment in new ways that expose openings for innovation. Inspiration can come from just about anywhere: clients, court rulings, contractors, clerks, research and development labs, support staff, disruptive technologies, seminars, competitors, opposing counsel, and so on. The point is that there is no shortage of sources for possible ideas. You must find ways to keep in touch with trends in your discipline and professional and industry marketplaces, with the viewpoints and perspectives of people from a variety of backgrounds and functions, and with ongoing social, political, technological, economic, and artistic changes. Do more than just meet the minimum, annual "continuing legal education" requirement for your jurisdiction; rather, take on the continuous improvement and development process that marks membership in a "learned profession." Be sensitive to even the fuzziest sign or weakest signal that something possibly new, novel, unusual, unfamiliar, and even strange is on the horizon.

In the legal business, skills at innovation and an "innovator's mindset" have allowed lawyers to seize opportunities to improve. These skills and mindset have permitted law firms to improve client relations, enhance attorney performance, create programs to increase diversity and inclusion, and institute other positive changes in how the law is practiced. Faced with a highly uncertain economic terrain coming out of the 2008 recession, law firms looked to innovation and creative thinking to spur changes in their use of technology, adding value to their clients' business and building the firm's strengths in the face of disruptive change. A good example of this mindset is the financial services group leader who studied the emerging field of cryptocurrency and blockchain, realized its roots in financial services and regulatory work, and persuaded the firm to open a new practice area, one of the first in the country. Similarly, the COVID-19 pandemic raised interesting and difficult questions about the future of appropriate locations for legal work (at law firm offices or remote) for law firm leaders.

Outsight is essential. As the managing partner of one national law firm explained, "While we don't know exactly what the legal profession will look like in five years, there's a growing sense that it won't look like it does today."[13]

EXPERIMENTING AND TAKING RISKS

For innovative processes to be successful, leaders must be comfortable with experimentation, which by definition involves risk taking. Learning only happens outside of your comfort zone, by doing things that you don't already know how to do (or do as well as you could yet). Risk is the chance or probability of something bad happening; you will be harmed or adversely affected if you take an action. Doing something new, because it has an uncertain outcome, brings some degree of risk. Still, as it is said, "nothing ventured, nothing gained," so leaders approach challenging the process with an experimentation mindset.

Achieve Small Wins

Innovation is often viewed as boldness, but boldness is not necessarily about go-for-broke, giant-leap projects. More often than not, it is about starting small and gaining momentum. Change conceived of too boldly or broadly can be so overwhelming that you can't figure out where or how to get started. It can defeat your capacity to even imagine what might be done and actually dampen motivation to do anything. Small, visible steps are much more likely to lead to early victories than big-bang efforts.

Consider the example of Ruth Bader Ginsburg, who, throughout her career as a lawyer, law professor, and jurist, continued to take risks, particularly on behalf of women in law, employment, and society, in pursuit of her ideals of equality and fair treatment. By breaking down each of the barriers in front of her, she worked her way, small win by small win, to her exalted position on the U.S. Supreme Court, where she could really make a difference for her lofty goals.[14] Similarly, banking and tax attorney Clarence Jones left his lucrative career to join the legal team for Dr. Martin Luther King Jr. By representing King in various legal challenges and embracing King's inspiring messages, Jones dedicated his legal career to many small but transformative wins for those seeking equality of treatment in the American legal system. Like many lawyers involved in public interest lawyering, Jones was able to use his technical legal knowledge and skills to achieve social change.[15]

Research confirms this concept of small wins leading to big changes. The long-standing understanding within scientific and academic communities is that major breakthroughs result from the work of scores of researchers, as countless contributions finally begin to add up to a solution. Researchers have shown that the sum total of all the "little" improvements in technology, regardless of the industry, contribute more to a substantial increase in organizational productivity than all the great inventors and their inventions do.[16]

This is also the case for individual change, as a small and unobtrusive nudge in the right direction of small actions can lead to long-term shifts.[17] To get people to *want* to change how they're currently headed, you need to nurture an experimental attitude and begin with a one-step-at-a-time approach, where each success builds people's commitment to pursuing a course of action. When you break big problems and projects into small, doable steps, getting people to say yes becomes easier.

This incremental change process has been called "small wins."[18] Small wins form a consistent pattern of accomplishment that attracts people who want to be allied with a successful venture, which builds their confidence and reinforces their natural desire to feel successful. Since additional resources tend to flow to winners, a small win means slightly larger steps or wins can be attempted next. A series of small wins contributes to constructing a stable foundation on which bigger risks can be taken, with each win providing information that facilitates learning and adaptation. This simple strategy of winning step by step succeeds more often than massive overhauls and gigantic projects. It's not just that it's easier; it's also because personal and group commitment is built in the process. Consider this in the context of planting trees. Planting one tree won't stop climate change, but planting one million trees, one at a time, can make a significant difference. Planting that first tree gets things started. The visible success shows others that they, too, can plant a tree and make a difference. Lawyers who built their own law firms from scratch did so one client or case at a time until they achieved a sustainable, profitable business.

Small, incremental, and consistent steps forward have a significant impact on both people's motivation and their self-confidence.[19] When people don't feel overwhelmed by a task, their energy goes into getting the job done instead of wondering, "How will we ever solve that issue?" Finding all the small ways in which people can succeed at doing things differently makes people want to be and stay involved.

Ensure Psychological Safety

Of course, when you experiment, not everything works out as intended. Mistakes and false starts are a natural and necessary part of the process of innovation and leadership. This means that as a leader, you have to make it "safe" for your followers not to feel they must get everything 100 percent correct the first time. Without feeling sufficiently safe, people will be unwilling, even unable, to experiment and take risks.

The idea of "psychological safety" is not a personality factor but a workplace characteristic—a hallmark of effective leadership and a highly functional workplace. Psychological safety exists in an environment where mutual trust and respect nurture candor and a sense of obligation to communicate when there are disagreements as well as opportunities.[20] It exists where people believe that if they make a mistake or ask for help, their colleagues will not think less of them, pick them apart, or ridicule or punish them.

Fear inhibits venturing outside of one's comfort zone and inhibits information sharing, asking for help, and experimenting. Due to fear, people remain silent even when they believe they have something to say that has the potential to add value. People do not do their best when they are afraid: research in neuroscience shows that fear consumes physiological resources, impairing analytic thinking, creative insight, and problem solving.[21] This situation has been likened to the difference between playing not to lose (avoiding losses) and playing to win (seeking gains).[22] Playing not to lose is a mindset that consciously or subconsciously focuses on protecting against the downside (i.e., embarrassment, ridicule, security) and thus necessarily involves fear. Playing to win, alternatively, is focused on the upside (i.e., seeking opportunity); although it involves taking risks, the environment is encouraging rather than fear inducing.

There is substantial empirical evidence that psychological safety matters both personally and organizationally, affecting everything from employee error reporting to return on investment.[23] A multiple-year study of over 180 teams at Google found that psychological safety was the critical factor in explaining why some teams outperformed others.[24] Similarly, a study involving more than 20,000 people worldwide indicated that when employees felt safe, there was a 347 percent increase in the probability of highly engaged employees, a 154 percent increase in great work, and a 33 percent decrease in moderate to severe burnout.[25]

Psychological safety for lawyers in law practice is particularly challenging since there is often a prevailing ethos of perfectionism, required autonomy over their work, and a reluctance to admit that a party in a case or a legal ruling has you stumped.[26] Fear of retribution or embarrassment inhibits many young lawyers, who then become afraid to admit their limitations to peers and supervising lawyers, which blocks their creativity and fosters mediocrity and complacency by those associates. The best law firm leaders are cultivating psychological safety among their young talent for greater workplace satisfaction, higher associate retention, and an all-around better work environment. One young associate relayed a story about an important moment in her career and credited a partner who made the difference. She received a call at home one evening from a partner leading a major transaction, and he asked if she would be willing to join his team. He added, however, that he realized she was a relatively new mother and had already been tasked with a few complex and time-consuming recent transactions. He assured her that she, not he, would make the decision on her joining the team and that there would be no repercussions if she declined. For her, it made all the difference in her relationship with him and the practice group because he "had her back."

Given its importance, leaders must be vigilant in creating psychological safety in their offices and workplaces. One strategy is to ask questions that invite participation and are especially directed at specific people who might not otherwise speak up (perhaps due to structural or cultural reasons). In asking questions, you create a space for others to contribute their thinking. This conveys your interest in their perspective and respect for their opinions. Show a genuine interest in what others are saying by asking them to tell you more about their thinking and experiences: "Can you say more about that?" or "Can you give an example?" Show appreciation rather than judgment for people taking risks; for example, say, "Thank you for speaking up about this matter [or option]."

Another strategy is asking questions to address what might motivate people's reluctant silence and possible defensiveness. For example, don't ask, "What mistakes did people notice when we did XYZ?" Instead, consider reframing the question: "Did we do everything as well as we could have when we did XYZ?" Test for consensus rather than assuming that silence means agreement: "Who has a different perspective?" or "What might we not be taking into account?"

Finally, you can promote a "humble mindset" among your colleagues and within team meetings by focusing on what can be learned rather than simply what didn't work and who might be to blame.[27] This means being willing to acknowledge your own fallibility and shortcomings. According to researchers, assuming a modest level of goodwill in your organization means that "most of the time your colleagues will respond well to genuine expressions of vulnerability and interest."[28]

Learn from Mistakes

There's no denying that change and leadership involve taking risks—and that when you engage in something new and different, you will make mistakes. Everyone does. That's what experimentation is all about. There are many trials and errors that occur when testing new concepts, methods, and practices. Keep in mind, though, that few mistakes are fatal—and success typically comes from quickly learning from experience and fixing mistakes rather than being able to get things perfectly right at the start.

Telling yourself to "get it right the first time" is a ridiculous standard to set because you won't. What's truly paralyzing about the too-often-voiced notion that "failure is not an option" is that it substantially increases the pressure never to experiment, veer outside one's comfort zone, or do anything risky. The fears and anxieties produced by this perspective are magnitudes greater than those experienced when your attitude is that the only way to succeed is to try. The real issues before you are, "How fast can you learn?" and "How quickly can you learn from your mistakes and failures before you get it right?"

Taking a page from the military's AARs (After Action Reviews) and health care's MMRs (mortality and morbidity reviews), consider how you and your colleagues can conduct a rigorous, systematic, collaborative, and transparent review of what happened (be it in the organization, in jury selection, in evidence preparation, in closing remarks, etc.) for the purpose of learning and to examine areas of improvement. A well-known plaintiff's lawyer in the Midwest, after learning that a federal appeals court had rejected a $35 million verdict in a major case involving sophisticated computer software, responded to a question from a young lawyer about his disappointment by observing that he had "never retried a jury trial without getting a bigger verdict on retrial." And he did.

The personal-best leadership case studies are testimony to how mistakes, setbacks, and even failures have played a role in leaders' eventual successes.[29] Without them, there would have been little to no learning, and leaders would have been unable to realize their aspirations or achieve momentous breakthroughs. Many reported that the overall quality of work improved when people had a chance to be tested, and possibly even fail. Regardless of the field or profession, studies consistently show little success without the possibility of failure.[30] This is reflected in the words of American author, entrepreneur, and humorist Mark Twain: "Good decisions come from experience. Experience comes from making bad decisions." The objective is never about deliberately making a mistake; the focus is on learning, and if you never do anything different from what you've always done, then learning (as evidenced by growth and development) simply doesn't happen.

Embrace a Growth Mindset

Unless you are willing to try something you have never tried before, you won't ever know what you can do. Let's say you are doing something right now that you know how to do. Then, someone comes along and suggests that there's a better way. Your initial reaction might be, "Well, that's okay, but the way I'm now doing it works well enough, and I'm comfortable doing it this way." You could continue with the status quo, but you need to realize that this is not how learning or progress happens. You can only learn and move forward when you experiment and experience doing something different from what you already know how to do well. Therefore, the best mindset for a leader is a growth mindset: "I don't know how to do this now, and I would like to be able to."

A growth mindset is a belief that people's basic qualities can be improved and strengthened through their intentional efforts—in contrast to a fixed mindset, which presumes that people's qualities are inherent and carved in stone. With a growth mindset, you believe that you (and other people) can learn to be better leaders, while those with a fixed mindset think that no amount of training or experience will make anyone much better than they already are.[31]

Those with a growth mindset embrace learning opportunities. Clinical education courses in law school allow students to learn essential lawyering skills and attitudes on the job. Skills development programs offered by bar associations and organizations such as the National Institute of Trial Advocacy, where young lawyers can experiment with behaviors under the guidance of skilled and experienced lawyers, are equally valuable. These programs provide opportunities for young lawyers to attempt the tasks that lawyers perform—preparing motions for summary judgment or voir dire examination of a witness, for example—and try out the comportment of being a representative of and advocate for clients.

Research has shown that individuals with a growth mindset demonstrate great tenacity and perform better when working on simulated business problems than those with a fixed mindset.[32] Other studies have shown that people with a growth mindset are more willing than those with a fixed mindset to embrace challenges, persist longer when facing obstacles, and sustain efforts even when confronted with resistance. These studies show that those with a growth mindset have a greater propensity to support experimentation and, unlike people with a fixed mindset, are open to feedback about their actions.[33]

Mindsets, not skill sets, make the critical difference in deciding to take on challenging situations.

Exhibit Psychological Hardiness

Uncertainty and risk come with any effort to improve matters and improve the status quo. What's critical is how you view change. In particular, psychologists have reported that people who experience a high degree of stress and yet cope with it positively have a distinctive attitude toward stress, which they call "psychological hardiness."[34] Psychological hardiness contributes to resilience, the ability to process stress so as to quickly bounce back (or, better yet, forward) from adversity.

In groups as diverse as lawyers, corporate managers, entrepreneurs, students, nurses, working professionals, artists, and combat soldiers, those high in psychological hardiness are much more likely to withstand serious challenges and bounce forward from failure than those low in psychological hardiness.[35] It isn't the stress of uncertainty and challenge that makes people ill—rather, it is how they respond to stressful events.

Healthy responsiveness to stress is critically important for lawyers because they often function in a high-pressure environment with long hours, schedules outside their control (managed by others such as court administrators and judges), and tremendous uncertainty. Many professional surveys and studies have documented the strong degree of work-related pressures on lawyers and how this frequently contributes unfavorably to their well-being.[36]

Commitment, control, and *challenge* are the three key elements of being psychologically hardy. First, to turn adversity into advantage, you must commit yourself to whatever happens. You have to get involved and engaged and be curious. You can't sit back and wait for something to happen.

When you commit, you find something interesting, meaningful, or worthwhile in whatever you are doing. Second, you have to take control of your own life. You need to make every effort to influence what is going on. While your attempts may not be successful, you can't sink into powerlessness or passivity or feel like a victim. Nor can you engage in denial or feel disengaged, bored, and empty. Third, to be psychologically hardy, you need to view a challenge as an opportunity to learn from both negative and positive experiences. You can't play it safe. Personal improvement and fulfillment emanate from the continual process of getting engaged in the uncertainties of life.

During the coronavirus pandemic lockdown, it was evident that psychological hardiness played an important role in determining who best handled the crisis. There were many examples of how resilient individuals responded to adversity—being able to maintain hope and find meaning and a larger purpose in the various individual changes required despite the unfortunate pain, loss, and suffering. They made a personal commitment to do something, even something very small, to take control of what they could: they volunteered to help others, shifted their small businesses to serve a need for food or equipment, picked up groceries for the most vulnerable, or found ways to express appreciation to caregivers and first responders.[37]

CHAPTER HIGHLIGHTS

- Leadership is not about maintaining the status quo but about challenging processes, rules, actions, and decisions.
- Challenging the process includes seizing the opportunity to improve and a willingness to experiment and take risks.
- Leaders don't simply wait for external factors to drive change; they proactively seek out what needs change.
- Small wins lead to big changes.
- Mistakes are part and parcel of experimenting and taking risks, so leaders must ensure the psychological safety of their constituents.
- Leaders learn from mistakes, have a growth mindset, and exhibit psychological hardiness.

CHAPTER 6

Lawyer-Leaders Enable Others to Act

"Partners owe it to associates to get them experiences on the front line. Helping them transition from timekeepers to revenue generators."

Leadership is not a solo endeavor. As we noted previously, a revealing clue to determining whether someone is a leader is looking around and seeing if anyone is paying attention to them and following their lead (or advice). Personal-best leadership experiences are never achieved by the leaders acting alone.

Teamwork is as critical in law as it is in sports, and lawyer-leaders are the "captains" of the team. Their job is to enable others to act—by harnessing their colleagues' talents and resources while fostering collaboration and encouraging discovery—for the good of the team. Heidi Gardner of Harvard Law School explained the significance of these roles in the law firms she studied:

> In sports, teamwork and collaboration are essential to the success of each athlete and every team. Depending on whom you talk to, the practice of law may not be a contact sport. What is clear [though] is that clients are keeping score on how well their lawyers and their law firms work and play together. Moreover, judging from the perspectives of legal practitioners from small, medium-sized, and large national law firms, they all agree that teamwork and collaboration are critical elements to achieving better outcomes for their clients and ensuring the financial wellness of their firms.[1]

Many similarities are also apparent from reviewing orchestra conductors. Most musicians are at least as, if not more, talented with their unique musical instruments; in fact, the conductor cannot play all the instruments and will never play a single note. The orchestra members look to the conductor to lead, through a clear vision, with infectious energy and passion, and to ensure that the musicians feel significant and appreciated. The conductor, like the most effective lawyers, creates harmony by getting everyone to play together, working through what otherwise might be dissonance as a result of anyone being out of sync by performing independently.

Enable Others to Act includes *building trust, fostering collaboration,* and *strengthening others.* Leadership is never a one-person operation. It's a team effort. Leaders create an environment in which the people on their team, in their department, or in their program can do their work collaboratively. They know that for others to act their best, they must build trust, facilitate relationships, and strengthen people's competence and confidence. The effectiveness ratings of leaders, the data reveals, increase in direct proportion to how often their managers and coworkers report observing them engaging in the leadership practice of Enable Others to Act.[2]

BUILDING TRUST AND FOSTERING COLLABORATION

Trust is *the* central issue in human relationships. Leaders need to trust their followers, and followers need to trust their leaders and each other. Without such trust, leaders will be unable to foster collaboration both with and among their followers. Collaboration is necessary to enable others to successfully implement a shared vision. Quite simply, without trust, you cannot lead.

When it comes to trust, the responsibility for anteing up first rests with the leader. When any leader says, "Trust me," but their actions don't demonstrate that they trust others or they don't take the time to listen and show that they are willing to be persuaded, then trust neither blossoms nor flourishes. Trust begets trust. The truth is that trust comes first; following and collaboration come second. The feeling of "us" is built into the word *trust.*

Collaboration Requires Trust

Without trust, collaboration will not happen. People unable to trust the words and work of others end up doing all the work themselves, or they supervise work so closely that they become overcontrolling micromanagers. These actions damage trust because members of the team feel they are not valued, and developing or enhancing their skills and career path is unimportant. As a consequence of not trusting others, such leaders are seen as untrustworthy themselves—and so others don't want to collaborate with them. Psychologists find that peers are more likely to listen to and get along with individuals who are capable of trusting people than with those who view the world with suspicion and distrust.[3]

Studies in which people are told they can trust their peers and manager consistently show that their discussions and decisions are significantly more positive than are those from group members primed to expect that their colleagues cannot be trusted. Members of high-trust groups are more open about their feelings, experience greater clarity about the group's problems and goals, and search for more alternative courses of action. They report having more influence on outcomes, satisfaction with the interactions, motivation to implement decisions, and closeness as a team than those in low-trust groups.[4]

Although these studies involved simulations, the participants behaved and responded in the way they did as a consequence of simply being *told* that they could or could not trust one another. Their actions demonstrated that trust or distrust can emanate from a mere suggestion.

Believing that one can trust others, and be trusted in return, is a significant predictor of how people will behave. Consider the experience of a third-year law student with a highly engaging and rewarding legal internship at a Silicon Valley startup. The deputy general counsel was responsible for most of the day-to-day operations in the legal department, and he created a culture of collaboration among the attorneys and the interns. Regular meetings were arranged where lawyers and interns would check in with one another, update their current projects, determine whether they had capacity for additional projects, and share insights into how matters were handled successfully. The purpose of the meetings was not just to discover if everyone was working hard but also to create a collaborative, efficient, and professionally engaging workplace. As a result, "Everyone in the office felt trusted and was able to learn from one another."

Another illustrative example involves the senior partner in charge of the intellectual property (IP) practice group of a good-sized law firm. She explained that she regularly had associates who were working heavily on a transaction or project take the lead in calls with clients (often general counsel of the law department) and explain how the work was being done and respond to questions. In explaining this practice, she told us her rationale was twofold: "To get someone who was deeply involved in the legal matter to explain to the client how it was going and to show trust and confidence in the associate."

Building trust through reciprocal relationships is often challenging because lawyers generally rank fairly low on the charts for social ability and high on the charts for skepticism.[5] Another challenge emanates because law practice is often adversarial, and so lawyers are not always open to others' views, especially those of their opponents. Notwithstanding these constraints, lawyers with a leadership mindset must work on building trust in order to collaborate, not just because it is financially advantageous (e.g., it reduces the costs of dispute resolution) but also because it is beneficial to clients and the "right" thing to do.

Demonstrate Trustworthiness

People say someone is trustworthy whose words and promises can be counted on, and people demonstrate trustworthiness in any number of ways. For example, trustworthiness is evident when you pay attention to what others are saying, consider alternative perspectives, draw on people's abilities, afford opportunities to make choices, and provide influence over the group's decisions. Nurturing openness and involvement, conveying empathy and compassion, and helping others address their concerns and solve their problems show trust. Such actions confirm people's belief that they can rely on you to do what's in everyone's best interests (not just your own!).

In fact, showing concern for others is one of the clearest and most unambiguous signals of your trustworthiness. For instance, you might volunteer to collaborate with people who are having difficulties completing an assignment, or arrive early to a meeting to greet everyone and inquire about how they are doing, or take the time to coach people who are taking on new jobs and responsibilities. When others know that you will put their interests ahead of your own, and they see this in your actions, they won't hesitate to trust you.[6] When people believe that you have their interests at heart—that you care about them—they're more likely to feel that they can talk freely with you about their aspirations, as well as their challenges. One managing partner told us that his job was "associate development"—that is, making sure they have experiences with clients and first-rate work products, and to help them transition from timekeepers to revenue generators.

A particularly salient way to show your concern for others is to actively listen to them. The more people feel that you listen to them and understand their feelings and perspectives, the more favorably they will feel about their relationship with you and the more likely they will be to trust you and be open to your influence. Studies reveal a strong empirical relationship between how people feel about their workplace and the extent to which their leader actively listens to diverse points of view.[7] Typically, in a high-stress work environment, such as a law firm, there is a tendency for people to listen for the least amount of information they need to complete a task so that they can quickly move on to the next assignment. Practicing active listening affords a deeper level of understanding, tapping into not just what the other party is saying but also attending to a host of nonverbal cues—for example, the tone, volume, and pacing of their speaking and their body language (facial expressions, gestures, eye contact, etc.).[8]

Some lawyers are simply not good listeners. Active listening, for example, is not asking your team members for input and then immediately responding back to them that the idea they put forward is unlikely to work or not relevant, or simply that you have a better idea. When your legal education has been based on criticizing ideas and coming up with counterarguments, these may be knee-jerk tendencies. When leaders and lawyers have this mindset and respond like this to their clients and associates, then people won't believe that they really want or care about their input, and they disengage. The situation becomes even more counterproductive when the leader assumes that a lack of input implies agreement or consent.

Active listening involves more than simply paying attention. The best listeners do much more than remain silent while the other person is talking.[9] They are focused on the other person and not on their own thoughts. Active listening is a conversation where both parties are more interested in trying to understand the other than in thinking about what they have to say in reply.

Active listening means asking questions that stimulate discovery and insight; being engaged in a way that makes the conversation a positive experience, causing the person to whom you are listening to feel supported and valued; showing appreciation for others' unique viewpoints to demonstrate respect for them and their ideas; and being empathetic to what others are going through, which creates bonds that make it easier for people to accept your guidance and advice. Great listeners don't try to solve other people's problems per se but are willing to offer suggestions and perspectives. Some have described great listeners as "trampolines" in that one feels that they can bounce ideas off them.[10]

It's important to remember that both parties in a conversation have filters through which all communication flows. Listening skills are particularly important for lawyers in their many roles—as counselor, negotiator, advocate, and especially leader—because of their responsibilities to clients.[11] Being constantly in touch with personal filters is critical to accurately communicating—especially with individuals and team members who have backgrounds and experiences different from yours. You will need to work through your own filters (and implicit biases) and appreciate the cultural identity lens of the other people involved when gathering input (verbal and nonverbal) about their interests and needs.

Collaborate for the Greater Good

Positive interdependence is the overriding mindset that facilitates trust and collaboration. It is the understanding that people have to rely on one another for their mutual success. With positive interdependence, everyone knows that it is the team's outcome that gets collectively rewarded and not merely each person's individual efforts. While each individual within a group has a distinct role, people on world-class teams know that if they only do their separate parts well, they are unlikely to achieve the group's goal. Positive interdependence nurtures the feeling that we're all in this together.

Lawyers frequently work in teams, so being a team player and understanding the leadership dynamic in building, serving on, and leading a team is a critical competence for lawyers. Fictional depictions of lawyers see them working in solo law practice settings, such as the iconic lawyer Atticus Finch in *To Kill a Mockingbird* or Perry Mason on the television show of the same name; and, to some degree, this may have been accurate at one time. But today, only about 10 percent of the lawyers in the United States practice alone, with another 32 percent practicing in firms of 2 to 100 lawyers.[12] Another 30 percent of American lawyers practice in government law offices and corporate law departments.[13] Teams, committees, practice groups, and other groups of lawyers make decisions about the firm or law department, serve on teams to service their clients, work with bar association and trade organization groups (like the American Law Institute), and participate on plaintiffs' or defendants' litigation teams in multidistrict litigation. Leading these groups and teams requires legal competence to be sure, but, more importantly, collaborative skills are essential.

Consider what was learned from a series of studies in which people were rewarded either for being the highest-performing team as a whole or for being on a team in which the rewards went to the highest-performing individual on each team. Though the latter (competitive) teams finished their tasks faster than the former (cooperative) teams, they were much less accurate, often simply because members withheld critical information from each other.[14] To boost the accuracy of these competitive teams, researchers had them complete a second task, where this time around, rewards would go to the entire team for high performance. Unfortunately, neither accuracy nor speed improved. People struggled to transition from competition to cooperation: once they had experienced their colleagues as competitors, they were no longer able to believe that they could trust them.[15] Completing even a single task under a structure that rewarded competition was enough to create win–lose mindsets, and these persisted even after the structure was removed.

Thus, the leader's responsibility is to make sure that the long-term benefits of working together are greater than the short-term benefits of working alone or competing with others on the team. In other words, you must ensure that people understand that by working together, they will be able to accomplish something that no one can accomplish on their own.

Organizational environments dominated by rainmakers and a culture of "eat what you kill" foster conflicts and disharmony, as also evident with hypercompetitive students who want to finish at the top of their class and tend to avoid participating in study groups or share resources. As we discuss in the context of building and leading teams, the set of outcomes associated with high levels of collaboration and positive teamwork is much more beneficial (for the lawyers and their firms) than legal workplaces lacking in those forms of interaction.

Leverage Reciprocity

When people collaborate for the greater good, norms of reciprocity permeate those relationships. In other words, there is a mutual, fairly equal give-and-take. If people know, for example, that you'll reciprocate, they realize that the best way to deal with you is to cooperate themselves and thus become recipients of your cooperation in return. Reciprocity leads to predictability and stability in relationships—in other words, trust. It's less stressful to work with others when you understand how they will behave in response, which keeps both relationships and negotiations from breaking down.[16]

The power of reciprocity in cooperative relationships is dramatically demonstrated in a well-known series of studies involving the Prisoner's Dilemma. As often dramatized on TV and in movies featuring police interrogations, two alleged lawbreakers are separated and confronted with a series of questions to which they must individually decide how to respond based on what they believe their colleague will say or do. There are two basic strategies: cooperate (don't say anything—i.e., cooperate with each other) or compete (blame the other party). And there are four possible outcomes based on the choices that they make: win–lose, lose–win, lose–lose, and win–win.

The maximum individual payoff comes for the person who selects a noncooperative strategy (i.e., places the blame on the other party) when their counterpart chooses to cooperate (i.e., to keep their mouth shut!). In this "I win and you lose" approach, one gains at the other's expense. While this might seem to be the most successful strategy—at least for the noncooperative player—studies show that it rarely proves to be successful in the long run, mainly because the other player won't continue to cooperate in the face of the first player's noncooperative strategy. This typically leads to both parties deciding not to cooperate (ratting out on each other), attempting to maximize their respective individual payoffs, which means that both lose in the end. However, when both parties choose to cooperate, both win, though in the short run, the personal payoff for a cooperative move (win–win) is often less than what it might be for a competitive one (win–lose).[17]

Dilemmas successfully solved by this reciprocity strategy are by no means restricted to the Prisoner's Dilemma. You face similar dilemmas every day, both personally and professionally. For example, if your spouse or partner is particularly busy and it's their turn to wash the dishes but you decide to do them instead, will they do the same for you next week when you are facing grueling deadlines? What are the long-term gains of inviting a colleague to coauthor a law journal article with you that you could just as easily submit as a solo author? Reciprocity turns out to be the most successful approach for even such daily decisions because it demonstrates both your willingness to be cooperative and an unwillingness to be taken advantage of. As a long-term strategy, reciprocity minimizes the risk of escalation: if people know that you'll respond in kind, why would they start trouble? Whether the rewards of cooperation are tangible or intangible, when people understand that they will be better off by cooperating, they're inclined to recognize the legitimacy of others' interests in an effort to promote their own welfare.[18]

Enhance Connections

In addition to reciprocity, another important factor in facilitating relationships and building trust is making sure that people feel connected to one another—and that these connections will endure. When people expect their interactions with one another to continue into the future—for example, they expect to run into one another at some event, continue to serve together on a contract or client litigation team for several years, or participate together on a subsequent task force—they are much more likely to cooperate in the here and now.

When you know that you have to deal with someone again, the consequences of today's actions on tomorrow's dealings are that much more pronounced. One of the enduring arguments made in lawyer civility training is that the lawyer you treated so poorly today may be on the hiring committee of a law firm you want to join or, worse yet, may receive a judicial appointment to a court you must appear in. In the end, enduring relationships, more than one-time or short-term ones, provide incentives to find ways to work together cooperatively to ensure mutual success in the future.

Consider ways that you can network with other lawyers in your workplace and cooperatively enhance opportunities to sustain those relationships over time. The relationships can often endure throughout your careers and provide a "network" of like-minded professionals whom you can count on when you seek a judicial appointment or a recommendation to a potential client. In this regard, it makes sense to remember the wise adage that "what goes around comes around."

STRENGTHENING OTHERS

While seemingly paradoxical, the most effective leaders are those who give their power away to others. That is, they don't make themselves strong by hoarding resources and keeping others weak, ill informed, and ill equipped, but they make those around them feel strong and capable. They listen to and credit others' ideas. They make sure that people do not feel left out of the loop when it comes to important decisions. They help colleagues feel ownership and a sense of responsibility for achievements. They enhance the competence and self-confidence of those they interact with. Law students uniformly tell us that the best thing about first-year study groups is that members challenge each other's research, thinking, and conclusions—but actively support and encourage one another in the process.

Traditional thinking promotes the archaic idea that power is a fixed sum; and, correspondingly, if you give away any of your power to others, you will have less power and be less powerful. Not surprisingly, people with this view hold tightly to the power that they perceive is theirs and are extremely reluctant to share it. This notion is wrongheaded and inconsistent with all the evidence on high-performing organizations.

When you give some responsibility to others, they become invested and passionate about the assignment because they own it. Feeling powerful—literally, feeling "able," which comes from a deep sense of being in control of life—they are better able to persist in their efforts to achieve. When you make other people feel powerful, in tangible and/or intangible ways, you are demonstrating profound trust in and respect for their abilities; this strengthens people's resolve not to let your trust and faith in them dissipate. Gallup surveys, involving millions of people around the world, decidedly show a close link between how powerful and engaged people feel at their workplace and their productivity, commitment, and retention.[19] Clearly, by strengthening individuals, leaders empower the entire organization.

Grant Choice and Discretion

The ability to make choices and exercise discretion is a key factor in what gives people the sense that they are powerful. Freedom is the ability to make choices. *Trapped* is the word that people generally use when they believe they do not have any latitude about how they can behave. When people feel stuck, they often act as rats caught in a maze, which, with no alternatives, typically stop moving about and eventually shut down. Having a feeling of genuine autonomy makes people powerful and increases their willingness to exercise their capabilities and meet their commitments more fully. Researchers have found that the perception of increased choice activates reward-related circuits in the brain, which makes people feel more at ease, enhancing their willingness to experiment and venture outside of their comfort zones.[20] Organizations are high performing when their employees are willing to work beyond their job descriptions. This happens when they have the latitude and discretion to make choices about both the work they do and how they do it. No one wakes up in the morning and gets excited about going to their workplace so that they can be incompetent and disruptive. People want to be responsible, productive, and self-directed; they want to exercise initiative. Constantly being told what to do by someone else and how to do it by some rulebook stymies these inclinations.

Furthermore, even if people think they know what needs to be done and feel they can do it, but they have to stop what they are doing and ask the higher-ups what to do, then the entire operation slows down. The only way to create an efficient and effective organization is by finding opportunities for people to use their best judgment in applying their knowledge and skills. Doing so is an explicit exercise in trust. There were abundant examples of how this worked during the coronavirus pandemic when, out of necessity, decision-making responsibilities were effectively pushed down to lower levels in the organization than ever before. Delegation generally demonstrates confidence and trust in another's capability, and providing stretch assignments also helps people develop and grow.

The experience of one third-year law student illustrates well the benefits of choice and discretion. He reported that in an internship with NASA's legal department, his supervising attorneys gave him broad discretion in creating "best practices" guidebooks, contract drafting handbooks, and communication guidelines for both the legal team's internal use and the office's correspondence with clients. "Through these actions, I was more heavily invested in creating deliverables that I could be proud of and that others would find beneficial." Trusting others paid more significant dividends than simply making the student feel valued—the benefits redounded to the entire organization.

Promote Accountability

With greater freedom of choice, the more personal responsibility people will accept.

Strengthening others necessarily entails people experiencing a greater sense of accountability. Accountability is a critical element in every collaborative effort. When people take personal responsibility and are held accountable for their own actions, their colleagues are more inclined to work with them. Specifically, the more that people believe that everyone is taking responsibility for their part of the project—and has the competence to do it—the more trusting and the more cooperative they will be. People will be more confident in doing their part when they believe that others will do theirs.

Furthermore, personal accountability is enhanced when the situation is structured so that people have to work collaboratively with one another. People are motivated to do well when they know that their peers are expecting them to be prepared and to do their job. The feeling of not wanting to let the rest of the group down strengthens each individual's resolve to do their best. The notion that you are accountable to others is a formative part of every attorney's professional identity.

Tellingly, the most frequent complaint about lawyers (right along with concerns about attorney fees and billing) is that they fail to communicate effectively with clients (such as being unreasonably slow to return calls or not doing so at all) and fail to keep their clients informed about the legal matter in question.[21] The source of lawyer malpractice claims are largely caused by rancorous attorney–client relationships and poor communications between the attorney and client.[22] Lack of accountability for these areas has reputational and financial consequences for attorneys and their firms.

Bolster Self-Confidence

But even if individuals are given the latitude to be accountable with choice and discretion to do something, it doesn't mean that they *will* do it. They may be reluctant to exercise their judgment because they lack the confidence to perform critical tasks in specific situations, fear making mistakes, or lack relevant information about the assignment.

Without sufficient self-confidence, people will not have the commitment required for taking on tough challenges. It's been said about would-be leaders that "it's hard to lead a cavalry charge if you think you look funny on a horse," and this humorous observation is supported by research. Lack of confidence manifests itself in feelings of helplessness, powerlessness, and often crippling self-doubt. In building your self-confidence and doing the same for those around you, you are bolstering what psychologists call *self-efficacy*—the inner strength necessary to forge ahead in uncharted terrain, face opposition, and make tough choices.[23] Self-efficacy is not a warmed-over version of the power of positive thinking. True strength comes from the self-confidence of knowing that someone expects you to succeed.

Research documents how self-confidence affects people's performance. In one study, participants were told that decision making was a skill developed through practice: the more they worked at it, the more capable they became. The researchers told another group of participants that decision making reflected one's basic intellectual aptitude: the higher their underlying cognitive capacities, the better their decision-making ability would be. Both groups worked through a series of problems in a simulated organization. Participants who believed that decision making was an acquirable skill continued, through several rounds, to set challenging goals for themselves, use effective problem-solving strategies, and promote organizational productivity. Their counterparts who believed that decision-making ability was inherent (i.e., you either have it or you don't) lost confidence in themselves as they encountered difficulties. They lowered their aspirations for the task in subsequent rounds, their problem-solving scores deteriorated, and organizational productivity declined.[24] Having confidence and believing in your ability to handle the job, no matter how difficult, is essential for positive end results.

Provide Skills and Knowledge, Training and Mentoring

As necessary as choice and discretion, accountability, and self-confidence are, they are insufficient by themselves to strengthen others. While you can communicate your confidence in others, people cannot do what they do not know how to do. This is where educational and developmental opportunities, along with access to mentoring and coaching, come in.

Without the knowledge, skills, information, and resources to do a job properly, people cannot, in fact, do that job proficiently. Providing increasing levels of responsibility and discretion requires an accompanying increase in training and development experiences, as well as the chance to learn on the job. For people to feel highly capable, they must continuously improve and develop their skills and abilities.

These are important reasons why some forward-looking law organizations emphasize the importance of leadership education and development for their lawyers, not just for their managing partners and practice group or office leaders. They are creating internal leadership development programs, often with the advice of consulting experts and former firm leaders but also by drawing expertise from business and law schools and private providers of leadership programming. Building leadership capabilities in early- and mid-career lawyers is often the primary objective of these programs because wise firm leaders know that this is the group from which future firm leadership will come.

Mentoring is another path toward improving competence and confidence. Mentors enable people to be their best by asking probing questions, providing constructive feedback, and modeling positive behaviors.[25] A three-year study of the impact of training revealed that high-improvement learners were four times more likely to indicate that they had mentoring conversations than individuals who showed little or no improvement.[26] In other words, improvement isn't merely about any particular or set of educational experiences; it's also the mentoring associated with those opportunities that matters. Unfortunately, research indicates that more than three out of five people promoted into frontline leadership roles report that they have never had a mentor.[27]

Being a mentor is not so much a job or position as it is a process—one that relies especially on an interpersonal relationship. The relationship doesn't need to be official or even formally acknowledged. You can mentor anyone if you have a sincere interest in helping enhance and enrich the other person's competence and confidence. Being a few semesters ahead in school, or a few years ahead in your legal career, often places you in a position to be more relevant, accessible, and available to your junior colleagues.

Law school students indicate that being mentored by an experienced judge or lawyer is one of the most important objectives of any clerkship or internship—even more significant than financial remuneration or academic credit. Another highly coveted position for law students is to serve as a professor's research assistant. Effective mentoring programs facilitate learning relationships so that you can acquire the skills, values, and professional judgment from those with more experience and wider perspective than you have. We've found that most lawyers are willing to be mentors, as they recall their own early years of working with a mentor, so they are eager to "pay it forward." However, we've also noticed a wide variance in their abilities and contributions in this regard. Keep in mind that it is unlikely that a single person can provide all the advice and counsel you might need. Consider several people, each of whom might provide wise counsel in different arenas. And mentoring programs are equally crucial for experienced lawyers.[28]

Law firms are increasingly creating mentoring programs for new lawyers to improve the likelihood of their retention and success. These are targeted generally for cohorts of young lawyers and, in particular, women, people of color, and LGBTQ individuals, who are most at risk of early departures from the firm. Often, these firms will ask associates who are progressing well in the firm to be paired with a new lawyer. Sometimes, the firm will permit new lawyers to request a particular partner or senior associate to serve as their mentor to help new lawyers navigate the complexities of law firm practices and social structures. Many of the most talented applicants for law firm positions will request information on mentoring opportunities and practices in the firm before agreeing to join the firm.

Coaching programs may supplement mentoring activities. In these relationships, usually between one attorney and a coach from either inside or outside the organization, what is explored are the behaviors and perspectives that advance (or constrain) progress, opportunities for professional growth and advancement, and the skills and attitudes needed for success and fulfillment.[29]

CHAPTER HIGHLIGHTS

- Leadership is ultimately a team effort.
- Building trust, fostering collaboration, and strengthening others enable people and groups to function most effectively.
- Trust engenders collaboration; collaboration will not happen without trust.
- Actively listening is an important way to demonstrate trustworthiness.
- A leader's job is to motivate others to collaborate for the greater good, encouraging norms of reciprocity and durable connections.
- Leaders who strengthen others bolster their own strength and that of their organization.
- Choice and discretion; accountability; self-confidence; and skills, knowledge, and mentoring are all factors that make people—and, in turn, their organizations—more powerful.

CHAPTER 7

Lawyer-Leaders Encourage the Heart

"Authenticity goes up when you get personally involved."

The chief counsel for a federal government agency made a point to set aside at least ten minutes in weekly team meetings to discuss the accomplishments of the individual lawyers as well as the support staff. The public acknowledgment of these contributions to the agency's mission, one young attorney told us, enabled "the lawyers and clerks to develop a sense of appreciation for one another, as well as the drive to continue succeeding, and motivated everyone in the agency to perform at the top of their game."

Encourage the Heart includes *expecting the best, getting close to people,* and *creating a spirit of community*. People need external inspiration and affirmation. Exemplary leaders are always there to help others find the courage they need to do things that they have never done before, and to recognize individual contributions and celebrate team accomplishments. In these ways, leaders figuratively give heart to others. The research from both managers and coworkers alike shows that the most effective leaders are those who most frequently engage in the leadership practice of Encourage the Heart.[1]

EXPECTING THE BEST AND GETTING CLOSE TO PEOPLE

Leaders must have high expectations, both of the people with whom they work and of themselves, because these expectations become the lens through which people view reality or the frames into which people fit reality. And to generate and communicate those expectations and form the bonds that motivate people to continue to meet those expectations, leaders must be out and about, getting close to others. This high-expectation mindset can be paradoxical for some lawyers because their work encourages them to be skeptical of their perceptions of people and legal situations; after all, they must anticipate risk and envision the multitude of ways things can go wrong, resulting in low expectations. Lawyer-leaders must be able to properly holster those traits and engage with their followers and constituents in a forward-looking and leading way.

Expectations shape how people behave, and there is ample empirical evidence that people act in ways that are consistent with the expectations that other people have of them.[2] People are much more likely to see what they expect to see, even when their perspectives differ from what actually may be occurring. If leaders expect people to be successful, they will treat them as if they are successful, and in this fashion, leaders' expectations trickle down to their followers. If you expect others to fail, they probably will. If you expect them to succeed, they probably will. Expectations also influence your own behavior as a leader. The high expectations that leaders have of others are based in large part on their expectations of themselves. This is one reason why it is so critical for leaders to Model the Way. Your own record of achievement and dedication and your daily demonstrations of what and how things need to be accomplished give credibility to your expectations of others.

Expecting the best of others manifests the greatest impact when leaders are out and about, getting close to other people. Without getting close to the people around you, how will you know them well enough to know what can be expected of them—and to communicate those expectations effectively? Without getting close to others, how will you give personalized feedback and advice to bolster and sustain the behaviors that meet expectations?

Expecting the best and getting close to people aren't hard to do, and you don't need to be seated on a hierarchical perch to do them. They cost you next to nothing and yet pay daily dividends. You can't ask for a better investment than that.

Treat People as Winners

Begin with the expectation that the people with whom you work are already winners. It's not that they will be winners someday—they are winners right now! If you believe people are winners, you will treat them that way.

Moreover, if you want people to be winners, you have to behave in ways that communicate to them that they are winners. It's not just about your words but also your tone of voice, posture, gestures, and facial expressions. No yelling, frowning, deceiving, heckling, or belittling. Instead, be friendly, positive, supportive, and reassuring. Admittedly, this can be challenging under high pressure and in stressful situations, underscoring how important this is to do.

To instill a winning attitude in people, treat them in a way that bolsters their self-confidence. For example, offer positive reinforcement, share lots of information, listen deeply to their input, give increasingly challenging assignments, and lend them your support and assistance. Research and everyday experience confirm that people with high self-esteem "feel unique, competent, secure, empowered, and connected to the people around them."[3] People are strongly influenced by leaders who believe in them and continually reinforce that belief through their actions and words. Feeling appreciated increases a person's sense of self-worth, which, in turn, precipitates success in both their professional and personal lives.

Positive expectations create positive images in the mind, which is where positive futures for self and others are first constructed. Unless you and others can see yourselves as being successful, it is tough to produce the behavior that leads to success. For example, people who had never participated in bowling were randomly assigned to different teams and instructed in effective techniques. Following these lessons, the bowlers were videotaped practicing. The teams were then shown selective portions of the videotapes: one team of the videotaped bowlers saw only the positive things they did; the other team saw only the negative. Those who saw only their positive moves subsequently improved significantly more than any of the bowlers on the other team, and they expressed the most interest in continuing with the sport in the future.[4]

In a series of studies, psychologists showed that by starting with the statement "I'm giving you these comments because I have very high expectations, and I know that you can reach them," the feedback they provided to their clients proved to be 40 percent more effective in subsequently changing targeted behaviors.[5] You can easily imagine what happens to participation in a meeting when every statement is criticized and ridiculed by those with the most seniority and position power.

Fortunately, legal education has moved away from the model provided by the fictional Professor Kingsfield in a novel about law school, *The Paper Chase*. Today, students benefit from considerable support from their schools in attempting to understand and adapt to the demands of law school and future entry into the legal profession. This same trend in treating the retention of junior lawyers as a return on investment for the law firm is seen in their engagement with professional development experts to assist with the maturation and growth of junior lawyers and improved formative assessment tools to measure associate performance. The old "look to your left and look to your right" approach to associate retention has firmly been replaced by a supportive, professional, and candid system for young attorney's development and retention.

The cycle of expectations and winning is a virtuous circle. When you believe in people's abilities, your favorable expectations cause you to be more positive in your interactions with those people, and those encouraging behaviors produce more winning results, reinforcing your belief that people can do it. What's really powerful about this virtuous circle is that as people see that they are capable of extraordinary performance, they develop that expectation of themselves and of the people around them, and another virtuous circle begins.

Establish Clear Standards

Positive expectations are necessary to generate high performance, but that level of performance isn't sustainable unless people are clear about the ground rules and expected outcomes. Without knowing the standards, assignments often just feel like busywork.

Clear standards give work a context, something that people believe they can work on together and be recognized for accomplishing. Standards help people keep their eyes on the target, focusing their attention and helping them ignore distractions.

Performance standards in law firms, especially large national firms, increasingly look to competencies that lawyers should be demonstrating in their work.[6] Firms identify the most important core competencies, or success factors, and then construct a system for evaluating the extent to which their lawyers are (or are not) meeting expectations. Commonly, these firms identify skills and traits such as legal excellence, client orientation, leadership, and commitment to business development.[7] On the other end of the spectrum, many smaller law firms do not have any systematic method of measuring associate performance, and, as a result, a critically important element of feedback is not available.

Seek Feedback

People need to know if they're measuring up to the standards or just marking time. The motivation to increase their productivity on a task *only* goes up when they have a challenging standard *and* receive feedback on their performance.[8]

Young lawyers will learn from their mistakes, but they learn more from positive interactions with senior lawyers as well as judges, opposing counsel, and others. While in law school, and as a new attorney, you sought information on how well, for example, you conducted a cross-examination of an expert witness or completed a draft of an SEC filing. Honest assurances about the quality of your work, or constructive criticism of your work product, are critical in developing your professional identity.

Unfortunately, feedback is not always forthcoming. Many senior lawyers or supervising attorneys were brought up in the "suck it up and just get your work done" era of law firm organization.[9] The most frequent complaint about internship and clerkship experiences is that little or no feedback was provided on projects that people worked hard to get right. The feeling, as many told us: "It's like the project fell into a black hole."

In a simulation of creative problem solving, participants were praised, criticized, or not given any feedback on their performance compared with how well hundreds of others had done. Those who heard nothing suffered as great a blow to their self-confidence as those who were criticized.[10] Clearly, no news has the same impact as bad news. One young lawyer wisely observed that "the fear of making teams complacent often leads senior lawyers to skip recognizing individual accomplishments, but in reality, the lack of feedback is highly counterproductive and diminishes morale."

Standards without feedback and feedback without standards have been shown to have little effect on motivation; however, together, they keep people on track. With clear standards *and* detailed feedback, people can self-correct and more easily comprehend their place in the bigger picture. You can no doubt remember how unnerving it was to go for months in a law school class without any feedback or sense of how well you were absorbing and comprehending the materials. While it is true that people might not always like the feedback (or, as students, the grade) they receive, being able to improve doesn't happen very easily without some sense of how they are doing now. With feedback, you can decide whether you are on the right track going forward and determine what help you need to be even more productive.

Get Out and About

Leaders must be out and about to provide timely and relevant feedback. They don't spend all their time in a cubicle, remain stuck behind a desk, glued to the screen, or fastened to some equipment. Leaders have to be mobile and visible. You have to get close to people and be curious about what is going on with them. This can be a challenge for lawyers, as they typically prefer more monastic or autonomous working situations.

Being out and about allows you to get to know others on a personal level and thus be more effective in how to provide feedback and determine ways to collaboratively work together most effectively. Since proximity is the single best predictor of whether two people will talk to each other, you have to find ways to get out of your office and get close to people if you're going to have any sense of what is going on with them. When you are working with colleagues in different offices or virtual workplaces, you have to make conscious efforts to spend time with people because they are not informally available to interact with.

You demonstrate that you care about others when you are *paying attention* to what they are doing as well as to how they are feeling. When you are clear about the expected standards and believe that people will perform as winners, you'll notice lots of examples of them both doing things right and doing the right things. When you pay attention to what's going on around you, especially with regard to how people are doing and feeling, you develop a sixth sense of what people need to know about how they are doing and are able to acknowledge and demonstrate empathy for their feelings and behaviors.

Another benefit of being out and about is increasing your visibility. As you get to know other people, they also get to know you. Paying attention and actively appreciating other people increases their trust in you. If people know that you genuinely care about them, they're likely to reciprocate and care about you. Furthermore, you can't improve as a leader if you're unable or unwilling to learn more about how your actions affect the behavior and performance of those around you—and you can't determine this if you aren't out and about and visible. Leaders who most frequently seek feedback, listen, and attend to it are significantly more likely to act fairly toward employees and be seen by their employees as acting fairly.[11]

You might be thinking that being out and about pushes against the oft-repeated refrains that leaders "shouldn't get too close to their people" and they "can't be friends with people at work." Well, set these myths aside! Over a five-year period, researchers observed groups of friends versus groups of acquaintances (people who knew each other only slightly) performing motor-skill and decision-making tasks. The results were unequivocal. The groups composed of friends completed, on average, more than three times as many projects and were more than 20 percent more effective in decision-making assignments than groups consisting merely of acquaintances.[12] Feeling a connection with others motivates people to work harder for the simple reason that people don't like to disappoint or let down individuals they consider to be friends. People stick around longer in jobs when they feel they have colleagues who know them and have their best interests at heart. People who report having a "best friend at work" are significantly more engaged, get more done in less time, have a safer workplace with fewer accidents, share ideas, feel informed, are innovative, and indicate having more fun on the job.[13]

There is an important caveat, however, in these findings. You and your friends have to be firmly committed to the group's goals. If not, then groups of friends may not do better. This is precisely why leaders must be clear about standards and create a condition of shared vision and values.

Personalize Recognition

People feel frustrated and seldom work to their capacity when their efforts and achievements are taken for granted. One benefit of getting close to the people around you is that it allows you to personalize rather than generalize both your expectations and appreciation. Of course, you have to do more than provide drive-by praise—you have to do more than simply walk around your organization or community saying, "Thank you, whoever you are, whatever you are doing." Realize that a one-size-fits-all approach to recognition feels disingenuous, forced, and thoughtless; and no matter how well-intentioned, over time these routines can increase cynicism. Because the most meaningful recognition experiences are personal, this requires that you get to know the people you are working with well enough to tailor the recognition to their needs, values, and aspirations. By personalizing recognition, you send the message that you took the time to notice an achievement, sought out the responsible individual, and delivered the appreciation in a timely, individualized manner. This kind of personal "touch" by a colleague or supervising attorney is particularly important to young lawyers who have excelled throughout much of their law school experiences and often link their success to the recognition and appreciation they receive from other people.

Don't make the mistake of assuming that people respond only to formal or monetary rewards; often, it's the simple, personal gestures that are the most powerful rewards. "A sincere word of thanks from the right person at the right time," researchers have noted, "can mean more to an employee than a raise, a formal award, or a whole wall of certificates and plaques."[14] In fact, personal congratulations rank at the top of the most potent non-financial motivators identified by employees.[15] (And an added bonus is that research has found that people who practice gratitude, as compared with those who do not, are healthier, more alert, more energetic and resilient, better able to cope with stress, and more successful.[16])

Creating a Spirit of Community

Human beings are social animals, hardwired to connect with others.[17] When social connections are strong and numerous, there's more trust, reciprocity, information flow, collective action, and happiness—and, by the way, greater wealth.[18] As we've maintained, leadership is all about relationships. Thus, a leader's job is to cultivate this spirit of community. Some of the most strategic methods for creating a spirit of community are providing opportunities for social support, making achievements public, establishing a fun environment, and prioritizing personal involvement.

Provide Opportunities for Social Support

Supportive relationships at work, characterized by a genuine belief in and advocacy for the interests of others, play a critical role in maintaining personal and organizational vitality. People just feel better about the work that they're doing when they enjoy the people with whom they're working. When people feel a strong sense of affiliation and attachment to those with whom they are working, they are much more likely to experience greater personal well-being and commitment to the organization, and they perform at higher levels.[19]

Research has consistently shown that performance increases in a socially supportive team atmosphere. In a study of twenty-five thousand call center agents, people were divided into two groups: one taking staggered breaks alone and the other taking breaks with their coworkers. In this latter group, those who had fifteen minutes to socialize and chat with colleagues had a 20 percent increase in performance over their peers who took breaks alone.[20] Furthermore, in top-performing teams, people give each other nearly six positive comments for every criticism. In medium-performing teams, this ratio diminishes to about two positive comments for every negative one. The ratio falls even more dramatically for the poorest-performing teams; members give nearly three negative comments for every positive one in those teams![21]

Likewise, motivation increases in an atmosphere that reinforces the feeling that "we are all in this together" because this makes the work environment a place where people want to be, stay, and work hard. An extensive ten-year study revealed that social support networks were essential for sustaining the motivation to serve. Service performance shortfalls in organizations were highly correlated with the absence of social support and teamwork.[22] Furthermore, service burnout decreases when coworkers support each other and share in mutual achievements because working with other people is not only enjoyable but also rejuvenating and inspirational.

The case for social support is further boosted by the fact that an exchange of information is more likely to be facilitated, whether in formal or informal interactions, when people like one another—and, of course, sharing information will bolster organizational success. Even in the age of social media, people are just more likely to share things when they're in a gathering with other people than when they're sitting alone at their workstations or on their mobile phones. When social support is lacking, individuals regularly ignore cooperative opportunities, as they distrust other people and their motives.

Social support is beneficial not only for organizations' bottom line but also for people's personal bottom line. Longitudinal studies in both the United States and Europe have found that people who make use of social support have higher incomes compared with those people who have not tapped into a social network. This was true both two and nine years after the study's baseline period.[23] This makes sense because people who feel distant and detached are unlikely to get much of anything significant done, and they will be compensated accordingly. It is worth speculating that this relationship between social support and financial success is a likely factor in the results of research involving more than three million people around the world, which found that social isolation is far worse for people's health than obesity, smoking, and alcoholism.[24]

Make Achievements Public

All over the world—in every country, in every culture, and in every organization and community—people stop working on certain days during the year and take the time to celebrate. Impromptu ceremonies are often convened to rejoice in a courtroom victory, making partner, the publication of a new marketing effort, the launch of a new service, the signing of a new contract, the opening of a new facility, the receipt of some civic or professional award, and the like. Banquets are organized to acknowledge individuals and groups who have accomplished the extraordinary. Colleagues get together with one another after working on an exhausting task force and give each other high fives for a job well done.

Why do people take time away from work to gather together? Sure, everyone needs a break from the pace and intensity of their jobs, but celebrating is not a frivolous excuse to goof off. Celebrations are among the most significant ways people have to proclaim their respect and gratitude, renew their sense of community, and remind themselves of their shared values and traditions. Celebrations serve as important a purpose in the long-term health of organizations and communities as the performance of daily tasks.

Performance improves when leaders bring people together to rejoice in their achievements. Recognition on an individual level increases the recipient's sense of self-worth, which improves performance—but public celebrations have this effect *and more.* Every time you can bring people together is a chance to renew commitment. Exemplary leaders in these gatherings and occasions seldom let pass the opportunity to make sure that everyone knows why they're all there and how they have been and will continue acting in service of that purpose.

Whether the occasion is to honor an individual, group, or organizational achievement, celebrations offer leaders the perfect opening to explicitly communicate and reinforce the actions and behaviors that are important in realizing shared values and shared goals.

By making achievements public, leaders build a culture in which people know that their contributions are not simply recognized but appreciated and valued. By making achievements public, leaders not only build an individual's or team's self-esteem but also enable others to vicariously experience a sense of accomplishment that allows everyone to feel part of one team. They provide a ready-made opportunity to reiterate shared values and common goals.

An important outcome of celebrations is reminding people that they are connected with others. Bringing people together in an atmosphere of trust, collaboration, and gratitude reinforces the fact that it takes a group of people working together with a common purpose to achieve the extraordinary. Such celebrations strengthen people's resolve to continue in times of turmoil and stress. In addition, celebrations are an opportunity to expose people to others in the organization with whom they do not usually interact. When celebrations cut across functional, hierarchical, and practice boundaries, people get a chance to exchange ideas with, and be stimulated by, people outside their own areas.

Because celebrating is not customary in many law firms, those that do happen take on special significance. Although celebrations should be enjoyable, entertainment should not be their primary purpose. Rather, their primary purpose is to create meaning. Celebrations must be honest expressions of commitment to fundamental values and appreciation for the hard work and dedication of the people who lived the values and achieved the standards. Elaborate productions that lack sincerity are more entertainment than encouragement. Authenticity makes celebrations not only fun but also purposeful.

Celebrations significantly affect how people feel about their organization and their leaders. On these occasions, it's vitally important to be clear about the behaviors that you want to reinforce. People will leave the event remembering and repeating what you say about what is being recognized and why.

Establish a Fun Environment

Leaders are on the lookout for every possible opportunity to inculcate fun into the work environment because fun isn't a luxury at work.[25] Every personal-best leadership experience was a combination of hard work and fun. In fact, most people agreed that without the enjoyment and the pleasure they experienced interacting with others on the team, they would have been unable to sustain the level of intensity and hard work required to achieve their personal best.

It has been said that "laughter is the best medicine." Neuroscientists agree and argue that laughter is really about social relationship and not so much about humor. The health benefits arise from the social support that laughter stimulates.[26]

Shifts in the psychological contract between employers and employees, workforce demographics, and the work itself are necessitating that people experience their organizations as places where they can do more than just work.[27] A fun work environment "intentionally encourages, initiates, and supports a variety of enjoyable and pleasurable activities that positively impact the attitude and productivity of individuals and groups."[28] Having fun sustains productivity, creating what researchers refer to as "subjective well-being" and contributing positively to affective, cognitive, and behavioral functioning of employees. In addition, studies demonstrate that having fun enhances people's problem-solving skills because fun makes them more creative and productive—which, in turn, fosters lower turnover, higher morale, and a stronger bottom line.[29]

In fact, fun and organizational success are deeply intertwined. The Great Place to Work Institute annually asks tens of thousands of employees to rate their work experience based on a number of statements reflecting workplace factors, including "This is a fun place to work." On *Fortune*'s 100 Best Companies to Work For list, which the Great Place to Work Institute produces, employees in the best organizations responded overwhelmingly—an average of 81 percent—that they are working in a "fun" environment.[30] Law firms regularly compete for "best place to work" recognition. They often tout their commitment to pro bono lawyering, wellness programs, mentorships, and support for associates, which reflects both the competitiveness of keeping top-notch talent satisfied and their efforts to enhance the work environment.

Prioritize Personal Involvement

When it comes to the leadership practice of encouraging the heart, in addition to providing opportunities for social support, making achievements public, and establishing a fun environment, it is essential that leaders be personally involved in order to create a spirit of community. Partners across several law firms reflected how a major part of their work was facilitating and promoting the success of their junior lawyers. They explained the goals of this effort in various ways: "To move the junior lawyers toward achieving partnership." "To turn them into exceptionally good legal tacticians and practitioners." "To help our associates achieve their own independence and competence on client development and financial freedom."

Often, being personally involved simply means making sure that you take the time and effort to "hang out" with the people you are working with, and extending yourself to others within your workplace office. One of the best ways you can show people that you genuinely care and that you appreciate their efforts is to be with them. Another way is to constantly be on the lookout for opportunities to "catch people doing things right," and this isn't done very well by staying behind a desk, counter, computer screen, or steering wheel. You need to see and know firsthand what's being done right—not only so that you can let individuals and teams know to "keep up the good work" but also so that you can tell others about the behaviors and actions that make a difference.

Telling stories about how people demonstrate their commitment to values is a compelling way to show your personal involvement, and it is one of the quickest and most effective ways to communicate how people are supposed to act and make decisions.[31] By sharing up-close-and-personal accounts of what it actually means in a real-time context to put shared values into practice, you create role models within your organization or community that everyone can relate to. And in this way, you make shared values come alive.

Storytelling accomplishes the objectives of teaching, mobilizing, and motivating better than bullet points in a slide presentation or tweets on a mobile device. Firsthand examples are more powerful and memorable than third-party examples (it's that striking difference between "I saw for myself" and "someone told me about").

Listening to and understanding the stories that you tell inform people more about the values and actions you most pay attention to than any company policy declarations or the employee manual. Stories communicate what really goes on within the organization. Well-told stories reach inside people, giving them an emotionally compelling way of learning what is really important about the experience.

Authenticity goes up when you get personally involved. You send a positive signal that you want others to be successful when you directly and visibly show them that you take the time to care and cheer them along. Moreover, you're more likely to see others take these same actions if you engage in them.

ENCOURAGE THE HEART: A COMPREHENSIVE FINALE TO THE FIVE PRACTICES OF EXEMPLARY LEADERSHIP®

Encourage the Heart is an appropriate final step in understanding The Five Practices of Exemplary Leadership operating system because it focuses on those who would follow you and how you make them feel valued in their relationship with you. However, it is important for another reason. Although each of The Five Practices is separate and distinct, there is overlap among them because they build on each other and often require many of the same leadership behaviors and foster similar positive sentiments and aspirations.

To Model the Way, leaders' high expectations of self are the basis for high expectations of others, as is true in Encourage the Heart. Furthermore, both practices feature setting an example, affirming shared values, and storytelling as leadership behaviors that engage followers.

To Inspire a Shared Vision, leaders must get out of their cubicles and listen to their followers, just as leaders must do to treat people as winners and express their gratitude to Encourage the Heart. In addition to Inspire a Shared Vision, leaders must exhibit energy and positivity, characteristics that certainly come into play when leaders make achievements public and establish a fun environment to Encourage the Heart.

To Challenge the Process, leaders must ensure psychological safety. This also features in the process of followers taking risks as they rise to meet expectations when leaders Encourage the Heart. Encourage the Heart comes into play in keeping people motivated through the small-wins process that is central to Challenge the Process.

To Enable Others to Act, trust and collaboration play key roles. To Encourage the Heart, leaders must get out and about to enhance followers' trust. Collaboration, connections, and reciprocity all play a role in creating a spirit of community and providing opportunities for social support. Furthermore, the choice and discretion, accountability, and self-confidence necessary to Enable Others to Act lay a foundation for the expectations needed to Encourage the Heart.

A similar case could be made for how Enable Others to Act requires providing opportunities to Challenge the Process, or how Challenge the Process makes the most sense when connecting with Inspire a Shared Vision, and so on. In sum, lawyer-leaders must engage in all five leadership practices not only individually but also in an intertwined manner. Together, The Five Practices of Exemplary Leadership create exemplary leaders who make extraordinary things happen.

CHAPTER HIGHLIGHTS

- Effective leaders show that they care by providing external inspiration and affirmation.
- By expecting the best and getting close to people and creating a spirit of community, leaders encourage the heart.
- If you treat people as winners, establish clear standards, and provide feedback, people will behave as winners.
- Encouragement is a personal form of feedback and strengthens trust within relationships.
- People who like the people where they work will stay at those jobs longer and be more successful and productive.
- To create an enjoyable work environment, provide opportunities for social support, make achievements public, inject fun into the mix, and prioritize personal involvement.

Part II

LAWYER LEADERSHIP IN ACTION: HOW AND WHERE LAWYERS LEAD

How is it that lawyers become lawyers who lead? In Part I, we addressed why leadership matters and when and how you can become a capable and effective leader. Moreover, that part of the book provides lawyers and their firms and law organizations with a blueprint, or as we refer to it, a model or operating system, to further the leadership development of lawyers and other professionals in your organization. Understanding and utilizing The Five Practices of Exemplary Leadership® framework provides you with a leadership operating system for being the best leader you can be.

In Part II, we take a look at leadership in action as lawyers. These five chapters examine the practice of being a lawyer—from individual associates and solo practitioners to managing partners and corporate counsels—and the exercise of leadership. The issues considered in these chapters are how lawyer-leaders create their professional identity as an ethical practitioner, make effective decisions, facilitate innovation, promote teamwork, develop emotional intelligence, handle adversity, and champion diversity, equity, and inclusion. Without question, those are the compelling challenges (and opportunities for distinctiveness) for today's law organizations.

CHAPTER 8

Personal Values and Professional Ethics as Lawyer-Leaders

"Can a good lawyer be a good person? Legal educators, lawyers, and professional ethicists often reverse this question and ask, 'Can a good person be a good lawyer?'"

You gain the title of *lawyer* by passing a bar examination, but the catalyst for becoming an effective, ethical lawyer is a transformational process you began in law school. This is where and when you learned new skills and abilities, honed existing ones, and integrated your personal value system with professional values. This transformation was accelerated as a new lawyer facing the challenges of being an entrepreneur, a businessperson, and charged with the well-being of your clients. This transformational process is the subject of new curricular focus in legal education toward recognition of the formation of a "professional identity."[1]

The process of forming a professional identity as a lawyer is essentially the same as the process of forming a professional identity as a leader. The two processes are not successive—they overlap. As a lawyer, regardless of your years of experience, nature of your practice, or hierarchical position, you *can* become, and be, a lawyer who exercises leadership.

PROFESSIONAL COMPETENCE AS LAWYERS (AND LEADERS)

People attracted to law school score well on standardized cognitive skills examinations (like the LSAT entrance exam) and have demonstrated academic success in their undergraduate studies. Admission to law school is highly dependent on both—a relatively strong score on a cognitive skills test and an undergraduate degree. However, neither of these factors has been shown to predict success as a lawyer, and some people have even questioned whether they significantly correlate with anything beyond grades in the first year of law school.[2]

What about the other skills, knowledge, and abilities that have been shown to predict both retention and success as a lawyer? Law students enter law school with some of these competencies and attributes associated with the probability of a successful law career. Still, even they have to be developed, honed, and tailored to the work of lawyering and the context of the law. Some of this development and training occurs in the modern law school curriculum, but most of it occurs in the first years of law practice through guidance and mentoring from more experienced lawyers and judges.

There are additional considerations, perspectives, and capabilities that shape the trajectory of a successful legal career, and you need to learn about and embrace these as early as possible in your legal career and even wherever you are right now in your journey of practicing law. You can learn how to play golf (or play chess, create ceramics, act, or write poetry) when you are in your forties, but you'll be much better off if you began to learn, and practice, when you were in your teens and twenties—and the same can be said for those engaged in the profession of law.

Lawyer Effectiveness Skills

Studies about the developmental process of new entrants to peer-reviewed professions (such as law, medicine, and engineering) show that every student in professional schools faces similar challenges. First, they must learn that profession's cognitive skills and abilities (i.e., knowledge about the profession and ways of thinking). Second, they must develop hands-on and real-world skills for being an effective professional in that field.[3] Third, they must internalize the norms and values of the profession. These three are foundational to successful entry into a professional field, requiring students' commitment to mastery and the preparatory professional school's commitment to providing learning and development opportunities (such as classroom activities, internships, mentoring, and coaching to assist students in acquiring these educational outcomes). This is how professional schools, including law schools, transform their students into competent practitioners.

In recent decades, many law schools have instituted courses to assist their students, commonly in their first year of law studies, in acquiring a clear understanding of what it means to think, act, and feel like a lawyer.[4] Many law firms and their professional development leaders have designed programs to assist their new lawyers in understanding and assimilating the demands and responsibilities of being a lawyer. To reach this point of personal identity as a law professional, students and new attorneys must understand and fully accept (1) their deep responsibility for the needs and requirements of their clients, employers, and the legal profession, (2) the development of sound professional judgment, (3) a commitment to their own well-being, and (4) "ownership" of their professional development throughout their careers. Developing an understanding of and competency in leadership is invaluable as part of the process of acquiring your identity as a lawyer who makes a difference.

How complicated is the effective, ethical practice of law? Surveys involving experienced lawyers who were asked "What is important for lawyers to be able to do?" reveal dozens of skills and behaviors that lawyers need to be effective as lawyers.[5] The list includes "technical" (or content) skills, like the ability to do legal analysis and reasoning, fact-finding, legal researching, speaking, and writing, all of which constitute a "baseline" for the practice of law. However, these pale in comparison, by a factor of nearly three to one, to critical interpersonal and organizational skills, which are typically associated with effective leadership—for example, influencing others, active listening, high levels of "emotional intelligence" and resilience, sustaining a passion and commitment to one's work, empathy, and continual self-development.

Such surveys of practicing lawyers and of law firm clients, asking about what lawyers need to be able to do, underscore the challenges to lawyers at every stage of their career.[6] Lawyers must be able to focus on and understand clients' business and legal needs, engage in sophisticated and creative problem solving, approach their work with an entrepreneurial mindset, manage projects, and be highly collaborative on teams and work groups. This extensive, and daunting, list of "necessary skills" to meet client and firm expectations should not be considered a superhero "leaps buildings in a single bound" role. Rather, these critical lawyering competencies, like the skills and behaviors of effective leaders, can be taught and learned by everyone who wishes to be at the top of their game, as a lawyer and as a leader.

Timetable for Acquiring Lawyer Effectiveness Characteristics

The long list of skills identified for an effective lawyer—most of which parallel the characteristics associated with effective leaders—can be intimidating and especially so to a law student and to any new lawyer. Like any new legal professional, you might wonder how soon you need to be able to do all of these after passing the bar examination. The simple answer is not immediately, but they can't be put off for too long if you expect to achieve both personal and professional success as a lawyer. Of course, some of them, such as analytical and writing ability, integrity and honesty, and a personal commitment to community service, are acquired (to some small or great extent, varying from individual to individual) prior to professional school. Many, such as persuasiveness and the ability to negotiate, are introduced and initially developed during professional school. Still others are more fully developed after becoming a lawyer, such as networking, business development, and mentoring. The important point right now is to determine how you can develop these skills in the formative stages of your life and career, or wherever you are in your career, because being a leader is not necessarily associated with a title (e.g., partner). The challenge is especially acute in the domain of leadership because the law school curriculum, and even the first few years as an associate, overwhelmingly emphasizes content skills (through classes and coursework) such as learning contract law doctrine, case analysis, and documentation.

Law firm leaders have additional demands on key management and leadership skills. A major law firm's chief talent officer described the essential skills and behaviors needed to lead law firms, as managing director or office or practice leader, as communication and people skills, such as relationship building and great listening abilities; emotional intelligence; the fundamental ability to persuade and inspire others toward a shared goal or future; the ability to drive execution; and "gravitas."[7]

Irrespective of whether these effectiveness factors are developed before, during, or after law school, lawyers must enhance and strengthen their abilities to demonstrate and use them. This is achieved through a process of personal and professional growth, which is based on a conscious effort to become an exceptional lawyer—and it is achieved in the same way, as discussed in Part I, for those lawyers who want to become exceptional leaders.

PROFESSIONAL IDENTITY AND VALUES

Using these professional effectiveness characteristics as a jumping-off point, how do legal employers, during the early years of new lawyers' "post-bar" development, assist them in forming their identities as lawyers and members of a profession? Following the publication of several influential reports on the state of legal education, the development of professional identity has become a required part of the foundational or core curriculum of law schools.[8] To the question of "What is *professional identity*, and how is it formed and shaped in students and young lawyers?" the answer is found in the integration of personal values with professional values. An important and very influential contributor to this discussion has been the Carnegie Foundation report entitled "Educating Lawyers: Preparation for the Profession of Law."[9] The report identified three "apprenticeships" necessary for the study of law and success as a lawyer: (1) substantive knowledge and analytical skills, (2) practice skills, and (3) ethical professional identity. The report argued that these are the central mission of legal education and, indeed, for the legal profession as it seeks to prepare its graduates for work in the legal profession.

This same framework provides the foundation for the legal profession and lawyer organizations' efforts at integrating new lawyers into the practice of law. Most modern firms emphasize the importance of mentoring young lawyers, often throughout their "apprenticeship" time as associates and senior associates, and the use of evaluation systems that emphasize the phased development of, and ability to demonstrate, key lawyer competencies.[10]

The formation of professional values requires a clear sense of the personal identity of the "lawyer in formation"—their values, priorities, goals, and insecurities. The identification and establishment of personal values continue to be subjects of great interest to educators, behavioral scientists, and human resources professionals. Research has generally found that the acquisition and formation of personal values come from people's life experiences, especially in their early formative years via modeling by influential people such as parents and other family members; teachers and coaches; societal "influencers" such as religious, political, and cultural role models (sometimes strong, positive ones—but sometimes not so much); and friends and colleagues.[11] By puberty, many of those values, perspectives, and traits have settled firmly into people's psychological beliefs, attitudes, and values.

Fortunately, people are not irretrievably locked into those perspectives. Through educational and other life experiences, new attitudes and behaviors can be learned. Law school provides rigorous and, for most students, novel educational experiences—invoking a challenging set of opportunities that is often described by graduates as "transformational."

CHALLENGES OF INTEGRATING PERSONAL AND PROFESSIONAL VALUES

The conflicts between professional demands (e.g., to clients, courts, and opposing counsel) and personal values are rampant in law practice, irrespective of the setting in which the lawyer acts as a lawyer. Law students and young lawyers will often find their personal values challenged as they are tested by the morals and ethics of their peers and teachers, as well as the clients and organizations they represent.

In particular, early in their legal career, young lawyers often wonder and are concerned about how well their personal value structure and orientation will align with their future professional roles, and how this affects their decision making in practice, exercise of professional judgment, and conception of the lawyer they want to be (and that their legal employers want them to be). The integration of personal values and perspectives with the values and expectations of lawyers is challenging to many. New associates will consider and reconsider their thinking about and discussions of such difficult questions for new law professionals as:

- "Will I be able to zealously represent a person accused of rape (or child molestation or war crimes) or a corporate client whose business is odious to me?"
- "How will I respond to a litigation client when this person insists that I overlook a damaging but relevant document in a discovery request?"
- "How candid must I be with a judge when I am questioned about contrary case authority? Do I conveniently ignore it, shade my description of its relevance, or something else entirely?"

These questions, and many others, arose in law school classes and will continue throughout your daily legal practice. The more you have embraced the professional ethics associated with being a lawyer and feel grounded in your professional identity as a lawyer and representative of the legal profession, the more clearly you will see the path forward through the many thorny and complex issues that you will be confronted with. Yet, they are quite important to the lawyer and their employer. Surveys show that Gen-Z and Millennial lawyers give significant weight to the moral values of their employers, with 60 percent saying that corporate responsibility programs were important in their selection of a potential or current employer and 63 percent reporting that a potential employer's social justice priorities would play a role in their decision-making process.[12]

Values, Inherent Aspects of Law Practice, and Psychological Issues

Many young lawyers have concerns about their ability to square their personal value system with the anticipated ethical decisions and behaviors in their roles as practicing lawyers. These concerns have been empirically linked with enhanced depression, anxiety, and unhappiness with their decision to become lawyers.[13] These conditions and disorders are exacerbated in young lawyers because now they move from conceptual anxiety to actually having to juggle the multiple, often conflicting, ethical and practice demands of lawyering. These psychological problems are created by inherent aspects of the practice of law, particularly those areas that law students read about and experience during law school—for example, the moral ambiguity found in many professional situations, the complexity of roles that lawyers are expected to play in their work, the legal ambiguity in practice situations, and the lack of effective mentoring and guidance by ethically centered lawyers.[14]

Moral Ambiguity

Young lawyers, in continuing the uncertainty formed in law school, often express concerns about their anticipated roles as lawyers, which revolve around the existential question "Can a good lawyer be a good person?" Legal educators, lawyers, and professional ethicists often reverse this question and ask, "Can a good person be a good lawyer?"

The question arises from the perceived tensions between being a public professional (or a "lawyer statesman") versus being an amoral technician of the law.[15] You may at times fear, as depicted by Rudy Baylor, the young attorney in John Grisham's novel *The Rainmaker*,[16] that your legal career will start down a path of cynicism, detached from the joys of work, and that you will constantly wrestle with differential morality in terms of your roles. Many are consumed by a nagging dread of operating in a value-conflicted occupational setting after law school, and for all too many these worries continue through their early days practicing law.

This concern is warranted. Many legal positions or lawyer roles, such as work in a government setting or in "cause lawyers" situations, involve dealing with how to integrate personal values into work.[17] Consider that Dr. Anthony Fauci, formerly director of the National Institute of Allergy and Infectious Diseases, described his experience on his first day as chief medical advisor to President Joseph Biden as "liberating" after serving in the same role in the previous administration. He no longer had to be stressed about his public comments, receiving pushback and second-guessing from his own team about them.[18] This expressed value—autonomy—is an aspect of law practice that attracts many individuals to consider law as a career, but it doesn't come easily in the first few years of legal practice. Private law firm practice settings, which for law school graduates constitute the vast majority of occupational positions, are viewed as less accommodating of personal values than other positions because those lawyers take their cases and their clients as they find them—they often don't have the luxury of selectivity in obtaining clients. Lawyers need to be able to find comfort in work that permits the integration of personal values and professional necessities.

Complexity of Roles

How do you get your head around understanding and accepting the many roles that you must undertake as a lawyer? Sometimes in the same week, if not the same day, a lawyer in private practice is expected to counsel clients; zealously represent them in legal proceedings, negotiations, and transactions; educate them on legal norms relevant to their business or personal life; recommend business actions that will help them avoid future legal problems and be more successful; and serve as a check on any possible "darker impulses." For the average twenty-four- to twenty-seven-year-old armed with four years of college, three years of law school, and possibly little work experience, that is a formidable list of activities at which to become proficient. The questions are not necessarily easier, by the way, at thirty or even forty years of age.

The complexity and uncertainty of these essential abilities often result in bouts of insecurity and fears of failure, malpractice, and peer embarrassment. Or it leads to a sense of apathy in that lawyers develop the attitude that if they don't care very much, setbacks and screwups are easier to put into some mental framework of accepting, forgetting, and moving on.

Legal Ambiguity

Another psychological barrier to feeling a strong sense of professional competence and well-being is the ambiguity inherent in many law situations. This ambiguity leads to young lawyers' omnipresent belief that "I don't know what I don't know" and makes them wonder whether that will result in embarrassment and professional errors.

The first introduction to this ever-present mental challenge occurs right at the beginning of law school with the common law tradition, involving, as it does, reliance on precedent and the indeterminacy of judicial decision making in cases. These materials in the first year of law school—as well as jokes about "whether you win or lose the case depends on what the judge had for lunch"—can result in feeling that there is just no way to accurately predict if your arguments to the court are enough to win the case, coupled with work in which there is most often a "losing side."

Mentoring/Support Issues

Another contributing source of psychological distress is the relative lack of mentoring and professional support, especially for young lawyers. Certainly, the increase in clinical and experiential law courses has improved law school student perceptions about "what the job requires and how I will perform as a lawyer" and has served to demystify some ambiguous and stressful areas of lawyers' work. However, mentors are still needed to help acclimate newly minted lawyers to the real-world challenges of law practice.

Traditionally, senior lawyers are expected to provide support to younger lawyers. However, in a survey of 1,200 lawyers (79 percent of whom were law firm associates), more than half (57 percent) reported poor support and weak or nonexistent formal mentoring in their firms, and only 50 percent reported that partners at their firms "genuinely cared about associate lawyer development."[19] Yet, the research shows that mentoring of associates, especially informal mentoring, makes a huge difference in their success.[20] While many associates reported that formal mentoring programs have less impactful effects, 57 percent of the lawyers who made partner reported having multiple informal mentors, while only 26 percent of those not making partner reported mentoring by colleagues. While the organized bar provides some mentoring opportunities (through, e.g., "Young Lawyer" educational programs that pair experienced volunteer lawyers with young lawyers), these cannot reach all the new lawyers who need and would welcome mentoring and guidance as they learn about how to be a good lawyer.

Consider taking the initiative yourself to cultivate a set of advisors or mentors you can approach for perspective when work gets challenging, even frustrating. A diverse set of perspectives can help you work through difficult issues and demands in practice. They may also remind you about the high aspirations associated with the law and its role in society and reignite your internal passion and sense of purpose. Keep in mind as well that there are likely multiple people who can support you, and each might be sought out for a specific rather than general reason.

Ethical Challenges in Real Life and Pop Culture

Conflicts in integrating personal and professional values are not only evident in real life but are also highlighted in films and novels. In real life, the theme of personal conflicts between a lawyer's individual values and the demands of the position or the practice of law was brazenly illustrated by former president Donald Trump's efforts to get Georgia's secretary of state to overturn the state's presidential election results in 2020 (which led to his subsequent indictment). Many depictions of lawyers in films and novels reflect the challenge of moral ambiguity and the conflict between individual integrity and the demands of the job. For example, Rudy Baylor, in

The Rainmaker, is enticed by an unscrupulous adversary (a prominent trial lawyer) to skirt ethical norms and behavior. He laments the challenge for young lawyers to avoid becoming another "bottom-dwelling shark."

Unfortunately, these frequent treatments of conflicts in values often appearing in daily newspaper and social media headlines and in popular culture provide neither a useful nor a dependable guide to young lawyers on how to align their personal values with the tasks they are asked to perform and the expectations of their clients, judges, and other lawyers. Adopting the perspective provided by The Five Practices of Exemplary Leadership® operating system provides vital guide rails to the challenges of successfully navigating the practice of law, especially clarifying your values and aligning actions with them. The next chapter also looks more directly at various perspectives associated with making decisions and fostering innovation on being an ethical lawyer-leader.

PROFESSIONAL IDENTITY AS A LEADER

An important way for lawyers to navigate the challenges in forming their professional identities, irrespective of the direction they wish to take in their careers, is to develop and strengthen their leadership competencies and attitudes. The process of becoming a lawyer shares many attributes and similarities with the formative process of becoming a leader—indeed, they are inextricably linked.

How do you come to think of yourself as a leader? How do you proceed to serve others as a leader in your personal and professional development? Answering such questions begins with the understanding that leadership is a deliberate choice. Self-education follows from that understanding: self-evaluation, which includes studying your own experiences as a leader and engaging in periodic self-reflection of your values—what's important to you—and reviewing your values' alignment with your decisions and revising as necessary; and evaluation of the behaviors of effective lawyer-leader role models. Such self-education is key to developing into a lawyer who successfully leads others.

Leadership: A Deliberate Choice

Previously, we explained that developing yourself as a leader and strengthening your leadership capabilities are not accidental processes or outcomes. You must want to lead; there are no (or very few) "accidental" leaders. Of course, some people are thrust into a leadership role or situation by unforeseen circumstances, but even then, becoming a leader and engaging in essential leadership practices and behaviors must be intentional if you expect a high probability of successful outcomes.

The pursuit of leadership is sometimes a matter of necessity within the lawyer's organization. Most legal organizations, even private law practices, are faced with the need for fundamental (and sometimes existential) change every four or five years.[21] The need to continuously improve and keep up with changes (be they technological, economic, political, judicial, local, or global) requires leadership across the organization, whether in a law firm, corporate or governmental counsel office, or judicial chambers. The most successful firms, regardless of their business, are characterized by high levels of leadership behavior across the many ways that one might slice up an organization.[22]

In the legal industry, success as a rainmaker is often treated as a proxy for effectiveness as a leader or demonstrating great leadership potential. To the extent that happens in modern law organizations, it is more coincidental than causally linked. Successful law leaders not only demonstrate exceptional skills as lawyers but also possess, and continuously strengthen, key leadership skills in their organizations.[23] These successful partners reach a point where they are making broad and significant contributions to the firm's success, often across practice areas and geographic reaches, in more ways than just their own practice areas. They are enmeshed in strategic issues facing the firm and spend more time helping other partners develop their practices, mentoring, and coaching other lawyers.

Often, the pursuit of leadership is a matter of personal goals. However, serving as a leader always reflects a desire not only to exercise influence in the pursuit of purposes greater than self-interests but also to feel a sense of satisfaction in the achievements of others. Both desires must be prominent regardless of whether others ask you to take on a challenge or situations occur where uncertainty, turmoil, and the need for fundamental changes push you to step forward and lead.

Self-Evaluation and Personal-Best Leadership Experiences

Self-evaluation is an important ability for forming a professional identity as a leader. Leadership of self is a fundamentally important lesson from law school, and it continues in the practice of law. After all, the very first person you have to lead is yourself! One of the most attractive attributes of practicing law is being a highly educated professional with a high degree of autonomy.

However, you are in a profession that is demanding and has high expectations for professional performance and integrity and where failure or inattention to duties can be costly in terms of professional malpractice and disciplinary actions. An ability to lead oneself toward appropriate conduct is critical to a young lawyer's success. Thoughtful consideration of your own life story is a highly useful way to pay special attention to the critical attributes of a lawyer's professional life. Appreciating the lessons (and blunders) resulting from your experiences and embracing a meaningful understanding of personal strengths and weaknesses in leading others shape how you learn to be an authentic leader.[24] Similarly, understanding the importance in professional life of the five key components of "emotional intelligence"—self-awareness, self-regulation, motivation, empathy, and social skills—can literally only come from a genuine and thorough "study of self."[25]

Reflecting on your personal-best leadership experience is a particularly powerful way to gain insights about yourself as a leader and the behaviors that matter. Describing a situation where you were at your personal best as a leader is an effective method for realizing that you are already a leader and capable of making a difference. Follow this up by taking the time to discern from this experience, determining what you need to learn so that you can be an even better leader and be even more comfortable engaging in the leadership behaviors that matter, building on your strengths, and taking actions to improve on areas of weakness.

We have used this exercise in law firm workshops on leadership development and have found that it is perceived as highly meaningful and helpful in attorneys' approach to their work in the firm, and it often gives them a greater appreciation for their colleagues. The ensuing discussions about their personal-best leadership experiences were among the most engaged for new associates, third- and fifth-year associates, and new partner leadership programs because of the realization that their leadership skills mattered to their work for clients and the firm and because their expressed pride in what they had done in that experience. The exercise is equally meaningful for young lawyers in firms with loose (or no) associate-level hierarchies. Often, these young lawyers sought outside experience or relied on mentoring relationships to guide their leadership of self in law practice. The development of these critical skills and attitudes, whether by horizontal education or vertical personal development initiative, was viewed as essential to their success as lawyer-leaders.

Leadership Role Models

Role models play an important part in the formation of leadership skills. Many lawyers understand the necessity of change and recognize the importance of being able to effectively lead others through change because of past leadership examples from school, social groups, internships, and previous jobs. They've witnessed good leadership examples and poor ones, and they have been able to gain and incorporate lessons from both. The same can be said about your time in law school. What were the behaviors of your best teachers, and how did they make you feel (e.g., respected, motivated)? In contrast, how did your least favorite teachers lead in the classroom? Think about your classmates who volunteered or were selected to chair various law school organizations and activities. Again, what behaviors differentiate the best leaders from the rest?

Analyzing the behaviors of those you admire as leaders is an important avenue for learning about how to lead—by emulating what these leaders do well and by avoiding those behaviors that result in mediocrity and disincentive. Pay attention when you can view, interact with, and work with lawyers (or judges) who manage or supervise lawyers, student clerks, and interns. The effective lawyer-leaders, regardless of the type of legal entity, manage themselves and their time well; convey a sense of mission and enterprise to everyone (including secretaries, paralegals, and law clerks); are truthful and respectful; and have ennobling ideals. This blend of competence as a lawyer and heartfelt commitment to service is inspiring.

We often hear from young lawyers about their observations and contrasting experiences with senior attorneys and especially managing partners: "I worked with one who was highly competent and patient, giving clear instructions and frequently explaining to everyone how important their work was for the cases and transactions that the office was handling. Another one I worked with was petty and sometimes mean to subordinates and often covered up his own shortcomings by blaming others." Certainly, there are takeaway lessons from both of these lawyers, but the lessons learned from the latter are both cautionary and, to some degree, damaging to morale and productivity.

It is true enough that sometimes a new law firm associate can learn useful practice skills from an assigned supervisor who is an ineffective or even a negative manager/leader (role model). However, lawyers who witness ineffective and negative leadership in their formative stage often form a negative opinion of the practice of law and of the legal profession. If this is your experience, then you need to balance the equation by finding opportunities to be with positive, inspiring lawyers who model effective leadership. Furthermore, though you may work for a poor leader, you don't have to be mentored by one.

Learning that leadership matters in attorney–client and workplace relationships is a crucial realization. By observing role models in action, you discover and envision how leadership skills and attributes coalesce into highly effective lawyering skills and attributes.

CHAPTER HIGHLIGHTS

- Developing skills for the effective, ethical practice of leadership mirrors the process of developing skills for the effective, ethical practice of law.
- It is essential for any lawyer, especially new ones, to reflect on who they are, what they care about, and the values and beliefs that drive their actions.
- Law practice is, in many respects, a retail business with various client demands and needs. You will often ponder and wrestle with the question "How can I keep focused on my personal values while facing competing and often inconsistent demands?"
- You must clarify your personal values and aspirations and thoughtfully examine the skills and attitudes needed for success as a lawyer. Then, you must figure out how to align those two perspectives in your personal and professional lives. Leadership development provides an effective way of beginning that analysis and preparing for a lifetime quest to integrate these twin demands.
- Law practice and the legal profession require practitioners who appreciate the connection between leadership and law practice and successfully model how to incorporate the two.
- You need to identify and connect with mentors, even without a formal mentoring program. Research shows that having mentoring relationships during formative career stages materially increases the likelihood of success in the practice of law.
- One important area in which lawyers become role models is how they view ethical issues and handle the inevitable choices that must be made in law practice. Learning to lead oneself is the best way to handle those issues.

CHAPTER 9

Making Decisions, Leading Innovation

"Good decisions reflect good judgment, which is literally the 'calling card' of the most successful lawyers and one of their most valuable abilities."

Lawyers constantly make decisions. And leaders, including lawyer-leaders, are constantly making decisions to implement a vision for their organization's success and to move change forward.[1] Lawyers make decisions in the practice of law, in the management of their firms, and in their personal lives. Decisions made in the practice of law frequently have great consequences for the lawyers themselves, for their clients, and for their professional organizations. Every decision means changes, and change is the province of leadership. Attorneys who are effective decision makers—based on the speed at which decisions are reached, the soundness of the decisions, and the ability to convince all parties involved that the decisions are the right ones to make—are valued highly. The decision to lead change, to become an agent of change, is a critically important decision for lawyer-leaders in their organizations, starting with the decision about whether and what changes are necessary or desirable.

On the one hand, lawyers make many routine decisions, even mundane at times. On the other hand, lawyers often have to make significant, even life-or-death, decisions for their clients, firms, and other legal entities. During the past decade, the law business has experienced dramatic challenges and market disruptions, and there is little reason to believe that these will dissipate or disappear anytime soon. They may, in fact, accelerate in scale and scope in the future, placing increasing importance on leadership. The decisions that lawyer-leaders need to make in the face of these extraordinary trends require a talent for innovation in adapting to and leading change.

SCOPE OF DECISION MAKING

The scope of lawyers' decision making is broad and closely connected to the roles they fill in their organizations (e.g., corporate counsel or district attorney), the clients they serve, and their relationship with those clients. The ability to ensure that good decisions are made is what lawyers, in large part, are paid to do as one of the fundamental or core services they provide to their clients.

Decision making, of course, varies by client and by situation. Cases involving clients facing substantial prison sentences or the death penalty introduce a different level of stress and consequences for making effective decisions than choices, for example, on handling incorporation for a new startup business or a complex real estate transition. Still, the individual and organizational consequences for a patent application error, a missed antitrust issue, an incomplete entertainment contract, and the like can be quite severe and consequential. Similarly, for many firms, the decisions made by partners and senior associates concerning the firm's "talent," especially new and junior associates, are among the most critical. Talent is often the firm's greatest financial commitment, and losing a fourth- or fifth-year associate is an expensive proposition, especially if it is preventable. Irrespective of the complexity of the task with which lawyers are presented and the severity of the consequences of their decisions, the process for making effective decisions has more similarities than differences.

Any discussion of lawyer decision making would not be complete without a reminder that there are certain decisions that lawyers make, and there are particular decisions that their clients make. This important distinction (or set of questions) consumes important time and materials, beginning with a professional responsibility class required for all law school students to complete and often reemphasized in continuing education programs on legal ethics. Some decisions in the practice of law are made only by the client. The attorney must accept that the decision was made solely by the client with or without the advice of counsel—for example, it is up to the client to accept or reject a plea deal or to go to trial in a civil case that could cost the client a great deal in litigation and business expenses.

Conversely, some decisions are made solely by the lawyer. For example, a trial lawyer doesn't ask a client if their case should be filed in federal or state court if there is no federal jurisdiction or if the proper motion is for judgment on the pleadings. The lawyer may advise the client on the decision the lawyer reaches, but it is a judgment call shaped by the lawyer's experience and strategizing and by the particularities of the case. Finally, there is a set of issues about which clients make decisions with the assistance of the lawyer—for example, where a decision must be made on a transaction, such as forming a business relationship or arranging a corporate acquisition, which calls for the client's business skills and the lawyer's legal judgment. Perhaps, technically, these are "client decisions," but the reality is that the lawyer serves the client's needs by shaping an understanding of the nature and complexity of the case or issue and guiding the client toward an appropriate decision that they both implement and accept. This is often referred to as "servant leadership" of the client.[2]

Although lawyers make many client-related decisions, it is evident that lawyers make many decisions that have nothing, or very little, to do with their clients. Law firms' decisions, for example, about hiring and firing matters, purchasing assets to support the law practice or business, and joining the local or national bar association are all decisions that lawyers frequently make that have no real connection to a client's needs or the lawyer's role in advising the client. In situations like these, lawyers function much like decision makers in any business setting.

A third decision-making arena occurs when a lawyer is in public service (e.g., a member of Congress or legal advisor to the governor). Decisions in these settings are often shaped by the lawyer's perception of the best interests of the public (citizens) and/or the governmental entity. These decisions are as influential as those made for or together with individual clients.

In all these settings and situations, decision making is complex because, typically, one decision leads to another decision, and so on. For leaders, there is no dearth of decision-making experiences, and each decision is as important as the next. There is an expression that "one bad decision leads to another," and this can, unfortunately, hold true in the scope of a lawyer's duties. Much like the experience of a sailor or engineer, a small error at the beginning of a voyage or a small error in software design will have huge consequences further down the line. These experiences—where sound or poor decisions at the beginning of a litigated case or a business deal affect the success of the legal matter—are common among lawyers and suggest the accuracy of the old saying "hindsight is 20/20." However, they also create a bank of experiences that lawyers can draw on and often share with junior associates to lead more successful ventures in the future. This sharing of past experiences, whether good or not, is essential to developing good, sound legal judgment in lawyers.

DECISION MAKING: JUDGMENT AND EXPERIENCE

Given that these settings are where lawyers make decisions and the scope of decision making expected of lawyers is broad, how do lawyers excel at making decisions for themselves and others? What are the characteristics of good decision making, and how can they be learned?

Lawyers develop and hone their capacity to arrive at effective decisions over time through education and intelligence, as well as the drive and motivation to succeed (win) and, in particular, judgment shaped by their on-the-job experiences.

Judgment Honed by Experience

Good decisions by lawyers and by leaders alike are reflections of good judgment, which is the "calling card" of the most successful lawyers and one of their most valuable abilities. Lawyers make judgment calls all the time. Whether or not to accept a particular client or agree to take on a case, whom to hire and to retain, and what advice to give a client about accepting a plea arrangement offered by the district attorney are all examples of the decisions commonly made by lawyers that are strongly shaped based on their judgment.

Law students and new lawyers often ask how exceptional lawyers acquire good judgment, and the straightforward answer is that it is gained through experience. Illustrating the point, presidential advisor and lawyer Ted Sorensen recounted this story about how lawyers acquire judgment:

> A new associate happens to be seated at lunch next to a senior partner and the younger person says to the veteran, "Tell me, why is it you have this big reputation for judgment?"
>
> "Well," the partner replies, "there are people who seem to respect my judgment."
>
> "If you don't mind my asking another question, why do they respect your judgment?" "Well, I guess I've made the right decision enough times," the partner says.
>
> "If you don't mind me bothering you, what was the basis on which you made the right decision?"
>
> "Oh," the partner replies, "that comes from experience."
>
> "One last question: What's the experience based on?"
>
> "Wrong decisions," the partner replies.[3]

Judgment, Experience, and Values

Experience will shape how leaders choose to apply their judgment to incorporate their values into their decisions. When lawyers are exercising leadership and/or are in leadership roles, their decisions are not made in a bubble; instead, those decisions are evaluated by their followers. For example, a decision to take on a controversial client (perhaps representing an alleged child molester or controversial organization such as the National Rifle Association or Planned Parenthood) may have implications on how others view you or the firm—in one direction or another. Of course, representing a client you disagree with might say a lot about your commitment to the legal process and doesn't mean you necessarily support gun ownership or abortion.

This is not to suggest that you should only take on cases, clients, and projects that are popular, but rather that the decisions lawyers make, large and small, send significant signals about their values and beliefs. Considering leadership as "values in action" means that every decision you make needs to be conscientiously aligned with who you are and what you care about; to do otherwise will damage your credibility.

It is important to note that you will be judged not only by the decisions you make but also by the decisions you deliberately don't make (as opposed to indecision, as noted below). These nondecisions will also clearly be decisions, albeit often invisible but nonetheless important in terms of getting a clear glimpse of your values.

Process of Making Good Judgment Calls

A great deal of making good judgment calls is a matter of a process that both leaders and lawyers follow in response to a particular situation. Most of these situations involve people (e.g., whom to hire and why), strategy (e.g., whether to add a new law office on the other coast), or a crisis (e.g., response to a sudden, challenging situation such as the loss of a major client). It isn't easy to imagine a situation in which the exercise of good judgment is not critically important.

The first part of the process for making a good judgment call involves preparation, taking the necessary time and research to size up the particular problem, situation, or person and understand the context in which the decision must be made. For example, is it a routine decision or an existential one? The second part of the process is making the call (thereby avoiding the pitfall of indecision), and the process concludes with executing or implementing the decision.

Deciding is important, but putting it into action is the critical point of the process.

One of the most essential attributes of lawyers who consistently exhibit good judgment is determining and focusing squarely on what is most important. They are not snookered or sidetracked. Their decisions go to the heart of the matter under consideration. This is similar to what constitutes great executive decision making: "[T]hey concentrate on what is important. They want to know what the decision is all about and what the underlying realities are which it has to satisfy."[4]

Judgment: A Learned Skill

Judgment is typically not something anyone is born with. Rather, it is an acquired skill and therefore one that you can learn and develop.

As previously noted, learning from your own experiences, especially stumbles and setbacks, is the primary way to hone your judgment. Experience, gained from both good and bad decisions, really does provide a foundation for the development of sound professional judgment. Not making the same mistake twice is evidence of learning and, as such, adds to your growing repertoire of judgment-related experience.

John Dewey, the American philosopher and educational reformer, noted that people don't necessarily learn from experience; they learn by reflecting on experience. Doing the same thing over and over again and expecting different results can be a sign of insanity. Reflecting on your experience is necessary for learning, and doing something differently the next time around, however slightly, is about leadership. Reflection is foundational to self-awareness and understanding yourself better. Mistakes and failures are the stepping stones to making progress, improving your judgment, and acquiring wisdom. The only people who don't make mistakes are those who don't do anything. Reflection provides insights into *why* some decision or action did or did not work out, and rather than feeling upset or embarrassed, generates ideas about what to do the next time. Reflection both provides and builds perspective and enables you to see what is happening in the moment in a larger context.

Another route to enhancing your judgment is through interaction with law firm mentors (whether assigned in a firm mentor program or an informal mentor arranged by the young lawyer) and practicing attorneys. Effective mentor arrangements encourage junior lawyers to ask those with more years of practice about how they approached difficult questions or problems—whether in client representation or matters of the firm's operation. Be sure to find out about the thinking process behind how they arrived at their decisions. Studying how successful lawyers in the firm and other highly seasoned lawyers have made tough calls and decisions is an invaluable way to develop your own judgmental ability. One benefit to the case-study approach in American law schools is that it permits a deeper understanding of why lawyers and judges made decisions in cases and encourages discussions, or brainstorming, about the thinking leading up to their decision making.

MECHANICS OF MAKING SOUND DECISIONS

As we have discovered in discussions with law firm leaders, practicing lawyers, and business executives, many people in managerial roles and positions have not sufficiently thought about the processes they use in making decisions. When asked about how they make decisions or why they made a particular decision, people often simply remark, "It seemed like the correct thing to do." This response fails to appreciate the effectiveness of the process they used (at best, it acknowledges only that the decision's outcome "worked out okay"—not even that it was optimal). Another frequent response is "I went with my gut," which means the individual decided without a conscious understanding of the factors underlying that intuition. Neither of these responses results in much insight into the learning process; the response might just as well have been "I got lucky," and that's not a ringing endorsement of one's capability to make good decisions and soundly exercising judgment. Clients don't hire lawyers because they "are the luckiest people they know" but because of their reputation for exercising good judgment and obtaining great outcomes.

Having clarity about the process of making good decisions is important to the practice of law, which is based on precedents. It is also critical to the practice of leadership, ensuring the consistency and trustworthiness necessary for building and sustaining authentic relationships.

Just like becoming an exemplary leader, effective decision making is a learned skill, not something that you either have or you don't. The skills associated with being a good decision maker can be learned and strengthened by understanding the elements associated with a sound decision-making process. That process involves a set of steps that can be used to make most decisions, beginning with an understanding of what type of decision is needed.

Classifying the Decision

At the onset, consider whether the decision you are being asked to make is primarily routine or substantive. Effective decision makers will approach these two types of decisions differently, even though they will employ a similar decision-making process.

Some decisions involve relatively routine choices and judgments—for example, what's for dinner or whether you want to buy the premium-priced pineapple rings in the grocery store versus the less expensive generic brand. While there may be qualitative and even quantitative differences in these choices, their consequences or outcomes are inconsequential—especially in the long run. Choices here seldom set precedents.

Other decisions have more substantive consequences, and the outcome of a case, a project, or a business initiative may hinge based on one correct or incorrect decision. Some Silicon Valley, Wall Street, and Pennsylvania Avenue lawyers describe the high stakes associated with some cases, and the clients' financial capability to support litigation, as "bet-the-company" decisions. In these instances, the decision may have existential consequences for the client. Other types of decisions might have strategic consequences for counsel. For example, "Should our firm open a new office, with all the expense associated with that, in Chicago (or some other location)?" or "Should the firm enlarge its practice fields to develop an intellectual property litigation department?" Understanding the type and importance of the decision to affected parties is the first step in arriving at an appropriate decision for the client, the attorney, or the firm.

Delineating the Problem

Once the decision has been classified, you need to consider the nature of the problem, which requires a decision. For example, does the problem involve a series of events—and, if so, is it necessary to formulate a policy or precedent that can be applied in future instances—or is this a one-off situation? Another consideration is whether the issue or problem indicates a need to fix a singular element or overhaul a potentially massive infrastructure, or something in between the two. A further consideration is determining for this problem who needs to be involved, whether from the perspective of bringing the requisite expertise and experience and/or from the vantage point of executing the decision. Generally, collaborative decision making results in better decisions for several reasons. Bringing a range of diverse voices to the table ensures that the necessary competencies are involved, but it also goes a long way to increase confidence that key perspectives were not missed, especially from those whom your decision is attempting to address, as well as those subsequently responsible for executing the decision.

Getting It Right

Often, delineating the problem to be solved will help establish parameters or boundaries for the type of answer necessary to resolve the matter at issue. At this point, an effective decision maker will ponder and focus on what is the *right* action or decision and not what is just *acceptable* or passable. Sound decision making requires a desire to "get it right." While associates and junior lawyers may be admonished, "don't let perfect get in the way of good" and "don't overthink it," it is essential for your reputation as an attorney and leader that you form an appreciation for the correctness of the decision that must be made. Your credibility and reputation are on the line.

A desire to get it right can present a personal challenge for all lawyers, but especially young lawyers who report feeling almost paralyzed by fear of making a wrong (or poor) decision, even in the face of a senior lawyer or mentor's assurances that "you're not expected to be perfect." Working through these challenges requires understanding your limits and strengths and being comfortable with doing the very best work you can do, irrespective of how it may turn out. Self-awareness and the ability to reflect on your strengths and limits allow a sense of grace, knowing that, inevitably, some mistakes will be made and preparing yourself to accept that fact, the associated consequences, learn and move forward.

Planning for Action

Another step in the process is to build into the decision the actual action necessary to resolve the matter. You know how frustrating, unmotivating, and wasteful it is to be engaged in a situation where a decision is made, only to discover that nothing subsequently happened or changed. For example, too often elected officials will pass legislation and then not provide the necessary funding and resources to implement the decision, or planning for a transaction fails to sufficiently remove contingencies, which hampers the timely completion of the deal.

Gauging Effectiveness

The final step is to gauge the decision's validity and effectiveness against the actual course of events. Ask yourself, "Did the decision make a difference? Did it accomplish its goals?" Take some time to reflect on the entire process, and consider what you did that is worth repeating and what you realize you would do differently in the future.

Stepping Outside of the Process

Introducing a deliberate process into making decisions, which some consider largely an intuitive action, can seem daunting and cumbersome. Yet, what the research finds, and what we've found from our own discussions with successful lawyers, is that attending to an intentional decision-making process is fundamental to leadership success. The best decisions, sometimes made under pressure, are not generally made when people are experiencing stress.

Making decisions with a clear head, based on principles, calmly, and not impulsively in reaction to pressure is very important. Still, it is true that effective decision making is not a simple list, a one-size-fits-all approach, or a specific step-by-step experience. You will need a blend of decision-making skills: part tactician, part therapist, part strategist, and part content expert. You will be required to provide clear-eyed analysis, and, on occasion, you will want the guts of a riverboat gambler.

CHALLENGE OF INDECISION

Some of the descriptions of the proper steps to arrive at a sound decision may sound unrealistic because they suggest that decision makers have all the time in the world to get to their decision when, in the real world, decisions often have to be considered, rendered, and evaluated in a relatively short time span—sometimes on the spot and under multiple pressures. One of the significant problems organizations face in moving through the effective decision-making process is dealing with the issue of "indecision"—the failure to make timely and sound decisions because of various real, imaginary, and self-imposed constraints on the decision makers. Sometimes referred to as "decision inertia," this is a trait to be avoided, but it occurs with some frequency among law firm leaders.[5] The inability to make a prompt decision is particularly troubling to young lawyers, who often lack the self-confidence to make a difficult decision due to their lack of experience. This has led some firms to give associates more client-facing opportunities to experience decision-making situations while still being mentored and educated by senior lawyers.

Causes of Indecision

Decision makers in law firms (and exemplary leaders) are busy and have an already-full agenda; they have the needs of their clients and cases to manage and move forward, as well as their own personal matters (e.g., family) that need their attention. Lawyers leading their firms are frequently challenged to prioritize an organizational matter when they are already juggling multiple issues presented by clients and other members of the firm.

Furthermore, many decisions require the consideration of external inputs (from experts and faculty reports to government findings and the like) and cannot be rendered very expeditiously. Decisions affecting groups of people and entire organizations and firms—for example, decisions about personnel retention and promotions, real estate, office acquisitions, and client practice areas—may sometimes, under unforeseen and unfortunate circumstances, have to be made quickly, but more often they will require extended deliberations, negotiations, even dispute resolutions, and the involvement of many parties (committees and departments within the firm or organization).

Solutions to Indecision

To preempt indecision, leaders must create a culture of decisive behavior, one that ensures that effective decisions are made promptly and correctly. Leaders must pay particular attention to how they act, and they must communicate that the importance of prompt and effective action is clearly part of the firm's DNA, as it is of each of the individual lawyers involved. Normative signals are sent via "social operating mechanisms" such as meetings, decision-making "trees," formal and informal emails, and similar communication systems to promote productive dialogue and influence the perceptions and actions of others in the organization.

In these ways, having an effective decision-making process in place creates an organization that is collaborative, efficient, and productive.[6] Moreover, candid feedback and strenuous follow-through characterize organizations that fully engage their people and teams, and mitigate against indecision paralysis.

EFFECTIVE CHANGE AND LEADERSHIP

You are very unlikely to get any better than you are right now without doing something differently than you are now doing. This truth applies to both individuals and organizations. If "better than today" is a desired end state, then change is required, and effective change is all about leadership and changing the business-as-usual environment. Don't get us wrong—there are no guarantees that change will result in improvements. However, without making any changes, the probability of improvement is quite unlikely. After all, the other truth is that if you are not growing, then, just like fruit on the vine, you will eventually rot. As former U.S. Army Chief of Staff Eric Shinseki observed, "[If] you don't like change, you're going to like irrelevance even less."[7]

Components of Change

There are a number of critical components for successfully initiating change. These include establishing a sense of urgency, selecting an appropriate "guiding coalition" to effect change, articulating a shared vision for change, identifying and communicating the actions necessary to address the challenge, generating an environment where it is safe to experiment and learn from experience (and mistakes), and integrating the changes into the organization's processes and culture.[8]

Need for Change

If an organization is doing well or a client's legal needs are routine, then the attorney's tasks are modest. However, if the challenges are great and the need to improve, modernize, or advance is critical, then those lawyers must implement a change process, and leadership will necessarily be required.

Law firms have experienced unprecedented pressures in recent years from several forces. These pressures include talent issues in the firm, such as hiring new lawyers and managing unproductive older partners; client demands for reduced costs of legal services; and the inability of senior lawyers and firm leaders to effectively manage technology, both their own as well as that of their clients.[9] In addition, the industry is facing increased globalization of legal services, a decline in the number of lawyers in law practice, and a growing number of alternative law service providers.

Such seismic fluctuations are endangering legal organizations these days, and most firms are neither effectively managing them nor leading transitions.[10] Surveys have found that over 70 percent of lawyers believe that the pace of significant change affecting law firms will continue to increase, yet only 38 percent of them indicate that their firms are actively engaged in rolling out innovative changes. They further report that the resistance to change efforts comes mostly from firm partners (ostensibly the leadership team).[11]

Clearly, responding to the trends and challenges of these times is necessary, and that won't happen without leadership. Those leading legal organizations are responsible for creating the energy and conditions for firm adaptation. In fact, in order to adapt to ongoing social, political, economic, and technological developments, firms must be making moderate changes annually and be prepared for major changes in the way they operate every four to five years.[12]

In the face of recurrent challenges and crises, the legal profession and lawyers have come to recognize that regardless of whether an organization is a law firm or nonprofit legal organization or corporate counsel office, change is a critical element of survival. For example, the need for decisive change hit many national law firms during financial crisis of 2008. Some firms were innovative and navigated the crisis but many failed and ceased operations.[13] Several firms found themselves needing to quickly understand the causes of the problem, inspire others to respond to these concerns, and enable their colleagues to implement the necessary innovations.

Law firm partners and senior associates, in lawyer leadership workshops, have described firsthand experiences when the law firms they have worked for have similar challenges—that is, motivating people to do more than show up, as well as perennial problems of retention. The process of moving others in the law firm forward is not all that different, in that every organization requires leadership for effective change.

Incremental versus Disruptive Change

Management is mostly about dealing with the status quo, while change and getting better than today (the status quo) requires leadership. The more significant and disruptive the changes, the more leadership plays a pivotal role.

Disruptive change occurs when a highly novel and unanticipated demand (often exogenous to the industry) or an immediate threat forces attention to the problem. An example of a disruptive change is the discovery of a radically new and different technology that renders many of a firm's assets obsolete (such as intellectual property or talent pools) or otherwise subject to a quick write-off.

Incremental change still requires leadership but at a much slower pace. It occurs when industries or market participants make continuous improvements—for example, making the firm's assets more efficient and productive or gradually increasing the demand for the industry's products. The client-driven demands for different billing practices (e.g., billable hours and value billing) are representative of more incremental challenges requiring subsequent changes in how law firms operate.

Regardless of whether the change is disruptive or incremental, all effective changes require leadership and begin with clear decisions and directions from leaders. Often, change creates new opportunities for those firms with creative, thoughtful leadership. For example, a firm's chair of the health care and regulatory practice groups saw an opportunity to build a new cannibus practice group as states began to permit the industry to grow legally and serve clients in that underserved market.

CHANGE AND INNOVATION

Approaching change in difficult and challenging circumstances requires leaders to be innovative and challenge the process. The need to innovate and demonstrate facileness is not solely the province of corporations; law firms and organizations face great challenges too and must have the capacity to respond to them. Leadership at the individual client or case level, or organizational level, will often require thinking outside the box regarding existing paradigms and precedents.

Leading innovation is a critical set of skills that lawyers need to master for the success (and perhaps longevity) of their law organizations and, equally important, for their clients' businesses. Simply put, innovation is defined as a novel idea that solves a problem, and it requires insight into the business environment and their clients' needs. In many business organizations, their legal departments are being asked to be drivers of innovative change, including leading the innovation process.[14] These skills are in great demand not only during times of great disruption to the legal community but also in addressing the normal, but recurring, challenges of changes to economic markets, practice areas of legal work (such as blockchain and AI), and changes in the market for law firm talent. They are skills that leaders have and that lawyers need.

Innovative Decision Making versus Traditional Problem Solving

People often confuse innovative problem solving and decision making with other, more traditional business thinking, such as strategic or long-range planning. These different approaches to problem solving have their place in legal organizations faced with ambiguity about future directions.

Traditional business thinking tends to be logical, requires evidence (proof), looks for precedent, is binary ("it is right or wrong"), is uncomfortable with ambiguity, and desires immediate results. There is nothing wrong with traditional business thinking in most organizations, but it is incomplete or inadequate for many situations that require more transformative action.

Innovative thinking is different from traditional forms of problem solving, being much more collaborative and value-added.[15] Innovative thinking tends to be intuitive and future-oriented, asking many "what if" questions. It is unconstrained by the past, embraces multiple possibilities, and relishes ambiguity. Innovation requires agility and quickness that are not generally prized in traditional planning and business decision-making routines and environments.[16]

In terms of incremental versus disruptive change, incremental change can usually be addressed by institutional strategic planning, while disruptive change often requires innovation to address the challenges presented by the threat. Nonetheless, innovation certainly can be—and might need to be—employed to address incremental change; although in terms of disruption, firms' response times are much shorter, and participants in the industry or market often may not understand all the factors that caused or led to the disruptive force.[17]

Importantly, providing innovative leadership entails creating an organizational climate where people are both free and encouraged to apply pioneering thinking and models for cutting-edge decision making. For example, design thinking and open innovation to address contemporary challenges for their clients and organizations.[18]

Components of Innovation

There are three components in the process of innovation that are particularly important to consider: (1) collaboration, (2) investments in people and processes, and (3) assessment and evaluation.

Effectively addressing change typically involves mobilizing a collective, rather than individual, response. Success at addressing the need for change, and implementing those changes, requires that you make sure an appropriate, diverse, and representative group of people is involved in the decision-making process. Frequently, this takes the form of creating a task force that is charged with generating ideas and alternatives.

Similarly, innovation occurs through team effort, when people are engaged with one another and share a common purpose, along with a sense that resolving challenges requires collaborative, rather than individual, efforts. To this end, leaders bring people together and create teams to process possibilities, which at the same time requires nurturing and sustaining a climate within the team and organization that values and pursues experimentation and risk taking.

Successful innovation needs an environment that fosters and permits not only experimentation but also learning, meaning that some setbacks, stumbles, mistakes, and failures will be an inevitable part of the experience. The people and teams charged with finding creative solutions to difficult problems must feel that they can consider alternative perspectives and try different solutions without fear of being embarrassed or penalized for not getting it absolutely right the first time. In this sense, perfection, as Winston Churchill best put it, is the enemy of progress.

Studies show that successful innovation processes involve participants who see themselves as pioneers and explorers. They are flexible thinkers, comfortable with ambiguity, and open to new ideas and ways of making things happen.[19] In harnessing this energy, leaders must build trust among the participants through building relationships, promoting cooperation, insisting on open communication, and inspiring a shared vision that builds commitment to persevere through setbacks and hardships.[20]

Effective innovation also means that leaders and their organizations must be prepared to make investments in both their people's abilities to innovate and in the tools and processes needed to be imaginative and creative. For example, an organization might try out new ideas in one office or region and iron out the kinks before launching any company-wide initiatives. Innovative processes can make a difference in the current era of legal services outsourcing, overwhelming technological advances and changes, and increasing client demands for greater law firm efficiency and better service delivery.

Finally, a successful innovation process doesn't stop with results but, similar to the after-action reviews conducted by the armed services, requires assessment and evaluation in order to foster learning and build future capacity. People will not struggle for long without knowing how they are doing and what progress they are making toward their shared aspirations. Researchers have found that feeling that progress is being made is one of the essential factors that motivate people and keep them focused on the target ahead.[21] Leaders create ways to provide milestones along the journey (and, certainly, litigation has many of these steps built into the process), as well as dashboards (modeled after automobiles) to give people a sense of how they are doing.

Roadblocks to Innovation

Many law firms, typical of most organizations, face internal challenges that inhibit support for truly creative action. Almost by their nature, organizations favor stability and are unprepared for, and perhaps even unaware of the need for, innovation and continuous process improvement. Global studies have found that only about 13 percent of employees are truly engaged in the work of creatively responding to major problems and that 50 percent of employees feel that they are too busy or otherwise blocked at work from being creative and innovative.[22]

These results underscore two critical issues for organizations facing the need for major change. First, for change to happen, a perceived urgency is necessary to spur innovative thinking. Second, this urgency needs to be so significant that leaders can essentially compel the creation of an innovation methodology that will get results (i.e., lead to substantive changes). The coalescing of these two elements is the special value that leaders add to the organization—they recognize and embrace the challenge and clearly articulate the need for change—and they persuade others to engage in creative steps to address the challenge.

Innovation and the Need for Leadership

Neither innovation nor creative change just happens on its own; inertia and continuation of the status quo are the default. Leadership is needed to drive the organization through innovative analysis, ideation, exploration of ideas for change, and adoption of the needed change.

Your aspiration to initiate and lead innovation will require expertise, commitment, and direction. The organizational climate for creativity is directly attributable to how leaders behave, with studies showing that 20 percent to as much as 67 percent of the variance in creativity depends on the example set by leaders.[23] If leaders inspire people in such a way that they can grasp both the need and the urgency for change, then people will more likely enlist in the cause and want to be part of the solution.

CHAPTER HIGHLIGHTS

- Decision making is a critical skill for lawyer-leaders—necessary for effecting change and inspiring innovation within an organization.
- Decision making impacts every aspect of the legal profession: clients, law firms, and public service.
- The foundation of good decision making is good judgment, and the foundation of good judgment is learning from experience.
- Decision making is a deliberate process, but not necessarily a rigid, step-by-step undertaking. Rather, it involves a blend of skills, abilities, and actions.
- Successful innovation requires collaboration and an investment in people and processes, as well as assessment and evaluation. Judgment and decision making, like leadership, are learned skills.

Chapter 10

Becoming a Team Leader

"There is a fundamental difference between working individually with a group of people and leading a team."

Popular culture films often portray lawyers as intelligent introverts who prefer the monastic life of poring over complex law provisions or as swashbuckling courtroom crusaders. These themes may make for good movies, but they do not accurately depict what lawyers do for their clients or how they conduct their professional and business lives.

In actuality, lawyers' work as counselors, negotiators, and advocates is quite people intensive and frequently involves working in groups to accomplish shared goals successfully. All law firms use, encounter, and participate in teams. Obviously, larger firms and corporate legal departments have more hierarchical structures, and the use of teams is more prevalent. Still, today's lawyers are often called upon to serve on and lead teams of peers, clients, and other lawyers. For lawyers to successfully build, participate in, and lead teams, they must effectively collaborate, not only within the firm but also with clients' teams.

COLLABORATION: WHAT IT IS, WHAT IT ISN'T

A truly collaborative work group or team comprises members who engage with each other toward a shared understanding and mutually beneficial resolution of the issues they address. A team can be defined as "a small number of people with complementary skills who are committed to a common purpose, set of performance goals, and approach for which they hold themselves mutually accountable."[1] Successful collaborative relationships require commitment and expertise to achieve the desired outcomes. Long-term collaboration may involve attention to or resolution of multiple projects (such as the foci of the management or litigation committee in a law firm) or address an ongoing issue (e.g., partner compensation). Litigation or deals may require shorter-term collaboration among a diverse group of professionals.

A fundamental difference exists between working individually with many people and leading a team. You could conduct your business by simply tapping into the experience and expertise of one or more individuals on a one-to-one-transaction basis. You seek an opinion on a specific matter of law, and the person you contact may not need to know about the actual case or the people involved. Although you consult with many people, none of them feel any sense of personal responsibility or accountability for the outcome. This group is composed of individuals who are each essentially independent of one another, and while you may be coordinating their efforts, they don't really constitute a *team*.

Collaborative groups, or teams, also differ from mere assembly projects wherein each participant prepares a report, and someone collects and collates them into a final statement. Collaborative teams are characterized by all members assembling together to work on all aspects of a project; by contrast, assembly projects are characterized by subject-matter experts working independently to contribute to a group report. These reports can be useful, but they are not the product of genuinely collaborative processes and generally lack sufficient joint input and consensus to be considered a collaborative effort.

Furthermore, a collaborative team effort differs from a sequential work situation wherein a series of successive groups each picks up a project where an antecedent group leaves off and carries the project further along. Such work groups have their own use but are not truly collaborative. Actual collaborative groups involve lawyers and other professionals working substantively together throughout a project rather than individuals or groups working separately on different project phases.

The power of a team (versus a mere assemblage of people) emanates from its strong sense of being an interdependent community that strongly influences people's attitudes and behaviors. Noncollaborative groups utilize individual strengths to get work done, with the members focusing on their own goals. In contrast, team members see themselves as connected and dependent on one another and utilize one another's abilities to achieve a common goal. The resulting products of these two groups are quite different—a reflection of the fact that more significant insights, knowledge, research, and thoughtfulness come from collaborating with others.

COLLABORATION: THE FOUNDATION OF THE LEGAL PROFESSION

From the very early stages in most people's education and socialization processes, they are expected to "play well with others." This dictate extends into all facets of adulthood, where collaboration is especially valued.

The legal profession is no exception. The foundation of the legal profession is collaboration. Teams are assembled for purposes that cannot be realized by a single individual or a group of individuals working either independently or sequentially with one another, including addressing an issue (e.g., partner and associate compensation), a problem (e.g., balancing the concerns and challenges of parenthood while practicing law), or an opportunity (e.g., moving into a new practice area). In addition to the work-product benefits of collaboration, research shows that when lawyers have strong collaborative skills on top of their technical skills, their firms earn higher profit margins, their clients remain more loyal to the firm, and their billing rates are higher.[2]

However, the importance of strong collaboration skills by lawyers transcends their impact on the bottom line of law firm profitability. The law firm practice group leaders we interviewed echoed the research findings. One partner described the team he assembled to consider the firm's addition of a new practice group and how their collaboration was essential to the firm's decision to add the group. Another partner described her firm's culture of cross-collaboration and ability to bring in partners with the right subject-matter expertise as the firm's "secret sauce" that permits a clear focus on clients' needs.

Areas of Collaboration

Collaboration is essential in all facets of lawyering: lawyer–client relationships, litigation, transaction work, and firm/organization administration/management. Lawyers must be able to collaborate with others to serve their clients best and get their work done. In today's complex environments, collaboration across disciplines requires lawyers to combine their knowledge and skills and tailor them to the clients' needs in a manner such that the outcome is more than the sum of individual participants' contributions. Law practice has become increasingly specialized, and lawyers are often selected because of their subject-matter expertise. They work in environments that are increasingly complex, volatile, and uncertain, and clients rely on their lawyers' abilities to help navigate those conditions. As the former general counsel to General Electric concluded, "[The] lawyer's core skill of understanding how values, rules, and institutions interrelate with social, economic, and political conditions is central to the demands of [their] leadership."[3] Research has found that lawyers who can collaborate across practice fields and clients are the ones who generate the highest revenues from client services fees.[4]

In particular, lawyers team up with others for litigation and transaction work, and lawyers collaborate in teams comprised of people with expertise that cuts across many technical and functional arenas. Much of the litigation and transaction work for business clients involves working across divisions or lines within an organization, involving, for example, accounting and engineering and, of course, general counsel or the legal department. On mergers and acquisitions work, lawyers with Securities and Exchange Commission and finance experience collaborate with functional specialists from the client's organization (i.e., marketing, finance, regulatory compliance) and technical experts from other fields. Regarding litigation, lawyers work on teams for settlement negotiations, trial preparation sessions, and client counseling meetings. Another common example is a team of plaintiff's lawyers from different firms who joined together in a multidistrict proceeding in federal court. These lawyers must collaborate on many tasks, including discovery scheduling, briefing of key issues demanded by the judge, and joint decision making on cases.

Furthermore, the work of most legal organizations—including midsized to larger law firms, corporate counsel offices, and risk management and compliance departments—is structured to be conducted by teams. Good examples of teams within a law firm are the firm's management, compensation, and associate committees. These teams are how the business of managing contemporary law firms happens. The reality for most law organizations is that teams function everywhere, are critical to their operations and success, and affect most aspects of lawyers' daily work.

Collaborative skills are also essential outside the firm in dealings with opposing counsel, where being candid and professional is critical to successfully completing the case. It may seem counterintuitive to view adversarial lawyers in deals and litigations as "collaborators." Still, the truth is that all lawyers must work together to conclude the transaction or contract for their clients or resolve the dispute in litigation. Many judges express their exasperation at the inability of lawyers in a matter of litigation to resolve seemingly routine discovery matters, forcing the judge to resolve motions to compel or for sanctions.

Collaboration: A Reflection of Societal Trends

The prevalence of teamwork in the law practice industry reflects broader economic and social influences because law jobs and legal projects are becoming increasingly complex, less time bound, and more global in scope. Organizations that cut across disciplines, industries, and businesses must rely on teams to handle multifaceted issues and the more mundane aspects of working in an organization. Work in mergers and acquisitions, for example, utilizes expertise and experience across fields of increasing sophistication and knowledge, and even a really savvy and technically proficient lawyer cannot individually demonstrate expertise in international finance, cross-border licensing requirements, and the economics of an acquiring firm's premerger and postmerger performance necessary to complete a complex deal. Instead, for that lawyer to successfully conduct the transaction or conclude the litigation, the principal skill is pulling together the right competencies and the best people to be on the team.

Furthermore, in a crisis situation, aggressive and collaborative work within the firm is needed to identify the objective and likely impacts of various scenarios and then devise appropriate ways to address them. Financial and economic pandemics in past decades have painfully shown how, when law firms reacted slowly and ineffectively, they subsequently failed.

Collaboration: A Learned Skill

Ninety-seven percent of the nearly 1,200 global leaders surveyed by the Center for Creative Leadership indicated that collaboration is essential to their organization's success.[5] Unfortunately, only 30 percent of these respondents felt those leading their organizations were skilled at collaboration. This gap between the perception that greater collaboration in the organization is necessary and the perception that the organization's leaders are not skilled at collaboration suggests that learning how to be more collaborative is an essential competency for leaders.

Collaboration is a skill that can be learned and honed. To that end, the most forward-looking law firms have been emphasizing the skills of successfully engaging in team projects and collaboration. Likewise, continuing professional development programming for lawyers increasingly focuses on collaborative skills such as negotiation, teamwork, and dispute resolution.

PERSUASION IN THE PROCESS OF COLLABORATION

Bringing people together requires an ability to be persuasive. Influencing the behaviors and decisions of others is a critical skill for any lawyer. Persuading people to work together for the common good of everyone involved is fundamentally similar to how leaders Inspire a Shared Vision (one of The Five Practices). Lawyers influence and motivate others, including clients, opposing counsel, and, importantly, judges, from whom a favorable decision is desired. Persuading others is central to lawyers' work in gaining support for a legal position or inducing a witness to provide the necessary information. People will follow a leader, just as clients will follow lawyers, when they clearly communicate a shared goal or purpose supported by common values and articulate why such a pursuit is in their best interests.

Persuasion and Communication Skills

Neither lawyers nor leaders are likely to be successful when they are inadequately prepared to persuade others. Preparation starts with identifying the key objectives the lawyer (leader) and the client (follower) want and need to achieve. This requires developing a heightened awareness of the situation and the message you need to send in that context, making it the right message at the right time.[6] In other words, lawyers and leaders must master communication skills in their roles as advocates and in their interpersonal interactions.

Success, regardless of profession or position, requires effectively communicating with a specificity of purpose and clarity of message. People in leadership and managerial roles spend 70 to 90 percent of their time communicating daily with others.[7] Leadership is very much a person-to-person business, and so often the messages must be at a personal level—for example, explaining how the proposed change or action will benefit people personally even when the change is at a group or organizational level. Persuading others to shift their behavior from one lane to another requires an appreciation that people find it challenging to give up what they are currently doing (even if they are unhappy) unless they can see how they will be better off by pursuing a different path.

Persuasion and Listening Skills

As we discussed in earlier chapters, excellent listening skills are also essential to being effective at persuasion and communication. Listening and understanding a client's or law firm associate's situation enables you to appreciate their goals authentically, empathize with the difficulties that the legal problem is causing, and articulate a set of shared objectives and a vision for moving forward.

Since persuading others to act differently may involve reciprocity, the importance of listening is highlighted. Reciprocity describes the situation where two parties agree that if you take this action for me now, I will, in the future, return the favor and benefit you. This is a common and essential form of persuasion between lawyers as they seek, for example, to resolve litigation or an impasse in a transaction. In these situations, the client's interest is advanced because the lawyer can move the transaction to a successful conclusion or garner something more beneficial to the client by trading off something less valuable.

Persuasion in Group Situations

Most situations where lawyers use persuasion to advance their clients' interests involve interpersonal interactions. However, sometimes you must persuade groups, such as a jury panel or a corporate board of directors, to reach an agreement or take a complicated, possibly less-than-optimal course of action. Situations like these require additional skills in (1) shaping a message that appeals to the group and (2) communicating that message to a group that may likely include some dissenting viewpoints.

To influence groups, you must be extra vigilant in developing a good sense of the audience's needs, wants, and interests and crafting a message that fosters meaning for them. As their lawyer and leader, you want them "to get it"; sometimes, that requires a nuanced message, while at other times, it may require a blunt message.

Persuasion: A Learned Skill

Given that most law school curricula lack developmental opportunities in persuasion, you will need to find ways to develop the skills to influence others effectively and ethically on your own. Persuasion begins with a firm, clear commitment to achieving the intended goal. You must muster cogent arguments for the sought-after goals, including marshaling sufficient and supportive facts, justifications, and reasons. You must consider how to communicate the rationale through skillful presentation, often in a face-to-face setting and sometimes quite spontaneously.

LAWYER-LEADERS: BUILDING TEAMS

By the time you pass the bar exam and enter law practice, no doubt you have had many experiences—some more successful and satisfying than others—with participation on teams, be they in school, sports, social and political organizations, or the workplace. Some of your most significant leadership experiences have come from these early occasions when you worked with others in groups to make decisions and take action—that is, to collaborate. For example, when a project team is led involving members from engineering, accounting, and legal, tasked with product development and rollout with a revenue projection of many millions of dollars. Or when several teams of lawyers and experts are led in handling class member notifications about litigation settlements and securing documentation of class members' agreements to settle.

Understanding and paying attention to what it takes to build an effective team in the first place is critical for leadership effectiveness. Building consensus, creating a clearly defined plan, and getting the right people on board are three essential considerations in creating high-performing teams.

Building Consensus

To start, there must be a shared understanding or consensus among the people involved regarding purpose—that is, why the team was formed—otherwise, it is just a group of individuals. Without agreement on purpose—that is, why people are being brought together as a team—the resulting collaborative efforts are likely to fail; they might simply be an answer in search of a problem. *Consensus* is more than a fancier word for *agreement*. It typically involves a decision-making process that seeks to ensure widespread support among the people involved for a specific course of action. Consensus also entails agreement on the goals or outcomes of the team's project. Like purpose as a guiding element for a successful team, the consensus of what a good outcome looks like is critical to the team members' acceptance of the group's work.

Reaching consensus is not a matter of just taking a head count to see where everyone is on a particular issue. Instead, it usually requires thoughtful persuasion to get everyone thinking the same way about how to solve a problem. This means setting an example by listening carefully to what everyone is saying, inducing silent members to speak, and incorporating and integrating multiple viewpoints into the dialogue. It also requires reflecting on points others are making, not just to win them over but to evaluate the validity of the ideas and arguments being advanced, regardless of their source, and how they will lead the team to successfully complete the task.

Clearly Defining Plans

Another essential, effective team component is a clearly stated plan of action to achieve the team's goals. Planning requires special attention from a leader early in the process. Effective teams will agree on and assign areas of responsibility to make the most efficient use of resources so that every team member knows what each is expected to contribute. Clear expectations are absolutely necessary to ensure commitment to (not simply compliance with) the project's achievement. Most team projects have expectations, whether developed internally or in their charge, about successfully delivering recommendations and reports.

A defined plan includes specifics about the project's timeline. Team members need to know that the project has a beginning and end—in other words, how to know when success has been achieved. You should begin with the endpoint in mind, effectively focusing the team on what information, data, and evidence will be required. Many projects require data evaluation before making a fact-based set of recommendations. For example, if the compensation committee wants to determine associates' compensation by national or regional standards, it needs sufficient information on the compensation levels of other law firms. Similarly, a law firm's efforts to assemble the most attractive associate hiring packages will miss the mark if they are not based on detailed marketplace information.

Another critical element of the action plan is clearly articulating follow-up steps and implementation actions associated with the team's conclusions. Unfortunately, this critical step is often overlooked because many teams' recommendations and action plans are not self-executing. The team, its leader, or the managing partner must ensure that recommendations and/or action plans are followed through.

Often, the defined plan includes an understanding of and appreciation for how the team's project fits within the organization's structure, of which the team is an integral part. A team viewed in the organization as strong, positive, and necessary is most likely to have its recommendations and conclusions accepted by others.

Getting the Right People on the Team

A third essential element is the composition and representativeness of the team. At a basic level, composition involves size and expertise. Is the team the right size to complete the task efficiently? Does the team include people with the necessary skills, experience, and clout?

Another critical consideration is how the team leader is selected, whether by statute, appointment, or election. Selection of the team leader by democratic methods generally fosters greater buy-in by team members. However, sometimes an individual, based on expertise, connections, or representation, needs to be brought in to lead the team.

Team composition also involves issues of representativeness. Do the people on the team reflect the diversity of the organization? Diversity can refer to whether there is sufficient participation from the affected parties and from underrepresented groups. Designing and leading successful teams involve considerations that stem from the uniqueness of the team's challenge. Sufficient and appropriate representativeness on teams is about more than "political correctness" or the organization's group dynamics. Diversity can bring essential perspectives, without which any proposed solutions may be doomed to fail, since the team simply missed and didn't consider issues necessary to the solution's eventual success.

In situations where the organization has multiple constituencies, the team's composition may need to reflect the interests and needs of many or all constituencies. For example, the American Bar Association's Section on Legal Education represents and responds to several interest groups within legal education, including law school deans and administrators, legal clinic directors and faculty, law students, law librarians, and others. The composition of that section's standing committees, task forces, and other governance or problem-solving groups often reflects these constituent interest groups.

Representativeness helps achieve commitment from the audience you represent or respond to, as well as provide the necessary expertise for the team's mission. In law firms, a cross section of participants from the major significant constituencies (senior associates, associates, senior partners, equity partners, etc.) are often included on teams, especially concerning internal governance issues. Representation considerations are important and sometimes more significant than the particular competencies brought to the team. Constituency-based selection criteria can also facilitate the implementation of the team's recommendations. A good example is the composition of a team addressing working-parent lawyer issues in successfully navigating toward partnership. A team assembled to address this set of thorny issues that doesn't include any members who have children at home would not be very credible to the employees at whom the firm's initiative is aimed. In addition, such a team will likely be insensitive to and/or miss many issues central to successfully implementing any solution.

Choosing and Developing Team Players

Research about high-performing teams has illuminated the essential traits of individuals and their actions that materially contribute to the team's success.[8] The more you understand the characteristics of strong team players, the more you can select the best people to be on your team. If you don't have any voice in membership selection, you must consider how to develop participants into strong team players.

There are five characteristics that matter in how people within a team behave: (1) having a shared mindset, (2) feeling invested in the outcome, (3) communicating respectfully, (4) accepting responsibility, and (5) experiencing appreciation. Of course, what is true about what others need is also true about how you must act, whether as the team's leader or simply as a strong team member, setting an example for others (and, in this way, providing leadership).

In putting a team together, select energetic and expressive people who generally interact positively with others. These characteristics facilitate trust, curiosity, confidence, and motivation within the teams with which they participate.[9] They encourage others to be open-minded, resilient, and persistent, and promote a sense that "we're all in this together." When team members feel respected by one another, they contribute more to the team's efforts by developing a shared mindset that fosters commitment to the team's purpose and goals.[10]

Similarly, you'll want to find people who are comfortable with making decisions by consensus and don't feel they need to win every point or argument personally. Obviously, teams are not successful when everyone is expected to be a "yes person" and "toe the line" or when groupthink becomes the dominant theme of discussion. However, the ability to disagree and then accept and commit to the team's decision is not only critical for every person but is also a clear indication that shared aspirations are embraced.

The best team players have a strong, positive connection to the team's goals. They will feel invested in the outcomes of the project. When those firms wrestling with the challenges of working parents achieving partnerships included one or more working-parent lawyers on the team formed to look into the problem, these lawyers became quite invested in the outcomes of the team's recommendations and how the firm followed through. This was not simply because they could personally benefit but also because they had become involved in and passionate about the equity aspects of those challenges.

Another vital team player characteristic is strong communication skills, especially the capacity for candid reflection. Engaging in respectful dialogue is necessary for highly effective team participation, and avoiding personal attacks and disruptive comments is crucial. Team members who monopolize the conversation during discussions, feeling compelled to restate a point or drone on, are oblivious to the impediments they are creating to effective communication among group members.

Emotional intelligence skills, such as self-awareness and empathy, generally accompany being a good communicator. Some people can sense discomfort or emotional difficulties from others on the team, and they act accordingly. They are good listeners and respect their colleagues on the team. Your leadership is required to identify when emotions are getting out of hand and becoming counterproductive, and you need to tactfully bring the focus back to the task at hand and reinforce the importance of collaboration.

On the most effective teams, people come to meetings prepared and on time. It sounds like a relatively simple matter, doesn't it? However, in our work with law students through senior partners, some of their top disappointments with their colleagues are voiced in comments such as "He is always late to meetings, and this is disruptive because we then need to catch him up with the discussion" and "She is always making meetings difficult because she didn't read the agenda or the other materials we were planning on discussing." Strong team members don't waste people's time. They stay on track and focus themselves and their colleagues on what the team is doing and why, the progress that has been made, and what lies ahead at the finish line.

Furthermore, on the best teams, people appreciate and recognize the contributions of their teammates. They not only express gratitude but also help find ways for the team to celebrate, both by achieving milestones along the way and publicly acknowledging the project's progress and completion. These actions reinforce the belief that "it is all for one and one for all" and that everyone contributes to the group's objectives. Without feeling that people care about one another's contributions and vice versa, the sense of being on a team, rather than simply a group project, is minimized and even lost.

LAWYER-LEADERS: LEADING TEAMS

Being a team means that the people involved see themselves as sharing a collective and common purpose, with mutual commitment and accountability to one another. However, this team mentality will fall apart without effective leadership, and collaboration will not occur. What constitutes successful team leaders is that they incorporate The Five Practices of Exemplary Leadership® (discussed in detail in Part I), and they address the common problems that plague teams.

Incorporating The Five Practices of Exemplary Leadership®

One of The Five Practices of Exemplary Leadership, Enable Others to Act, specifically focuses on collaboration. This practice stresses the importance of collaboration for implementing a shared vision. Certainly, this practice is necessary for leading a team—but it is not the only one. Leaders inspire team members to collaborate toward a common goal by employing a variety of leadership behaviors, which run the gamut of The Five Practices.

Model the Way

Lead by example through your decisions and actions. Be the first person to follow you, and don't undermine your credibility by mismatching your actions with your words or not keeping your commitments and promises. Let people know why you care about the team members and their work and why they should also be willing to put in the long hours required for success. By sharing your own thinking, you can set the tone for others to share their thoughts and ideas more freely and search for shared aspirations.

Inspire a Shared Vision

In envisioning the future, imagination, which has often been touted as even more critical for success than intelligence, is likely to be the factor that helps you and your colleagues see what is just beyond the horizon and get there ahead of others. Curiosity goes hand in hand with imagination. Be contagiously curious about what is happening—and do so in a way that gets others interested in knowing how all the parts fit together. Being curious sets an example of being open-minded and interested in more than just what you are thinking and doing.

You also need to get others on board, and you can do this by showing them how they can make a difference. Keep people focused on the purpose behind the work and the higher meaning involved with the tasks being performed. Ensure that the team understands the difference their efforts and outputs make toward the bigger picture, as their contributions may not be realized for several years.

Challenge the Process

When you encourage your team members to "think outside the box" and experiment, you should mean it by fostering a team environment that supports such creative thinking and rewards it where appropriate. Creating psychological safety allows people to take risks and innovate. You need to provide support and encourage supportive behavior among your team members. Team members need to feel respect from their peers and affirmation that they are competent and making contributions to the greater good. People become more open-minded, resilient, motivated, and persistent when they feel safe participating in a group.[11]

Research has found that positive emotion and interaction modes help establish trust, curiosity, confidence, and inspiration in team participants.[12] Feeling psychologically safe, people will share their experiences for the benefit of others, admit their mistakes, be open to feedback, and look for ways to help others. In such an environment, people will stretch themselves and encourage their teammates to "reach high" in discovering new knowledge and creative ways of thinking about problems and their resolution.

Enable Others to Act

You have to build relationships based on trust in order to foster collaboration. And the trust must flow both ways. People on your team must be able to trust your word and believe that you have their best interests at heart, and you must extend the same trust to the people on your team. Leaders demonstrate trustworthiness by showing empathy. Being empathetic means understanding and appreciating the needs of others and what they are experiencing (although it doesn't necessarily mean always agreeing with how they see things).

Empathy has always been an essential interpersonal skill for leaders, and its importance gained increasing attention during the coronavirus pandemic and accompanying economic and social unrest. Empathy during these challenging times was demonstrated by those leaders who were knowledgeable about and sensitive to what their colleagues were experiencing in their day-to-day lives, and the importance of doing so continues. Get yourself into the habit of listening attentively to those around you, paying attention to their verbal and nonverbal cues. Be so attuned that you can provide the support and assistance they need to press ahead and deal with the challenges and setbacks that might be holding them back.

Take actions that engage people, where you can give them choices and latitude in making decisions. What responsibilities can you share and even delegate? Look to the full range of talents, interests, and knowledge that individual team members bring. The best-performing teams have an evident appreciation and inventory of their members' competencies as a group. They are most likely to use their knowledge to devise problem-solving strategies because gathering information from all team members about their interests and competencies increases their understanding of the task and the range of alternatives and strategies for dealing with it.[13]

Encourage the Heart

You can't take team members for granted. You have to expect the best of them, be willing to get close to people, and create a community spirit.

In particular, you need to ensure that people feel their contributions to the team matter and are critical to their mutual success. Express your commitment to and enthusiasm about both the team's capability and their goals. Public acknowledgment of achievements, including in the form of celebrations, is optimal for ensuring that people feel appreciated for who they are and for what they contribute.

Addressing Problems That Plague Teams

Unfortunately, any number of problems can derail even the best-constituted teams. Exemplary leaders, though, can anticipate, recognize, and be prepared to handle at least three common problems that often plague teams: unproductive team dynamics, irresponsibility, and insufficient direction.

Manage Team Dynamics

Some impediments to collaborative teamwork result from poor group dynamics. A familiar problem to which some otherwise effective working groups fall prey is groupthink. Groupthink means that everyone agrees with or otherwise parrots the first speaker's comments, resulting in a *cascade effect*, and no new or additional insights come from the participants—even while it is apparent that diversity of thinking and sharing of experiences will lead to better decisions. Repetition of a well-made point doesn't make it any better, and repetition of the same point can impede new and creative thoughts.

Team members can also fall into a pattern of focusing on the insights, data, and conclusions they had when they started their participation on the team rather than offering unique data and insights or challenging one another's perspectives. By focusing on what everybody already knows, team members can fail to assess and evaluate critical insights and information held by others in the group.[14] Involving people with diverse backgrounds on the team pays dividends in accuracy because these individuals tend to process information more carefully.[15]

In addition, team members may become polarized and consequently dig into their positions with firm and unyielding conviction. The best decisions may not emerge because of the persistence of a few dominant (or "elite") group members. Another shortcoming to watch out for is when teams amplify their members' errors rather than correcting them. As the old saying goes, those who do not learn from past mistakes are doomed to repeat them.

Exemplary leaders confront issues such as these by deftly moderating meetings to ensure that they are robust, with open and respectful discussions to which everyone contributes and listens to one another. Leaders who have earned the trust of their colleagues will more easily extract optimal performance from group members.

Address Irresponsibility

Let's face it: Some (sometimes many) team members are irresponsible. They don't turn in their work on schedule, show up for meetings on time, or come prepared. Such irresponsibility needs to be acknowledged and dealt with.

You earn the team's respect when you make the most of their time and ensure that meetings are efficient and well run. When you are leading the team, formulate a work plan. Carefully plan workflow and meetings, and work around team members' individual schedules when possible. Make work assignments that ensure that people are engaged and remain positive. You must be fearless about directly confronting difficulties and, where necessary, having candid conversations with underperforming team members. Holding slackers accountable is how others understand that the standards and shared values of the team are taken seriously.

Provide Sufficient Direction

Another problem affecting successful team performance is insufficient direction and governance at the top—from the team leader or leadership group—which causes dysfunctionality, mistakes, false starts, conflicts, and possibly failure. The team leader's importance in this regard cannot be overstated.

Clear and effective leadership at the top of the team is especially critical in cross-functional teams that span the organization—for example, teams from across multiple departments in a law firm or teams that include disparate membership (i.e., from the law firm, various departments within the client's organization, a marketing research firm, an outside expert). A study involving 95 teams across 25 leading companies revealed that nearly 75 percent of cross-functional teams experienced serious problems.[16] They could not get the job done because they lacked "governance support," that is, being able to prepare budgets, stay on schedule, or follow specifications and requirements. Even project teams with moderate governance support were still four times less successful than teams with strong governance support.

Effective teams do not just happen. It takes concerted leadership efforts to reap the benefits of teams and achieve the synergies of teamwork over individual efforts. The good news is that leadership, like collaboration and persuasion, is a skill you can learn and a set of behaviors that can be cultivated and honed through leadership development classes and experiences.

CHAPTER HIGHLIGHTS

- The ability to collaborate is a critical skill for today's lawyers because so much of their work involves collaboration on teams, with clients, and with many internal and external parties.
- A truly collaborative team is one in which members work together toward a common goal. Groups of individuals working independently or sequentially with one another are not collaborative teams.
- Persuasion is a critical competency in fostering collaborative efforts. It requires the ability to communicate a shared purpose and articulate why pursuing it is in people's best interests.
- In building collaborative teams, lawyer-leaders must attend to the components of effective teams (such as consensus, a defined plan, and composition/representativeness). They must also select strong team members and develop them as necessary.
- Leadership is essential to the success of high-performing teams. These skills, behaviors, and attitudes can be identified, and lawyers must learn and apply them to their organizations' most critical collaborative activities and initiatives.
- In addition to incorporating The Five Practices of Exemplary Leadership®, lawyer-leaders must address the problems that plague teams (unproductive team dynamics, irresponsibility, and insufficient direction).

CHAPTER 11

Developing Emotional Intelligence and Handling Adversity

"Lawyers with strong indicators of emotional intelligence generally outperform their less emotionally intelligent colleagues."

It is widely recognized that success, however defined in today's complex world, requires more than strong cognitive abilities. One estimate is that only 15 percent of people's financial success is due to technical ability, with the remaining 85 percent due to personality and the ability to negotiate with and lead people.[1]

Emotional intelligence (emotional quotient, or EQ) is the facility for identifying, processing, and regulating emotions within yourself and others. It is the ability to recognize and appropriately react to your emotions and to those of others around you, and emotional sensitivity is a critical component of effectively interacting with others. While technical skills and cognitive abilities are quite crucial in law practice, EQ skills, especially during times of adversity, are the accelerant taking a good lawyer to an exceptional one—just as they transform a good leader into an exemplary one.[2]

Given its significance in achieving personal and professional success, we have been surprised by how many lawyers just "don't get" the substance of EQ. Lawyers, being high in analytic traits and skills, tend to view EQ as "soft skills" (as opposed to the "hard skills" of reading and discerning meaning in case law) and, therefore, at a lower level of skills needed for success. Our research, as described in this chapter, suggests the opposite—solid and empathic people skills, coupled with thoughtful introspection and a mindful self-management temperament, are fundamental keys to success as a lawyer.

BEYOND INTELLIGENCE (IQ)

You will need more than content "tools" in your toolkit to succeed in law practice. You need to be able to think and act beyond the day-to-day tasks performed in litigation, client advising, and transactions and employ leadership skills, which will carry you forward to success both as a lawyer and a leader.

Prior chapters have emphasized many critical practice-specific capabilities required of lawyers and how these are especially important and necessary for providing exemplary leadership. Leading a team of peers or direct reports, effectively making timely and appropriate decisions, navigating crises with creative and innovative processes, and persuading others to follow your vision are all preeminent skills for today's lawyer-leaders.

Still, there are additional abilities that lawyers need to possess, develop, and demonstrate to be successful, especially in volatile, challenging, and uncertain environments, as is the case with much of the work that lawyers do. A survey of hundreds of senior lawyers, corporate counsels, and law firm leaders regarding the most important skills lawyers need to lead their law organizations revealed a demand for five specific strategic leadership skills.[3] The first two are relevant for lawyers just entering their firms, and while the latter three concern more senior members of the firm, it is worthwhile to keep them in mind as you envision moving ahead:

1. Intensely understanding clients' needs and effectively responding to them in a timely manner. Law is a *people business*, and the emphasis of the firm and its members must be on client satisfaction.
2. Taking care of oneself while also caring for the firm and its members.
3. Effectively managing the organization's "talent," including new and existing members. The primary cost on the balance sheets of most legal organizations involves people, their care, and retention.
4. Making sound decisions and establishing the organization's strategic direction. Respondents agreed that this is a core function of leadership and is especially crucial in uncertain times.
5. Responding to change and addressing the need for growth in the organization and its personnel. According to the survey, the ability to anticipate economic, legal, and law practice changes is a critical factor in fast-changing times. The organization must be committed to responding to those changes by developing new and existing markets and practice areas.

These findings help highlight the behaviors, attitudes, and abilities required of lawyers to effectively lead, guide, and develop their organizations in challenging times. While "knowing more law" and "developing greater mastery of the rules of civil procedure" are important, they are not at the top of the list. In fact, nearly all the top-of-mind concerns require emotional intelligence, not greater legal competency.

EQ AND THE LEGAL PROFESSION

Social science research has identified factors essential for success in professional positions and careers: cognitive abilities, technical skills, and interpersonal (EQ) skills.[4] Cognitive abilities include intelligence, reasoning, and analytic skills. These skills are often the most immediately valued and the primary "evidence" for hiring decisions, as well as entrance into professional degree programs such as law school. Technical skills, such as job knowledge and law practice abilities (e.g., taking a deposition and preparing a strategy for litigation discovery), are also often valued in placement and career promotion decisions. The third area of professional skills is emotional intelligence, including understanding one's strengths and limitations, self-confidence, and the ability to work with and lead others.

This latter area is often undervalued as evidence of a lawyer's worth to the law firm or practice group. However, many law firms view coaching and developing emotional intelligence as a competitive edge.[5] Research shows that lawyers with strong indicators of emotional intelligence generally outperform their less emotionally intelligent colleagues.[6] For example, surveys show that lawyers with the EQ skills needed to effectively collaborate generate the highest revenues within their firms.[7]

Emotional intelligence sharpens abilities to assess risk, as evidenced by a greater understanding of ethics, recognizing when and how others make ethical choices, and consciously strengthening personal ethical choices. EQ makes lawyers better communicators, especially during difficult conversations with clients or colleagues in which tough choices must be made. People with strong emotional intelligence are also more empathetic, which is critically essential for lawyers in their client-counseling role. Moreover, lawyers with strong emotional intelligence are more credible to their clients, adversaries, colleagues, and judges because they are aware and in control of their emotions and place a premium on positive interactions with others.

The findings from a study conducted in a large, nationwide insurance company have important implications for practicing attorneys. The sales agents who were strong in emotional areas such as self-confidence, initiative, and empathy sold policies with an average premium of over 50 percent more than those of their weak counterparts.[8] People want to do business with a person they like and trust rather than with someone they don't like, which is significant for lawyers regarding interactions with clients and juries.

The challenge, notes Ronda Muir, author of *Beyond Smart: Lawyering with Emotional Intelligence,* is that while lawyers score high in cognitive abilities, they tend to score poorly in emotional intelligence—which has a massive impact on the public's low opinion of the legal profession overall.[9] Our leadership classes have impressed us with how law students grasp the importance of EQ behaviors and abilities. Still, they often reach this conclusion, unfortunately, by pointing to the poor interpersonal and self-management skills of lawyers they have worked with. The legal profession, the students readily concede, needs considerable improvement in emotional intelligence.

EQ AND LEADERSHIP

The linkage between emotional intelligence and effective lawyering is clear, but does emotional intelligence help in leadership too? Research shows that emotional intelligence is the barometer of excellence in virtually any job,[10] and the most successful lawyers and leaders have well-developed EQ capabilities.

Expert Views

In speaking about lawyers' need for more and better EQ skills, one renowned expert on lawyer leadership reported that "though technical excellence and intellect are critical factors for success as a lawyer, emotional intelligence is the differentiating factor for successful leadership."[11] As well as being essential to lawyers in their personal and professional lives, EQ skills influence and advance your ability to engage in The Five Practices of Exemplary Leadership®.

Daniel Goleman, an internationally prominent psychologist, has studied and written extensively about emotional intelligence in the workplace, and he indicates that technical abilities and cognitive skills provide a "threshold" capability or capacity for success but that EQ skills are twice as important.[12] He contends that the ability to use emotional intelligence is one of the hallmarks of truly effective leaders. Self-aware people know that their feelings, beliefs, and abilities affect others and use those feelings and beliefs to inspire and implement change in the organization.

EQ and Organizational Success

Emotional intelligence on the part of leaders contributes mightily to an organization's performance and productivity. For instance, emotionally intelligent supervisors and managers can sense how direct reports feel about their work situation and intervene effectively when those employees feel discouraged, dissatisfied, and frustrated. When supervisors are self-aware and able to manage their emotions, people will trust and feel good about working with them. Studies show that employees who rate the quality of their immediate supervisor as *poor* are four times more likely to leave their organizations than those who rate their immediate supervisor as *excellent.*[13] Retention is directly tied to the EQ of the organization's leadership.

EQ is the "driver" of a healthy, productive, and effectively functioning workplace. Look deeply at almost any factor that influences organizational effectiveness, and you will find that emotional intelligence plays a role:[14]

- *Opportunity for growth.* People seek a work environment where their position has potential for development; employees desire the freedom to innovate and grow personally and professionally. Second- and third-year law firm associates voice this same refrain about the importance they place on the opportunity to grow their skill sets, influence firm decisions, and develop their professional skills with clients.
- *Responsibility.* Employees who believe they are responsible for getting things done in their organizations feel the most invested and favorable about their workplace. Delegation shows that their supervisors trust them and value their work.
- *High standards in terms of integrity and quality work.* Employees who believe that their organization has high standards and that those standards are clearly spelled out report the highest levels of satisfaction with their organization.
- *Reward systems.* Employees who perceive a transparent, achievable, and relevant system of rewarding good performance are much more motivated and satisfied with the organization than those who aren't confident about how their work is valued. Lawyers who work hard, are thoughtful, and "win" expect their organization to reward them accordingly.
- *Clarity of organizational purpose, values, and goals.* Employees who are most clear about whom and what they are working for are most likely to express pride in telling others about their organization. Likewise, employees who have the most favorable feelings about their workplace are the most committed not only to their clients but also to their company.

All these drivers of workplace motivation and retention are relevant to most professional workplaces, especially law, where there are significant mutual dependencies on other lawyers in the firm to maintain high standards of ethical conduct and professional comportment. The key point is that workplace satisfaction does not happen by accident or without effective leadership, and such leadership reflects the characteristics associated with strong emotional intelligence. Research abounds that high levels of emotional intelligence "create climates in which information sharing, trust, healthy risk-taking, and learning flourish."[15] In contrast, "[L]ow levels of emotional intelligence create climates rife with fear and anxiety . . . their organizations may post good results, but they never last."[16]

We have asked law students and junior associates in law firms alike to reflect on the exceptional leadership skills demonstrated by a lawyer or judge, and, without exception, it was their EQ skills that made the most significant impact on their perceptions of a desirable, effective workplace. For example, when we talked with lawyers on a particular district attorney's office staff, they commented on the DA's strong leadership: "He told the truth to us and to the public." "He was highly ethical, and his principles were evident and inspiring in how he led the office." "His value-driven leadership and his highly effective interaction with everyone in the office made it a place that we wanted to be associated with." Similarly, junior associates in another firm we interviewed were considerably more likely to comment on and compliment senior associates on their "people" or "interpersonal" skills than their technical skills in the law. What mattered to the newer lawyers was the ability of their leaders to put themselves in the young lawyers' "shoes" (empathy), their encouragement of self-reflective skills, and their measured approaches to junior associate errors and lack of knowledge on particular topics.

EQ: Leading Self and Others

Consider for a moment the attributes of colleagues, supervisors, or organizational leaders with whom you have worked and whom you highly admire. What behaviors and personal attributes characterize them and make your work together positive and productive? We suspect that your list will include, in some fashion, the characteristics associated with emotional intelligence. Some of those characteristics relate to a leader's ability to lead oneself; others relate to a leader's ability to lead others.

The first two aspects of emotional intelligence—awareness and regulation—focus on the individual and the ability to lead oneself. If you do not know who you are and what you stand for, or if you don't know how to control your impulses and harness your emotions for the group's good, then why would someone choose to follow you?

Self-awareness requires a deep understanding of your emotions, strengths and weaknesses, and needs and wants. Being self-aware means that you understand how your feelings and attitudes not only affect you but also impact other people. For example, if working on a tight deadline brings out the worst in you, you adjust your work routine to finish your work ahead of schedule. Self-aware attorneys will know what difficult or demanding clients do to their moods and frustration levels and act in a manner that moderates or avoids those feelings and situations. They have developed the skill of self-reflection—the ability to examine how their own motivations, beliefs, and values affect their thoughts and actions, and the capacity to adjust or change them in light of others' actions and thoughts and to do so in future experiences.[17] When you experience intense emotions, slow down and think about why you are feeling what you are feeling, and be more intentional in how you choose to react.

Self-regulation requires continuous attention and personal growth because most people are impulsive and emotional about things that are relevant and important to them. People generally learn at an early age that they must control many of these impulses and emotions to function well in their classes, jobs, and personal relationships. For lawyers and leaders, this ability is critical because people who are in control of their feelings and impulses can create an environment of trust and fairness, which coworkers, direct reports, and others highly desire. People who can regulate their behaviors also tend to avoid improper conduct (e.g., rarely verbally attacking others) and demonstrate higher integrity (e.g., not stereotyping people) than those who succumb to temptation and take the "low road." Lawyers with high self-control are generally reflective and thoughtful and comfortable with ambiguity and the need for change.

EQ's second dynamic—the ability to work well with others—has an outward focus, and it is evident in lawyers' efforts to attract and keep clients, retain talent in the firm, and work with others who actually want to interact with them. This aspect of emotional intelligence addresses your ability to lead others and has two critical *social* attributes: social awareness and social skills.

Social awareness is your ability to sense and respond to the feelings, difficulties, and attitudes of those around you. When you say that someone doesn't have a clue about what's going on, you are really saying that they are unaware of how their behavior and statements affect others. Saying that this person is "tone deaf" is another way of saying that they cannot put themselves into someone else's situation. Both expressions refer to a lack of empathy. Active listening is an antecedent of empathy—that is, thoughtfully considering the feelings and concerns of others. Take the time to look at situations from other people's perspectives (not just argue for your own). Respond to, rather than avoid, feelings, and seek to understand the *why* behind how people are expressing themselves and their viewpoints.

Social skills refer to your ability to manage relationships with other people and are closely associated with communication skills. Leaders and lawyers with strong social skills build common ground and can develop rapport with a wide range of people. Many of these skills are the team-building skills described in the previous chapter. Be purposeful and attentive when networking, making connections, and creating projects and situations that bring people together. Generate alternatives when disagreements arise, and promote a cooperative climate in which everyone feels welcome and invited to contribute.

EQ is a necessary part of any effective leader's portfolio. You have to lead yourself first, and then you need to be able to lead others while recognizing that success in any endeavor comes about through the intersection of these two facets of EQ and leadership. Because leadership ultimately involves doing something that has never entirely been done that way before, developing the mindset of an entrepreneur also has particular relevance to lawyer-leaders.

The coronavirus pandemic saw a premium placed on lawyers who understood the importance of empathy and the ability to demonstrate it. They tended to make it clear by their words and actions that "we're all in this together," and they were constantly looking out for their team's or employee's best interests. Empathy places the welfare of others above the leader's own self-interests, and it "normalizes the practice of caring about how those around you are doing."[18] Law firms that most successfully navigated the coronavirus-related challenges, and are today effectively dealing with hybrid and virtual workplaces, have their primary focus and attention on the people in the organization and on their welfare.

EQ: An Entrepreneurial Mindset

We heard variations of the following reflection from young attorneys across the spectrum of legal settings and organizational sizes: "I wish that someone had told me in law school about how I would need to be an entrepreneur in order to be a successful lawyer." This lament echoes what a growing number of practicing attorneys and law firms are also coming to terms with.[19] As with successful corporate entrepreneurs, lawyers with strong EQ can leverage empathy, handle ambiguity, and see challenges from various perspectives, which improves problem solving, creates strong relationships, and ultimately wins people over. A meta-analysis (looking at nearly 40 studies involving more than 65,000 entrepreneurs) found that while both IQ and EQ were essential for entrepreneurial success, EQ had twice the influence of IQ.[20]

Entrepreneurship, defined as "the pursuit of opportunity beyond the resources you currently control,"[21] requires an internal drive to make the most of possibilities, a willingness to experiment coupled with the ability to pivot and adapt as circumstances change quickly, and the ego strength to overcome and learn from setbacks. Assessing an entrepreneurial opportunity requires discerning how to capitalize on that prospect, candidly calculating what resources you will need and how to gain control over them, and determining the best structure to use to take advantage of an opening.[22]

Like successful entrepreneurs, lawyers should have a growth mindset and believe strongly in themselves. What follows is being unafraid of making mistakes, being in touch with your feelings, and carving out your own path forward. This self-awareness contributes to a bias for action. It favors decisiveness—taking to heart the wisdom of one entrepreneur who claimed that he hadn't ever met a rich person who had never lost any money but had met many poor people who had never lost a dime.[23] Adopting an entrepreneurial mindset means believing more in the possibilities than in the probabilities, becoming comfortable with discomfort, and proactively looking for problems so that you have the "opportunity" to fix them.[24]

Bring these entrepreneurial qualities to your legal practice and to the organizations you associate with. This entrepreneurial spirit and process are essential to how lawyers effectively turn adversity into opportunity within their legal firms and environments.[25] The most successful lawyers have an entrepreneurial mindset as they evaluate and seize new business opportunities, including market expansions, adopting innovative technologies, developing novel practice areas, and launching a new law practice group.

EQ SKILLS AND MANAGING ADVERSITY

Lawyers make their living dealing with adversity. From your earliest days in law school, you are educated to anticipate conflicts and disagreements and deal with setbacks and disappointments. In the legal profession, you can't take anything for granted; you must expect the unexpected, and wild cards are in every deck. Of course, such observations apply to everyone, no matter their occupation or status. Still, they take on particular importance when you are a lawyer-leader dealing with significant circumstances, such as handling a client's liberty or wealth—and another reminder about why emotional intelligence is essential for lawyers and lawyer-leaders.

Adversity and the Legal Profession

In a powerful scene in *The Paper Chase*, the iconic Professor Kingsfield dryly remarks to a classroom of new law students, "Look to your left, look to your right. One of you won't be here next year." This comment highlights the fact that law is a profession rife with adversity. Perhaps no one knows this better than junior lawyers and associates in law firms when confronted with multiple requests for work products and participation in projects by their more senior colleagues in the firm.

Lawyers' professional lives are complicated by regular setbacks, unanticipated circumstances, challenging people who disrupt an established plan or strategy, and the vagaries of luck. Drawing a judge with a history of opposition to a significant element or point in your case is a modest example of adversity; having the entire mergers and acquisitions department in your corporate defense firm leave (with associates) to form a boutique firm is a more significant example. The sudden, unanticipated death of the top rainmaker in the firm is another noteworthy situation, as would an economic recession that causes the firm to seek protection from federal bankruptcy laws.

Law organizations have been experiencing significant changes and challenges from various sources in recent years.[26] They have to overcome or manage serious threats to their business, including competitive pressures from international law firms and alternative legal services providers; a dramatic escalation in the use of technology in the practice of law; challenges associated with attracting and retaining young, as well as experienced, talent; and increasing demands from clients for reducing the cost of legal services.[27]

On an individual level, too, adversity is ubiquitous. Setbacks such as an adverse jury decision, a case dismissed on summary judgment, or an inadequate arbitration award all create stresses on the attorney of record. Additional pressures to succeed, to name a few, come from law school debt, possible new family responsibilities, managing people (e.g., administrative personnel), and exploding overhead costs.

Methods of Coping

Lawyers and leaders need to understand and plan for adversity and crisis. Whether from a leader's or a lawyer's perspective, the issue is not whether you will face adversity but rather how you will deal with it when it happens.

A great deal of research on mental and emotional hardiness and coping has shown that every person has a distinct, consistent pattern of thinking about life's ups and downs and also that most people are unaware of their particular pattern.[28] A classic study examining how different people reacted to an identical challenge found that stress does not affect every person similarly.[29] During the coronavirus pandemic, for example, while everyone experienced the same storm, they were not all in the same boat, and so the hardships from the health crisis were experienced in different ways.

Some people easily handle a crisis or lousy outcome, while others experience great difficulty coping with it. The difference is not attributable to a character flaw but rather to the variances in how people process, manage, and rebound from a challenging episode or situation. For some people, adversity is viewed as an opportunity for change and growth rather than a situation warranting anger, disappointment, and despair due to the challenge or failure.[30] Those with the strongest EQ skills cope most successfully with adversity.

Trial lawyers, for example, know that in litigation, there is always one side that wins and one side that loses, so some appreciation of how to handle a defeat and help a client understand a loss is vitally important. Much of lawyers' work involves a stark divide between winning and losing, and more than "tough skin" is needed. What's required is a finely tuned ability to manage oneself, built by experience and strong EQ skills.

EQ Skills and Crisis Leadership

There is little question that lawyers are living in tumultuous times—economic upheavals, health pandemics, social unrest, political polarization, and climate calamities are likely to continue. Thus, lawyer-leaders need the skills and attitudes that will permit them to function well in those uncertain times, and equally important, they need to survive and prosper with their spirit and self-confidence in good shape. In other words, they need strong EQ skills to lead through crises and adversity.

A volatile, uncertain, complex, ambiguous (VUCA) world does not favor taking a business-as-usual attitude, even though people are looking to their leaders to set the path forward, providing "marching orders" through a vision for the future. More is necessary, especially for lawyers, when a change in the law or legal practice is necessary. Law firm experts explain that in times of uncertainty, confusing disruptions to the status quo, and challenge, legal professionals look to leaders for a vision of a positive and realistic future and the ability to lead change.[31]

You need to understand and consider the following six EQ-inspired strategies in reframing crisis and adversity as opportunity:[32]

1. *Broaden the context* in which you find yourself by reminding people that the situation is not personal and that many others are trying to cope with the same disruption and dislocation. While that doesn't address the steps that must be taken to deal with the crisis, it does provide a mental framework for considering the problem.

2. *Be candid* with your colleagues and/or team about the situation, what actions must be taken, and what is or is not working. Many Americans saw this played out poorly with the federal government's early reaction to the coronavirus outbreak: confusion, obfuscation, disregard for medical science, and intentional misstatements of fact. People don't blame leaders for adverse outcomes over which they had no control, but they do blame them and cease to trust them if they don't tell it like it is.
3. *Reach out to others and engage* more than ever with them. If you perceive that difficult times lie ahead, then your colleagues are also experiencing those challenges, uncertainty, and possibly even isolation. People experience those feelings and reactions in a crisis, and you must be fully engaged in leading your team through it. Get started by asking people about their conditions and situations; express empathy but also ensure that by "working together," this calamity can be turned into a positive opportunity to improve the team or organization. Demonstrate compassion and caring for others so they know you have their best interests in mind and will do your best to get everyone through the crisis.
4. *Act quickly and boldly.* Prompt action is usually necessary and expected depending on the nature of the crisis; strive for strategic decision making with speed over the precision of impact.[33] Speed over precision is preferred because people become cognitively overwhelmed during a crisis, helpful information is incomplete or unavailable, and there is a tendency to shut down. Therefore, effective crisis leadership requires prompt but thoughtful action to assess the threatened harm's scope and extent (and cause) and then engage in active decision making and responses.
5. *Do what you say you will do*—don't make promises you can't keep. People admire and follow those who stick to their commitments and set an example for others to emulate. Be both candid (realistic) and optimistic in offering a pathway forward. Demonstrate progress in small increments, and keep reminding people about the improvement that is being made. One of the most disappointing aspects of the federal government's initial handling of the COVID-19 pandemic was that there was no national mandate or plan of action, and each state and municipality was on its own; consequently, when government agencies eventually took action, they appeared to be chaotic and quixotic.
6. *Prepare yourself to lead in a crisis.* Many of the demands of leadership are predictable, but most crises spring on the leaders and their

constituents with little notification. In such circumstances, prompt, confident, responsive action is needed. It will be helpful if you have identified how you will communicate and how roles and responsibilities will be allocated in a sudden and significant event. Think of this as a fire drill, or liken this to the emergency response exercises that first responders conduct. Each challenge requires its own playbook, but leaders can prepare in general ways for a crisis and then adapt to the challenge that prompts action by the group.

Resilience and Grit

Life doesn't come with a road map, and there is no freeway to the future. Every life path (personal and organizational) has twists and turns, roadblocks and delays, and unexpected detours, some of which will be graver, more challenging, or even more joyous than others. Each change affects people differently, yet people generally adapt well over time to life-changing and stressful situations—partly thanks to resilience and grit. While resilience involves getting back up when you've been knocked down or coming back fighting stronger after a loss, grit is your passion for and perseverance in reaching a long-term goal. Lawyer-leaders can use their EQ skills to transform adverse situations into opportunities by fostering and promoting both resiliency and grit in themselves and their teams.

Psychologists define *resilience* as the process of adapting well in the face of adversity, trauma, tragedy, threat, or significant sources of stress—such as family and relationship problems, serious health problems, or workplace and financial stressors. Resilience can be considered a kind of solitary internal "grit" that allows individuals to rebound, often stronger than before, from setbacks and sustain their drive and commitment over time.

As much as resilience most often involves bouncing back from these difficult experiences, it can also involve profound personal growth (actually bouncing forward).[34] Resilient people look at the world in a very realistic way, and, as such, they act in ways that permit them to face head-on the problems, challenges, and opportunities that come their way. They may be disappointed with their situation, but they have prepared themselves for adversity and even great success. Resilience positively influences people's work satisfaction and engagement, lowers their levels of depression, and improves overall well-being. Resilient people are generally healthy, productive, and dependable. They can respond "quickly and constructively" to crisis and adversity, and resiliency has been shown as a critical factor in explaining the differences between highly successful and unsuccessful people.[35]

Grit helps to explain why some people accomplish more than others despite similarities in talent and resources.[36] Grit is the motivational drive that keeps you going, for example, on a complex case over a sustained period of time. Research involving a large, international sample found that grit was related to The Five Practices of Exemplary Leadership®, with the grittiest more likely to lead by example (Model the Way) and to support others in challenging the status quo (Challenge the Process). From a practical view, grit enables you, as a leader and as a lawyer, to be more willing to stick with, stand up for, and live by your principles, as well as be comfortable taking risks and learning from experience.[37]

Building Resilience and Grit

How you envision situations and explain setbacks to yourself can build resilience and grit. For example, resilient people view difficulty as a challenge, not a paralyzing event. They see the effects of setbacks as temporary rather than permanent and view them as experiences from which to learn and as opportunities for growth and development. Resilient people recognize that they won't win in every situation, so they don't blame themselves or consider themselves victims when that happens. Instead, they focus on what they can learn to propel themselves forward the next time.

Furthermore, you build and foster resilience and grit when you have a purpose for what you are doing and a commitment to make the most of every relationship and the causes you care about. Focus your time and energy on situations and events over which you have some control and where you can have an impact, because this strengthens your resolve and confidence, overcoming feelings of helplessness, loss, and powerlessness.

One of the most potent ways to build personal resilience and grit is to forge connections and relationships with others. This helps you remember the meaning of your work, maintain perspective with confidence, and focus on the path forward so that your colleagues and team members share your confidence and strategic vision for solutions.[38] Look at the Grit Project, created by the ABA Commission on Women in the Profession, to develop and enhance women lawyers' grit and growth mindset. The articles, videos, case studies, and activities are all foundational for lawyers of any race, ethnicity, or sexual orientation.[39]

EQ: A LEARNED SKILL

While identifying and describing the significant pressures and demands on themselves and their law firms, a substantial percentage of law firm leaders readily admit that they and their firms are not undertaking substantive actions to handle these challenges and, consequently, are losing talent, clients, and market share.[40] Firm leaders report deep concerns about the large number of American law firms that have experienced an existential crisis caused by an economic recession or a collapse of a practice area and have gone out of business in the past two decades.[41] The causes for law firm closings and failures are varied, but most can be traced back directly to the failure of leadership.

To adequately prepare for adversity, lawyer-leaders must develop EQ skills. Strong EQ skills and aptitude are very important in lawyers' work. However, they are not genetic, meaning they can be learned, developed, and mastered. While emotional intelligence often increases with age and maturity, a conscious commitment to advancing these abilities can considerably improve your effectiveness as a lawyer and a leader, even early in your career. Like building up muscle, doing so takes time and intentionality. As with building muscles, though, building EQ skills is worth the time because the end result is strong and healthy leadership.

CHAPTER HIGHLIGHTS

- Cognitive and technical skills are necessary for success as a lawyer, but emotional intelligence (EQ) skills are even more essential. This is true for any lawyer and even truer for lawyer-leaders.
- EQ skills are essential for leading self, others, and organizations.
- The legal profession is characterized by adversity, but lawyer-leaders can best handle adversity and crisis situations with EQ skills.
- EQ helps leaders foster resilience and grit—two critical factors in handling adversity—in themselves and their followers.
- Leaders with EQ provide leadership that turns adversity into opportunity, diffuses conflicts, and builds greater harmony and cooperation in the workplace.
- EQ abilities are not innate and may not come naturally to many lawyers, but they can be learned and developed so that all lawyers can add this skill to their toolkit of effective leadership.

Chapter 12

Leading the Charge for Diversity, Equity, and Inclusion

"Lawyers interpret for their clients the national policies promoting equality in opportunity for all Americans—yet they have often failed to lead their own organizations to meet those goals."

The American Bar Association (ABA) recognizes that the legal profession has a diversity problem. They have led initiatives promoting greater diversity and have established goals for enhancing diversity in the profession and eliminating bias throughout the profession and the judicial system.[1] The ABA's goals stress three fundamental components to achieve a more diverse profession and the elimination of bias: greater efforts to diversify the legal profession, more significant consideration of equity in compensation and status, and expanding inclusion and belonging in the profession and its institutions. These are collectively known as diversity, equity, and inclusion (DEI); together, they require leadership in law organizations to succeed.

The ABA has established a center for advancing diversity in the profession and sponsored programs to assist law organizations in achieving their goals of greater diversity and inclusion. The ABA's Diversity & Inclusion 360 Commission articulated its commitment that "all providers of legal services, including law firms and corporations, . . . expand and create opportunities at all levels of responsibility for diverse attorneys" and urged "clients to assist in the facilitation of opportunities for diverse attorneys, and to direct a greater percentage of the legal services they purchase, both currently and in the future, to diverse attorneys."[2] Particular challenges for women and people of color were highlighted by the coronavirus pandemic, which makes DEI efforts all that more significant.[3]

A strong institutional commitment to greater inclusiveness in the profession is an excellent starting point, but more must be done. Leadership is what will move the legal profession and its institutions and organizations (from the organized bar to law firms and schools) toward a state of equality in opportunity and equity in outcomes.

Lawyers' work requires great awareness of the need for a more inclusive society and far more diverse workplaces (usually expressed in terms of racial, ethnic, gender, and sexual orientation). Lawyers are at society's front line in addressing problems of discrimination and justice. They routinely advise clients on legal and business problems stemming from their less-than-inclusive workplaces—yet lawyers predominantly work in those same workplaces. Lawyers interpret for their clients the national policies promoting equality in opportunity for all Americans—yet they have often failed to lead their own organizations (e.g., law firms, corporate counsel offices, and government legal departments) to meet those goals.

In recent years, law firms and organizations seeking to advance their own diversity and inclusion initiatives and to support their clients' DEI objectives have been challenged by political headwinds and strong objections to these initiatives in some quarters. Whether the political challenges are short term or are to remain for a while, lawyer-leaders must navigate the challenges and the shifting political climate while remaining focused on the instrumental importance of the benefits of diverse and inclusive workplaces.

DIVERSITY PROBLEMS IN THE LEGAL PROFESSION

Many Americans aspire to become lawyers. Surveys show that many people have this career goal, and in recent years, more than 60,000 people annually apply to American law schools.[4] Accordingly, you might think that the ranks of lawyers are as diverse and representative as the United States at large. However, the facts suggest that the legal profession is mainly White and male; this is also true for the federal and state judiciary.

Although about 42 percent of law school applicants identify as *not* White/Caucasian,[5] demographics of practicing lawyers tell a different story. Black people constitute 12 percent of the U.S. population but only 5 percent of American lawyers.[6] Hispanic/Latinx people constitute 18 percent of the national population, yet 6 percent of its lawyers. Asians comprise about 7 percent of the U.S. population and 6 percent of American lawyers.[7] Notably, White people in America account for 60 percent of the population but an overwhelming 79 percent of lawyers.[8] Furthermore, according to contemporary surveys, males in America account for only 49 percent of the population yet constitute 61 percent of practicing lawyers.[9] Even a cursory examination of the factual data indicates racial and gender disparities in the legal profession.

The diversity gaps are again quite apparent among the most venerable and prominent group of lawyers—those who serve on the bench in the judgment of others. The judiciary is the most significant segment of American lawyers due to judges' impact on setting national policy and providing a face for the civil and criminal justice systems and the overall legal profession. Some illustrative data on the diversity issue: Approximately 80 percent of all sitting federal judges in the United States are White.[10] Only one in three federal judges are female.[11] And more than half of all state court justices are White and male, while only 15 percent are people of color, even though White males constitute only about 30 percent of the U.S. population.[12]

In addition to the diversity calculus in the legal profession, there is the problem of some people questioning whether a diversity issue even exists. In any legal environment, there will be a range of opinions, with people holding polar opposite positions. Some will exclaim, "We don't have a diversity problem; everything is okay" or "All this diversity stuff is just political correctness!" Others will look around their firm and point out, "Everyone here looks the same" or "There aren't many people in this agency who look like me" or exclaim, "The data indicates that we don't very well mirror the population, do we?"

Surveys have highlighted substantial differences in perceptions among lawyers about the extent to which the firm's professionals experienced or perceived bias and uneven access to opportunities and benefits. For example, in one survey, only 11 percent of White male lawyers believed that diversity efforts were failing to address subtle racial or gender bias, compared with 40 percent of White women and about 50 percent of women of color.[13]

The diversity and inclusion problems of the U.S. legal profession affect the leadership of the profession and its law firms. White attorneys are almost twice as likely to reach partnership status than other racial groups, and men are twice as likely to become partners than women.[14] People of color account for about 10 percent of partners at large firms, and women comprise only 25 percent. While the opportunity to ascend to partnership status for women and lawyers of color is limited, some firms are signing the "Mansfield Rule," which requires firms to confirm that they considered pools of candidates that are at least 30 percent diverse, including women and underrepresented racial and ethnic groups.[15]

Clearly, there is a need for greater diversity and inclusiveness in the legal profession, and to address head on the pushback and skepticism surrounding this issue. Organizations' efforts to support all their workers by instilling a great collective sense of belonging have been challenged by the politicization of DEI by elected officials who seek division and separateness. Yet the reasons to promote greater diversity and inclusion within law organizations remain clear and, moreover, are expected by firms' clients. These needs highlight the necessity for lawyer-leaders.

FOUNDATIONAL CONCEPTS

It is critical to grasp some foundational concepts to understand how to address diversity issues and how leadership can help. Mastering key terminology is the beginning point for any discussion of diversity, and understanding the problem of implicit bias is the starting point for finding a solution to the diversity problem. Understanding that discrimination is systemic, often inheres in the structures of the American legal profession, and is not simply the product of individual animus is also fundamental to increasing diversity in the profession. Finally, the concept of belonging is the key to understanding how more significant attention to DEI efforts in the organization will improve performance and outcomes. A core goal of DEI programs and initiatives is to create a culture and climate of belonging so that everyone in the organization contributes to its success because they belong and believe in it.

Diversity, Equity, and Inclusion

What the terms *diversity* and its close cousins *equity* and *inclusion* mean and entail is often misconstrued. Each of these terms plays a vital role in combating bias and discrimination in the legal profession and the practice of law, and in strengthening an organization's vitality and culture.

Diversity is the presence of differences within a given setting. A single individual is not diverse; diversity is a relational construct based on some collective whole. It is typically described by a numerical representation of different types or groups of people, such as how many Latinx people are admitted to law school, how many females are recruited to a firm, and how many Black people are getting promoted and advanced in an office. The measurement of diversity is usually captured in fairly traditional characteristics, such as age, gender, and ethnicity, or people's identities (such as by disability or sexual orientation). The representation of women lawyers in a firm or the percentage of Asian American lawyers in a particular office, for example, permits comparisons over time or with various organizational factors (e.g., compensation and rates of retention and partnerships). This data is valuable to the firm's leaders, who are interested in advancing diversity goals.

Equity recognizes that in most settings, there is no equal starting place; it's like a Monopoly game where someone doesn't get to begin playing until most other players have already purchased properties and built houses. Equity acknowledges this context, commits to addressing the gaps and imbalances, and takes corrective actions. Equity refers to institutional efforts ensuring that all people, especially historically marginalized populations, have access to opportunities, resources, and support from the organization. Equity does not mean equality—as in each person is treated equally—but rather strives to eliminate any constraints on individuals' ability to access an open position, a promotion, or the organization's resources to support their personal goals and ambitions.

Inclusion focuses on the "how" of diversity—the behaviors and social norms, along with policies and decisions that contribute to or hinder the involvement and sense of belonging that people feel about the group, team, or organization. Inclusion can be tangible and visible, such as who gets invited to meetings, whose opinions are heard, how offices are physically organized and allocated, or even who gets access to particular information and resources. Inclusion is what new lawyers are thinking about when asking themselves questions such as the following:

- How well do I fit in this place?
- How welcome do I feel in this situation?
- How valued does this place make me feel when decisions are made?

An analogy is often used to describe the relationship among these three concepts: diversity is invited to the party, equity is asked to plan the dance, and inclusion is asked to dance. Stated another way, equity is a goal for the organization, with diversity being a first (and quite significant) step and inclusion referring to the effort, actions, and environment necessary to achieve the goal. Belonging is when everyone knows the words to the songs; they all share the sense of a community of shared goals and aspirations and feel included and valued.

Implicit Bias

Perhaps the greatest challenge to lawyers and their organizations is the underlying reason that DEI efforts are necessary in the first place: "implicit bias" and its effects on the structure and operation of law firms and law organizations.

Social scientists have firmly established that people employ two cognitive reasoning systems—one that is rapid, intuitive, and prone to errors, and a second that is more calculated, deliberative, and more likely to be error-free.[16] It is the first type of reasoning in which implicit perceptions, attitudes, and stereotypes occur and affect social judgments without conscious awareness or control. These implicit thoughts and feelings leak into many behaviors and attitudes, including how you perceive others and what you value. Within this type of reaction, behavior results from unconscious mental processes based on these implicit attitudes and stereotypes formed by life experiences. They occur below the surface of your conscious thinking.

Researchers have documented certain almost-spontaneous perceptions by particular groups when they encounter members of other particular groups—for example, perceptions by White males when they encounter African American males or Asian American women. These biases and prejudices, if unchecked, cause a great deal of discrimination and exclusion directed toward—and a resulting lack of opportunities for—racial, gender, and ethnic group members as well as other groups of marginalized and disadvantaged people.[17]

The inability to corral implicit bias has dramatic, and usually negative, implications for law firms. Consider the well-documented case of a national law firm that actively recruited (at considerable expense) and hired more than thirty African American associates in an eight-year span but could not retain any of them. These associates cited implicit bias as the reason that they left.[18] The legal profession is concerned that implicit bias affects attorney hiring practices and evaluations of "minority" lawyers by senior colleagues.[19] These forms of bias in hiring, retention, and promotion make it challenging to ensure fair, equitable access to the benefits of the law firm for diverse associates.

Implicit bias also affects other areas of the law and the administration of justice, such as the noteworthy perception in many communities of color that the court systems are racist, treating Black and Latinx parties adversely compared with White parties in the system. Furthermore, recent events have shown that implicit bias is a persistent problem among law enforcement personnel, leading one group of researchers to conclude "that [police] officers might be *implicitly* biased against minorities and more likely to use force against them as a result."[20] The researchers noted that although there is a perception of a disproportionately more significant number of police killings of people of color, there was no centralized database of officer-related deaths until the police killing of Michael Brown in Ferguson, Missouri, in 2014.[21] The negative impact of these perceptions of racism and bias is decreased trust in these crucial institutions of justice.

There is clear evidence that law firm leaders tend to underestimate the impact of unconscious bias in their firms and overestimate the effectiveness of their current policies.[22] However, research has shown that efforts to mitigate the perceptions of unequal treatment of diverse parties can successfully ameliorate the effects of implicit bias.[23] Overcoming inertia or complacency about identifying implicit biases often begins by collecting data and actually looking at various metrics connected with diversity, equity, and inclusion within the organization and by being familiar with the research studies on these issues across the profession as a whole.[24] Thoughtful and appropriately aggressive measures by a firm's leadership can improve the working environment for diverse lawyers and level the playing field regarding hiring, retention, mentoring, pay, and promotion.

Lawyers and law organizations must remain vigilant in their efforts to combat expressed or implicit bias not only in their own workplaces but also in the "halls of justice" and the legal profession in general. Lawyers have not been blameless in the centuries of systemic bias and racism in the United States: they drafted racial and ethnic exclusion clauses in millions of real property deeds, helped landlord clients implement redlining practices, and actively counseled clients on racist, and often illegal, practices that held back communities of color for many years. Indeed, lawyers should aspire to learn from that history and strive not to repeat it. Even more, it is incumbent on them to lead toward positive change now.

One area that lawyers can begin to attack is the problem of systemic bias toward women and minorities in their own law organizations. There has been considerable analysis of how hiring, retention, and partner decisions have discriminated against women and lawyers of color within the firm and how discrimination occurs in myriad ways.[25] The pyramidal structure of attorney hiring and progression in the firm is often insensitive to the demands placed on women lawyers who need personal leave time for children and are often called on to provide caregiving to other family members. These individual and personal interests of many lawyers are challenging law firms to adopt more flexible structures for promotion and retention policies reflecting these demands of the law firm's talent.[26] Solutions to these challenges require thoughtful attention and leadership across the organization to harmonize the firm's interests with the personal needs of their staff.

ADVANTAGES OF GREATER DEI

While it is fair to conclude that the legal profession has a diversity problem, it is more accurate to state from a leadership perspective that the legal profession has a diversity "opportunity." Why are diversity, equity, and inclusion in the legal profession and the judicial system important from an opportunity standpoint? The answer lies in examining the institutional and professional benefits of more inclusive law organizations—for example, the increasing importance that young lawyers and even corporate clients place on greater diversity, and the acceptance and embracement of differentness in the institutions with which they choose to associate.

Performance Benefits

There is considerable research that supports DEI institutional goals. Advancing diversity and inclusion ameliorates many primary organizational goals, such as optimizing recruitment, increasing retention, enhancing institutional reputation, and driving client development.[27]

Why aren't law firms more diverse and inclusive if doing so would improve them? Diversity can create conflicts because there is a broader range of perspectives shaped by people's upbringing, cultural differences, and biases, which are hardwired into their thinking and beliefs. Studies show that efforts to promote diversity and a more inclusive workplace environment may "simultaneously produce more conflict and employee turnover as well as more creativity and innovation."[28] Cultural, racial, or ethnic biases, often implicit, are powerful headwinds to overcome to achieve diversity's positive influences.

Despite the challenges, the evidence clearly establishes that diverse teams and organizations perform better, generating more creative thinking and innovation. Most senior executives, including law firm managers, indicate that organizational policies and practices promoting diversity and inclusion are essential for several reasons, but mainly because they improve the organization's performance.[29] This same conclusion was reported in a Boston Consulting Group study: "[I]ncreasing the diversity of leadership teams leads to more and better innovation and improved financial performance."[30] Research into team performance has generally concluded that diverse and "nonhomogeneous teams are simply smarter."[31] They are smarter because people on these teams generally bring more information, carefully scrutinize the available data, don't rush to judgment, listen to one another, generate more alternatives, and reach better decisions.[32]

Studies also show that people working in diverse organizations tend to be more aware of their own biases. Unsurprisingly, rates of discrimination and harassment claims decrease directly proportional to positive assessments of DEI workplace culture.[33]

Cultural Draw

A law firm culture characterized by inclusiveness appeals to today's prevailing cultural landscape. In particular, it is a draw for young lawyers and corporate clients. Like many enterprises, law firms are undergoing a significant transition in their ranks from older, Baby Boomer generations to younger, Millennial employees. These generations lack an overlap in everyday life experiences (just think how law school studies have changed from spending hours in the library stacks tracking down documents to streams of information now accessible directly at one's desk), an understanding of each other's needs (e.g., today all law school graduates are seriously impacted by student loan debt, causing nearly half of them to delay or abandon marriage plans and starting a family, and correspondingly putting more emphasis on work–life balance), and different ways of communicating (with Baby Boomers preferring face-to-face conversations, while graduates today favor "speaking" via text or email).

Millennials represent about 50 percent of the U.S. workforce, and they rate the culture of the workplace, and its acceptance of their specific work and lifestyle preferences, as extremely important.[34] Reports indicate that they are happier working in creative and inclusive cultures compared with authoritarian, rule-based ones.[35] Young lawyers want to feel included, valued, and listened to, and they respond more favorably to workplace culture than to financial rewards. In fact, organizational culture and fit are rated as more important than compensation in their decisions regarding which firm to join and whether to stay rooted in that firm.[36] A law firm that responds to the interests and values of its younger lawyers, especially as the Baby Boomer partners are moving toward a less active status or retirement, will best utilize and retain their talent.

Consider this experience: we learned about a law student struggling with whether, as a Latinx, she should seek an internship with the district attorney's office. She posed this question to a BIPOC (Black, Indigenous, and people of color) deputy district attorney, who impressed on her the importance of having a more diverse group of prosecutors. While he admitted at times to struggling with the loneliness of being a person of color working in a predominantly White field, he was actively engaged in the recruitment process to help other people of color join the team. His explanation and encouragement convinced her to accept the internship. If individuals do not see people who look like them in the classroom, in the firm, or in the profession, they neither aspire to be part of that occupation nor envision a path to leadership and success.

This cultural appeal, which applies not only to Millennials but also to corporate clients, is interwoven with questions about the purpose of diversity. In approaching issues of equity and inclusion in the workplace and society, some lawyers question why efforts to enhance diversity are necessary. Their reasoning begins with a legalistic approach: does the law require a broadscale effort to create more inclusive and diverse organizations, or does the law simply prohibit discrimination and exclusion from public rights? They may ask if the firm should increase diversity because it is a priority of the national organization of lawyers (i.e., the ABA) or because it is the "right" thing to do in a moral or ethical sense. In other words, should the firm promote equity and inclusion goals because it has to or because it wants to? An expedient landing point for this decision often comes down to "because it is good for business."

Indeed, many large corporate clients require that their law firms have active diversity plans and outcomes, and often the corporation's general counsel will be driving efforts to improve diversity in law firms through their selection of outside firms. By having a diverse organization that values differences across several dimensions as well as accommodates them, a law firm increases the likelihood of retaining its younger lawyers—the firm's talent of the future. This is a substantial boon considering that, according to one estimate, losing an associate can cost the law firm between $200,000 and $500,000.[37] So, the right thing to do becomes the smart thing to do.

Besides being the right thing to do, supporting and advancing greater efforts at inclusion and diversity has legal and policy implications for law firms and lawyers. Rule 8.4(g) of the American Bar Association's Model Rules of Professional Conduct prohibits lawyers from engaging in conduct that discriminates against another based on protected categories (e.g., race, sex, religion, sexual orientation, gender identity) "in conduct related to the practice of law."[38] About two dozen states have adopted rules like Rule 8.4(g) prohibiting discriminatory actions by licensed attorneys. This remains a complicated and controversial area regulating lawyer conduct. Still, the key takeaway is that lawyers must be mindful of the barriers to inclusion and equity in society, and particularly in the practice of law.

LEADING DEI CHANGE

The talent (human resources) of a law firm is the most important asset in their path to success—and that talent is more productive, successful, and satisfied if they feel that they are included, that the organization values their opinions, and that decisions are fair and equitable. Finding a solution to the diversity problem is essential—and that solution lies in leadership. Leading legal organizations to enhance inclusion and promote equity is not unlike leadership efforts around many other major initiatives. Exemplary leadership skills, behaviors, and attitudes are required in order to influence the organization constructively, and strong emotional intelligence abilities are what leaders need to lead themselves and others in the organization toward more inclusive workplaces.

The pernicious influence of implicit bias makes this a daunting task. For example, a leader committed to positive change must perceive the need for change and persuade others of that need and how to accomplish it. Consider the leadership challenge implicit in surveys that indicate only 27 percent of White males feel strongly that improving diversity in their law firms is important, compared with 87 percent of women of color and 61 percent of White women in those same firms.[39]

Nonetheless, there are several actions that leaders can employ to effect changes in their organization's culture of inclusiveness. These include assessing and addressing one's own biases (identifying blind spots in one's own thinking and behavior); determining the current level of inclusiveness in the organization, which entails being open to feedback from others; extending diversity training throughout the organization; and creating and articulating a vision for change. In addition, as described above, law organizations can sign on to and commit to the goals of the "Mansfield Rule," which indicates a commitment to generating more diverse pools of candidates for associate and lateral hires.

Self-Analysis of Implicit Bias

The first, and perhaps most obvious, step for lawyers leading change in their organization's culture is to address their own biases, implicit or otherwise. It is difficult to lead change if you don't believe it's needed and can't acknowledge how you have been complicit in the problem. Racism scholar Ibram X. Kendi explains that everyone is either racist or antiracist. There is no room for neutrality, and there is no such thing as a "non-racist."[40] Antiracism is an active and conscious effort to work against multidimensional aspects of racism. Similarly, becoming an "ally" is being recognized by the people for whom you are being an ally by involving yourself in promoting and advancing an inclusive culture through positive and intentional action.[41]

Because everyone has biases, law firm leaders need to set an example in identifying and dealing with them, beginning as leaders do by "going first" before asking others to step forward. They should seek implicit bias training to indicate their sincere interest in these issues, acknowledging their potential shortcomings and demonstrating that the issues involve everyone in the organization. Self-administrated tests are readily available—such as the Harvard Implicit Association Test,[42] which can form the basis for efforts across the organization to assess the extent of implicit bias and take measures to address it.

Part of assessing and addressing implicit biases involves identifying blind spots in interactions with others and being open to both new and challenging information. For example, more than conceptually acknowledging that everyone doesn't think like you, you must appreciate the value that perspectives and experiences different from your own have. Reflect on your interactions with others, much like viewing a videotape, to evaluate how your unconscious biases may have led you astray in your understanding of what they were saying. Leaders must also determine whether they are trapped in a bubble of thinking and consequentially only hear preprocessed messages from their experiences. People generally hear only what they want to hear (not unlike children's "selective hearing" when their parents admonish them), which blocks critical thinking and more rational or realistic evaluations. Escaping this trap demands deep listening and really hearing and understanding what others are saying and feeling.[43]

Current Level of Inclusiveness

In addition to assessing themselves, leaders determined to enhance the team or organization's culture must assess what level of inclusiveness currently exists. It's been shown that the "behaviors of leaders (be they managers or senior partners) can drive up to 70 percentage points of difference between the proportion of employees who feel highly included and those who do not."[44] Taking stock of the organization's culture requires a commitment by the firm's leadership to find out how others feel about their workplace environment. Indeed, leaders interested in improving the culture of inclusion and equity must actively seek input; they can't work in their offices while waiting for someone to make an appointment and let them know what is going on. Leaders are out and about; to quote John le Carré, the British author of numerous espionage novels, "a desk is a dangerous place from which to view the world."[45]

Many law firms have increased and often improved the sense of community and belonging by minority and female lawyers and staff by creating affinity groups. These groups bring together junior lawyers with more senior lawyers to collaborate on projects and intra-firm activities that advance younger lawyers' connections with the firm members and with other younger lawyers. Sharing a bond as a Black associate in the firm, as a military veteran, or as a "first generation" college or law graduate is a powerful way to find a place and friends with similar backgrounds at the firm, to belong with others in the organization. One law firm's "first-gen" lawyer group teamed up to sponsor community-based initiatives to support Black and Latinx students' efforts for admission to colleges, and its veterans group reached out to a veterans support group, providing legal services to unhoused or recently incarcerated vets.

For leaders to be successful in gathering feedback about inclusiveness, members of the organization must feel that their leaders are approachable and interested in learning about how their behavior is impacting the performance of others. They must take steps to determine the extent to which people believe they are treated with dignity, respect, civility, and decency. They must also determine whether people feel a sense of belonging in the organization, feeling valued and appreciated for who they are and what they contribute. Law firm leaders and their firms can move the inclusiveness needle by actively promoting mentoring opportunities for women and lawyers of color. Mentoring relationships, whether formal or informal, can give junior lawyers access to people who can help them learn the ropes and navigate the organizational culture.[46]

One of the best and most straightforward questions to ask others is, "How can I (or the firm) do better?" You might not like the feedback you receive, but it is the only way that you (and the firm) can improve. Listen carefully—and without judgment—to what others say, especially if you disagree with some parts or premises of the others' viewpoints. Also, listen to what people are not saying, and make sure that the really important clues are not being overlooked. For the famous detective Sherlock Holmes, in one case, the "dog not barking" completely shifted his perspective. No matter what the initial data reveals, feedback is always "friendly" if the intention is to use the information to make improvements. The data becomes the foundation on which to build, and it offers a forward-looking perspective rather than a backward descent into the past, assigning blame or shame.

Ubiquitous Diversity Training

Another step in DEI leadership is extending diversity training beyond the formal hierarchical ranks. An organization won't benefit if only the most junior or most senior people engage in training to address biases. It will profit tremendously if implicit bias training and education about the advantages of greater workplace inclusion are extended throughout the organization and as appropriate to the needs and experiences of various constituencies. Many law firms have realized tangible benefits from creating a diversity function, often a chief diversity officer or a diversity committee. These firm leaders develop and promote diversity and inclusiveness goals and strategies, assist with recruiting more diverse lawyers and staff, and provide guidance and expertise to other firm leaders in advancing a more diverse and inclusive environment.[47] Midsized and small law offices do not have the same level of resources as large firms in initiating and sustaining a solid DEI function. Those intent on improving the climate of inclusiveness have brought in outside experts and organizations to work with the firm's members to increase awareness of bias and achieve a diverse and inclusive workplace.

Recent studies have shown that efforts to enhance corporate "belonging" and "bridge building" between racial, ethnic, and gender groups lead to greater benefits to the organization, and, according to the Society for Human Resource Management, three-quarters of the surveyed firms planned to invest more in belonging initiatives.[48] These initiatives are being implemented in addition to those groups' DEI programs and activities.

Vision for Change

A critical step in leading the move toward DEI is creating and articulating a vision for change, including why it is essential to the organization and its members and how they and the organization will be better off due to the change. Two critical aspects are a "recognition of leadership *for* diversity, which would increase the range of people who are leaders, and leadership *with* diversity, to ensure that leadership is beneficial to everyone and the organization as a whole."[49] Effective leadership in law organizations requires thoughtful attention to both dynamics of leading change—with and for diversity toward a more inclusive workplace.

Lawyers and their firms often overlook the need for visionary leadership because they have concluded that "vision" is not in their wheelhouse; this is something that others, including their clients, do—but not them. This is a relatively narrow and limited perspective on the roles of lawyers—in all positions, but especially in managerial and leadership roles. The top-performing and most effective lawyers (especially those in their organizations' senior hierarchical positions), according to a survey of a cross section of many types of law firms, are "more visionary, provide their teams with much-needed perspective, and engage associates and peers in critical discussion and decisions."[50] These leaders can accelerate their firm's transformation to a more inclusive work environment because they can provide perspective and persuade others to embrace the change.

DEI Change: A Win–Win Situation

Initiatives to create a more diverse and inclusive workplace generate equitable opportunities, and enhance the organization's legitimacy internally and externally. Of course, simply instructing people to be respectful of others does not necessarily result in a workplace where people feel respected; rather, leadership must be proactive about inclusion. And leaders themselves must display inclusive behaviors and manifest attitudes that suggest they highly value the inclusiveness of others; without that, diversity efforts are perceived as simply window dressing. It is important to note that inclusion is not a zero-sum game where losses to another offset any gains by one group of employees. Everyone wins when the workplace culture becomes more inclusive, welcoming, and fair to all employees. The organization is more profitable and has greater retention, and people are proud to say that this is the organization to which they belong.

CHAPTER HIGHLIGHTS

- Diversity in the legal profession is a problem—but also presents a leadership opportunity.
- Diversity, equity, and inclusion are related concepts. Diversity refers to differences in an environment. Equity refers to efforts to ensure an even playing field of opportunities for all team members. Inclusion refers to the ways in which members of a group are accepted and feel they belong.
- Efforts to increase associate and junior lawyers' sense of belonging and inclusion are among the most rewarding initiatives law firms are taking to attract and retain a diverse workforce of professionals.
- Implicit bias is a roadblock to achieving DEI in legal organizations.
- Law firms benefit from DEI in terms of performance and their ability to attract and retain talent and corporate clients because of the many benefits, the right thing to do—greater DEI—becomes the smart thing to do.
- Lawyers and law firms must lead the incorporation of DEI into their environments. The leadership effort begins with a self-analysis of implicit bias, moves on to an assessment of the current DEI culture and diversity training for everyone in an organization, and culminates with creating and articulating a vision for change.

Afterword

Looking to the Future: Leadership Development to Produce Better Lawyers

"To move forward successfully, lawyers must develop their professional and personal leadership abilities to thrive in a turbulent and complex world, sustaining their growth as lawyers and as individuals."

This afterword brings together two crucial "lawyer as leader" themes along with the "imperative" to further and advance your leadership skills. Strong leadership skills create opportunities for lawyers and law firms to build relationships with their clients, and, at a fundamental organizational level, they are essential to the success of all legal organizations in these ongoing, challenging, and turbulent times.

Complexity is not a recent phenomenon but rather a long-standing conundrum that began with your entrance to law school, with the challenges presented by adapting to the study of law ("thinking like a lawyer"), navigating the bar exam, and, without question, extends into your practice of law (irrespective of the practice field or setting). Likewise, the legal profession has been subjected to a turbulent environment over the past decades, including major financial meltdowns, mismanagement and alleged fraud, technological disruptions, a catastrophic global health crisis, social and environmental justice rallies, and increasing political polarization. These days, the demand is that "lawyer-leaders must be as agile as white-water guides in treacherous rapids."[1] The more than one million practicing lawyers (as well as tens of thousands who work in law-related fields) have been experiencing a succession of challenges that have dramatically affected every lawyer and the legal profession itself. Unprecedented shifts and conundrums are the reality of the contemporary practice of law.

As the old adage goes, "Extraordinary times call for extraordinary measures"—and that speaks directly to the necessity of paying greater attention to leadership both for lawyers and their organizations, regardless of size or setting. Lawyers must navigate their environment and grow as professionals in whatever context they practice law, and enhancing their leadership skills will contribute substantively to their success in the legal profession overall. We have maintained throughout this book that leadership education and development are essential to lawyers and their organizations. Leadership development is the single and most substantive tool for today's lawyers to align their aspirations for success and happiness with the realities of law practice's very complex and uncertain environment.

Becoming a lawyer in a leadership position is not the objective, though. The aspiration is to become a lawyer with leadership skills, attitudes, and behaviors. Being a lawyer with solid leadership abilities provides some real opportunities for success as a lawyer. This afterword aims to provide a path for your personal and professional development as a lawyer and as a leader—and, consequently, as a person who makes a difference.

LEADERSHIP DEVELOPMENT IN CHALLENGING TIMES AND CIRCUMSTANCES

There are several guideposts to pay attention to and understand in your leadership development journey: the context in which leadership should occur, the environment in which leadership must be exercised, and why leadership skills are necessary to address the challenges and opportunities in that environment. Once you've recognized and understood the landscape in your path, the process for leading forward begins with creating a plan for leading yourself and others through resolving those obstacles, switchbacks, and detours associated with being a lawyer and practicing law.

To move forward successfully, lawyers must develop their professional and personal leadership abilities to thrive in a turbulent and complex world and sustain their growth as lawyers and individuals. Law school was a great place to have already started on this journey; however, the opportunities for leadership development don't begin and end with law school graduation. There are hopeful signs—such as leadership development programs and partnership criteria emphasizing demonstrated leadership—that legal firms are stepping up their interest in leadership development by organizing various educational programs and workshops for everyone in their organizations. A systematic leadership development program strengthens internal leadership structures, enhances client retention and billing rates, demonstrates the firm's commitment to the long-term development of junior talent, and benefits from succession planning. Even in the absence of some formal leadership development program in law offices, lawyers, especially junior lawyers, lawyers of color, and women lawyers, must act proactively to advance their abilities to lead themselves and their law organizations.

Professional Challenges

A second-year associate with a national law firm aptly described the challenge facing every new attorney: "I'm navigating an extremely complex environment, which, in many ways, lacks transparency. The firm hasn't caught up to the leadership needs of new lawyers like me, so it is definitely a struggle." This statement reflects a common and profound concern: more leadership, both individually and by lawyers in their firms, is required to address the complexities of modern law practice. Moreover, the consensus is that "law firms can no longer assume that leaders will simply emerge from the ranks."[2] Rather, attention to the development of leadership must be intentional rather than implicit, and this is true not only for law firms but also throughout the entire legal profession, including the judiciary.

Law Firms in a VUCA World

A **V**olatile, **U**ncertain, **C**omplex, and **A**mbiguous (VUCA) environment is an apt description of the practice of law and much of the legal profession.[3] These past decades have prompted clients to reassess their need for legal services and become more selective in choosing their service providers, thus increasing competition among law firms.

For example, the 2007–08 economic recession and the 2020 coronavirus pandemic presented grave challenges to the legal profession, law firms, and even law schools. Law school job postings dropped, associate and new attorney hiring dwindled, and lateral hiring in law firms declined appreciably. Preceding these catastrophic events were ongoing threats to law firms from the growth of alternative service providers offering lower-cost service models and the introduction of services from international law firms. Similar threats to the law practice organization model stemmed from a decrease in the overall demand for legal services and a glut in the number of lawyers, which created an oversupply of providers. In addition, clients have been demanding cost efficiencies and more value in the delivery of legal services.

These sudden, complex, unanticipated events and recent trends in law practice constitute significant VUCA demands, some disruptive and some incremental. Disruptive changes occur, for example, when a new technology renders most of the firm's current technology obsolete. A recent disruptive change occurred when the COVID-19 pandemic closed down most in-person law practices, which required a sudden shift to remote lawyering and more significant, more complicated interpersonal interactions. The movement from hourly billing to value billing by law firms is an example of an incremental change, which has been occurring slowly over time. Disruptive changes require quick, innovative responses, while incremental changes require institutional and strategic planning and action. While leading a law organization through disruptive change or incremental changes requires different approaches, the fundamental, and at times existential, question is whether the firm has leaders who can step up to take the reins and lead others through the tough decisions that must be made.[4]

Change is what leaders eat for breakfast, and leadership is what is required to respond to both disruptive and incremental challenges and trends. Unfortunately, as noted previously, law firms in particular, as well as other legal organizations, have too often failed to step up to these challenges—the result being that many of those groups suffered, some gravely, by moving into bankruptcy and insolvency. Many of these woes can be traced back to insufficient or failed leadership at the firm level. At the same time, some firms during this period, through innovative leadership, have been able to take on those challenges and difficulties and build new opportunities for their legal teams and firm growth.[5]

These complexities of modern law practice are manageable and provide inflection points for lawyers and their organizations to innovate, develop, and thrive through effective leadership. The currents and headwinds that lawyers must face have been described at several points in this book in the context of acquiring the leadership skills needed to handle these blustery conditions.[6]

The greatest challenge in these times is whether lawyer-leaders are developing their skills and attitudes quickly enough and in the right ways to handle VUCA environments effectively.[7] A survey of law firm leaders by the Center for Creative Leadership asked what skills were needed to lead contemporary law firms. Respondents generated a list of more than thirty skills that lawyers need to have or must develop, ranging from "how to motivate underperforming partners" to "how to be a more effective communicator."[8] The survey results identified the skills that today's lawyer-leaders needed while highlighting the urgency that law organizations face in finding ways to develop these skills effectively. Many have commented that the needed response is entirely personal: "No matter what role you play in your legal organization, you are being called upon to exercise leadership as we try to navigate through these completely uncharted waters."

Personal Challenges

Being a lawyer and practicing law are seldom mundane or easy. Clients make unreasonable demands, documents multiply, and workloads are often unending. The dread of being unprepared, making a mistake, and losing a client's case, as well as costs ranging from livelihood to life itself, add tremendous pressure. Frequent travel, late evening and weekend sessions, and nights away from home augment the stress many lawyers experience. Then there are the financial challenges: paying off law school debt, covering overhead, and managing the administration of the firm.

These ingredients make for a potent, sometimes deadly, cocktail, resulting in lawyers experiencing a very stressful occupation and lifestyle. However, leadership can be an effective antidote.

Wellness Problem

Due to the combination of stresses inherent in lawyering, the legal profession has a well-documented wellness problem. There are rehabilitation centers that specialize in working with lawyers who are substance abusers and in treating the stress, depression, disability, and addiction that are prominent in the legal profession. In every state, there are Lawyer Assistance Programs that provide confidential services and support to legal professionals who are struggling with substance use or mental health issues.[9]

A report sponsored by the American Bar Association and the Betty Ford Foundation found that 21 percent of licensed, employed attorneys qualify as problem drinkers; 28 percent experience depression, and 19 percent have anxiety symptoms.[10] The Centers for Disease Control and Prevention found that lawyers have among the highest rates of suicide as well as drug and alcohol abuse. Lawyers also rank high in divorce rates as well as illnesses exacerbated by stress.[11] Furthermore, nearly 70 percent of legal malpractice suits are associated with substance abuse.[12]

These problems often begin in law school and are exacerbated throughout many lawyers' careers.[13] Significant stress is reported by 96 percent of law students, nearly 40 percent higher than medical students and more than twice that of graduate students in general. Depression rates at the end of the first semester of law school are approximately four times higher than that of the general population.[14] Postgraduate, younger lawyers, those in their first ten years of practice, have the highest incidence of these problems.[15]

Addressing the Wellness Problem

There are steps or approaches that lawyers and law firms can take to alleviate the challenges of stress in the profession of law. Leadership development is one undervalued and underutilized tactic. For instance, one of the first steps in addressing wellness—or thriving, even better—is evaluating your values, goals, strengths, weaknesses, passions, and the like. Regardless of the profession, when people are in jobs that align with who they are, they are more satisfied with their lives, happier, and generally more productive. Again, leading yourself is a necessary precursor to being an effective lawyer-leader for others.

Another wellness step in a legal career is preparing for a lawyer's work by creating a realistic mindset for practicing law. Wellness programs offered at law schools, at some law firms, and through bar associations are a preventative for sliding into the core causes of lawyer unhappiness that may lead to unhealthy behaviors and attitudes. National, state, and local bar associations have implemented steps to identify and address lawyers' wellness problems, such as substance abuse and depression, and their implications for clients and the legal system.[16] Furthermore, opportunities for public service outside of the law firm, such as pro bono representation, peer support, and advice through sections of bar associations and groups, provide avenues for lawyers to address many of the underlying causes of distress and dissatisfaction.

Leadership training and development are robust avenues for addressing the wellness problem. Throughout this book, we have stressed the value of leadership training for lawyers and the many positive benefits of leadership skills. Early career leadership development of positive traits and competencies has been identified as a positive way of dealing with the harmful aspects of lawyering. For similar reasons, law schools have been increasing the amount of leadership development and training for their students because those abilities are in demand by law firms. This is because "leadership training often includes competencies such as collaboration, teamwork, problem-solving, inspiring others, creativity, transparency, humility, healthy conflict, goal setting, self-promotion, and marketing."[17] These educational experiences are instrumental in preparing lawyers for a healthy, professional work and life balance.

Finally, self-care is essential to your ongoing ability to make a difference as a lawyer and as a leader. Doing so, one law firm partner told us, "is not a luxury, it is a requirement." If you aren't in a good place yourself, this will inevitably affect your relationships with others and your work. By analogy, if you do not refill your car's tank, you will run out of gas and never reach your planned destination. You need to ensure that you have seriously thought about and reflected on your future as a lawyer and a leader. It is never too early to identify your aspirations and develop a perspective of how you want to live your life, who you want to serve, and how you want to be remembered.

LAWYER LEADERSHIP DEVELOPMENT OF THE FUTURE

The contemporary practice of law and legal education has changed dramatically due to both disruptive events and incremental trends. Lawyer leaders must be committed to developing the necessary skills to lead and prosper in such an environment.

Leadership development efforts must be directed toward complex and adaptive competencies such as greater agility in learning, robust self-awareness, increasing comfort with ambiguity, a better facility for strategic thinking, and an entrepreneurial mindset.[18] Looking to the future, surveys of law firm leaders and managing lawyers who were asked about what lies ahead for lawyers and, more particularly, what the main challenges are for lawyers who lead organizations and teams are in agreement that law practice will be very different in at least three ways for the coming generation of lawyer-leaders.[19]

First, law firms and legal organizations will invest less in developing their human resources in traditional ways, such as hiring consulting experts and holding management and leadership workshops. Instead, they will encourage their employees to take greater responsibility for developing themselves as leaders and preparing to take leadership responsibilities and roles in the future. Firms probably will not abandon their associate professional development programs or succession planning for more senior lawyers. Still, you can anticipate that more individual initiatives on your part will be expected in developing your individual leadership abilities. Consequently, lawyers will have more "vertical professional development" as they seek to achieve greater levels of personal, professional, and leadership development.

What does this development look like, and what should young lawyers today be thinking about to prepare themselves? One of the principal areas that will distinguish exceptional lawyer talent is the ability to enhance the range of their cognitive and emotional intelligence without being forced or instructed to do so. In terms of adult learning theory, this means moving through stages of cognitive development from being "socialized" to a more advanced level with the capacity for self-growth and transformative thinking.[20] Lawyers, more than ever, must possess high levels of self-awareness, empathy, and social skills to inspire others through their leadership and move organizations forward in complex, uncertain, and volatile times.[21] These are key competencies and abilities that you need to demonstrate. Preparing yourself to lead others through the organization's challenges requires a clear and deep knowledge of what others need and what it takes for the team to face those challenges.

Second, along with changes in how leaders are developed in legal firms, organizations will value leadership that is more "networked," focusing on leading through a collective process. Much of today's work is performed in highly networked environments. Hence, it makes sense that those networks and collective groups will be the medium in which leadership is exercised. Leadership in law organizations will become less linked solely to one individual and will be distributed throughout the organization to many others. Leading teams and departments, great "followership," collaboration and teamwork, and excellent communication skills will be the characteristics that distinguish lawyer-leaders in this contemporary environment.

Third, the exercise of leadership will place a premium on creative thinking and the ability to innovate around problems. Strategic planning skills will continue to be important for those charged with leading legal organizations, but there will be less and less top-down command-and-control tactics. Rather, the ability to lead change through a process of innovation that taps collectively into the talents of people at all levels will be a vital competency of these up-and-coming law leaders.

The legal profession got a glimpse of why these skills are in high demand during the 2007–08 recession. While law firms were hit hard, the hardy and nimble firms were able to focus intently on their clients' needs in the recession, address gaps in knowledge and utilization of technology within their firms, and adapt their hiring and retention practices to strengthen the commitment of their lawyers and staff to the pressing needs of the firms and their clients. The pivot to virtual work demanded the same agility during the 2020 coronavirus pandemic.

These events also hit many lawyers personally, as they required a great deal of entrepreneurial skills and behaviors. Many law school graduates saw their plans for the future (e.g., securing a position in a law firm) suddenly evaporate, and they shifted their thinking to opening their own law offices. Starting your own law firm demands entrepreneurial abilities that law school graduates don't often have, nor do law schools necessarily prepare them for that possibility. In VUCA environments, everyone must think like an entrepreneur.

This new vision for leadership in law organizations is neither fantastical nor cynical. It reflects the ongoing changes in the complex environments that all professionals and their companies face.

COMBINING LEADERSHIP SKILLS AND CLIENT DEVELOPMENT SKILLS

Most law firms, irrespective of size or practice specialty, emphasize client development skills and practices for all their lawyers, especially associate and junior lawyers. Building relationships with existing and potential clients is the foundation for the firm's long-term success, whether a small firm or a national law firm with a dozen offices. They often guarantee the success of new lawyers who show promise at sustaining those relationships.

The practice of law is much like practicing leadership: they are both "retail businesses," highly dependent upon nurturing personal connections and relationships, are built on trust and respect, and deliver a high-quality product. A lawyer's credibility is critical to building and sustaining that relationship, just as a leader's credibility is essential to their relationship with constituents and followers. How do successful lawyers build these relationships? The same way leaders do.

Credibility is rooted in perceptions of the lawyer's competence, trustworthiness, good judgment, and commitment to fully and ethically represent the client's interests. That relationship begins with the lawyer's honest evaluation of the client's problem and the development of effective strategies to address that problem. Lawyers who demonstrate their knowledge of the legal issues and who can formulate possible strategies to resolve them have high credibility with clients. Then, the lawyer's ability to engage in practices that help the client in resolving the problems—we contend through the practices of exemplary leadership—is likely to maintain the client's trust in their lawyer and their recommendations and actions. In these situations, the lawyer's ability to guide the client toward the resolution of the case or transaction collaboratively is essential to sustaining the relationship, even if the ultimate outcome of the case or transaction is less than desired.

Of course, clients are not mere followers but the object of the representation; their cause is the lawyer's duty. A high degree of collaboration and candor between the lawyer and client is much more likely to result in favorable outcomes and, importantly, sustain a relationship that may endure beyond the initial case or transaction.

APPRECIATING LEADERSHIP STYLES

Regardless of how leadership development evolves in the future, one thing that will not change very dramatically is the importance of how you behave as a leader, as characterized by The Five Practices of Exemplary Leadership®. The Five Practices constitute a valid conceptual framework and a set of operating principles that "are universally relevant and effective across various cultures, environments, settings, and populations."[22] A study involving more than 71,000 leaders and 200,000 of their direct reports from 77 countries concluded that this framework "is a 'safe bet' for how leaders should behave."[23]

Still, context matters. This framework's robustness derives from its focus on behavior and adaptability to various personalities and circumstances. That said, it is incumbent on you to reflect on and diagnose the situation and setting in which you find yourself and engage the various leadership practices appropriately—often referred to as leadership styles—with which you utilize The Five Practices.

The most effective leaders can use multiple styles, choosing those that suit the demands of the situation and the needs and interests of the people involved (be they colleagues or clients). There is no one-style-fits-all or all-encompassing approach to providing leadership or utilizing The Five Practices. Consider, for example, how the leadership behaviors associated with Challenge the Process would vary in "style" (and probably scope) if you were engaging with a law school intern versus a senior partner in the firm. Likewise, as a litigator, how would you Inspire a Shared Vision (tapping into the hopes and dreams of your constituents) when engaging with a client facing a misdemeanor versus engaging with another facing a first-degree murder charge? As realized during the coronavirus pandemic, we were not all in the same boat while trying to ride out this storm. No one can describe and prescribe what to do in every situation, whether referring to the law or leadership. Depending on the situation, you'll be responsible for scoping out and determining how best to apply the various leadership practices and behaviors. Both adaptability and flexibility on your part are required.

Scholars have suggested a variety of "styles" for how an individual might behave while leading a group.[24] Each style is only effective when it appropriately matches the requirements of the situation, and demonstrating flexibility is often the key to success.[25] You will find it informative to consider which of these styles described below seem most like you and appreciate that one style doesn't fit all situations. You will always want to Model the Way, but how you do that in person will vary with how you do that virtually, just as it differs when dealing with someone you've had a long relationship with versus a new colleague or client. Here's a brief look at several styles, and you can think about how well they reflect various personalities, including your own, and how to adapt your style and leadership behavior to the demands of the situation and nature of your audience.

Authoritative Style

In some circumstances, lawyer-leaders may rely on their status or rank (such as managing partners) to employ an *authoritative* leadership style. There are legitimate circumstances in which hierarchical relationships require compliance—one person must make critical decisions and expect acquiescence from everyone. Meeting a tight deadline on filing merger or acquisition documents is an example of when the partner calls the shots and others fall in line.

While a leader may need to resort to coercion (as in "it's my way or the highway"), this approach doesn't occur frequently in legal professional settings. Even when required, exemplary leaders will still explain the thinking behind their orders rather than being autocratic and simply saying, "Do as I say." Otherwise, trust will be eroded over time.

Affiliative Style

Another style in legal organizations, at least among lawyers working on a litigation or transaction project, is *affiliative.* This style relies on strengthening interpersonal relationships, building mutual trust and respect, and using persuasive strategies to guide colleagues toward agreed-upon objectives. Affiliative leaders believe that "people come first." With this style, the leader is often up close and personal with people, establishing team bonds, attending to emotional needs, clearly communicating goals, seeking buy-in, and encouraging everyone to work cooperatively to achieve shared objectives.

Democratic Style

In some workplace settings, especially with a highly educated and seasoned group, the leadership function is widely diffused, perhaps among a network of professionals, and the person in charge as the official leader will utilize a *democratic* style for taking action and making decisions. In this reasonably participative approach, the leader will ask people questions such as "What should we do?" and "What do you think?" and use their input to make choices. For example, in a session of lead counsel in a multidistrict litigation proceeding or a meeting of class action counsel, the most appropriate approach to making decisions is likely to be more collaborative and inclusive.

This leadership style requires a high degree of trust and confidence by all group members, not only in the leader but also among themselves. Everyone needs to be prepared and committed to the task and goal and comfortable with rewards distributed based on interdependence rather than independent contributions. The leader emphasizes collaborating, obtaining buy-in, and soliciting input and feedback from everyone involved.

Pacesetting Style

If a lawyer-leader's leadership style is *pacesetting*, then in this approach, the leader literally says, "Do as I do, and come along with me." This method can often achieve results quickly, especially if the team is highly motivated to accomplish the task.

This style can be constructive when, for example, a partner is attempting to mentor a group of associates in a transaction, and the explicit message is "If you want to know how to do this, then pay attention to what I do and how I handle this." This approach is also commonly seen when a chief litigation partner leads a group of associates in learning, for example, the ropes of trial preparation and witness cross-examinations. However, this style can fall short if the team members sense that the leader is arrogant or unapproachable or if the people involved don't share a common sense of purpose.

Coaching Style

Another approach to leading others is a *coaching* style, in which leaders are prone to saying, "Consider this," and then they provide attention to individuals by mentoring and offering advice. This approach has value, for example, in succession planning, where the leader wishes to prepare a person (or several people) for possible future leadership responsibilities in the firm. One downside is that this leadership style can be quite time-consuming and challenging, requiring considerable interpersonal competence, especially as a role model. It is most appropriate, however, when seen as investing in the future of an individual and/or organization. This is why coaching junior lawyers is highly valued by many firms, especially midsized and large firms. Experienced coaches can provide more one-to-one or individualized development, signal areas for the junior lawyers' skill development, and help shape their career paths in the firm. They can also work to develop strong emotional intelligence skills in their younger counterparts, thereby helping build relationships with clients and colleagues at the firm.

The coaching style is not the same as mentoring. Coaching tends to be more directive than mentoring and often involves expressed goals for the individual being coached. Mentoring is frequently accomplished in a more question-and-answer method. For instance, a new associate is encouraged to bring issues, concerns, or problems to their mentor for discussion, with the ultimate resolution left in the hands of the person being mentored.

Mix and Match

There are many typologies of leadership styles in the academic literature; the previous presented just one continuum, ranging from authoritative at one end to coaching at the other, with various styles in between. Each style has its place in your leadership toolkit, just as carpenters need several saw blades and varieties of screwdrivers in their toolbox. The most effective leaders can use more than one style, especially as situations shift and change. The Chinese proverb wisely proclaims, "The wise adapt themselves to circumstances, as water molds itself to the pitcher." Armed with The Five Practices of Exemplary Leadership®, you have a framework for going both wide and deep in how you behave as a leader.

SELF-DEVELOPMENT: BASIS OF LEADERSHIP DEVELOPMENT

Wanting to lead, believing that you can lead, and understanding your style are applicable as guidelines on your road to becoming an exemplary leader. However, you are the driver, and being an exemplary leader comes from being the best version of yourself. In the art of leadership, leadership development is fundamentally a process of self-development.[26]

Inner Quest

The quest for developing your leadership skills and behaviors is first an inner search to discover and be in touch with who you are. Through discernment and self-reflection comes the confidence needed to lead. Self-confidence is awareness of and faith in your own powers. These capabilities become clear and strong only as you work to identify and develop them—and own them.

As you begin this inner journey, you must wrestle with some difficult yet fundamental questions. For example:

- How much do I care about making a difference, justice, fairness, wealth, influence, and the people who are like me or different from me?
- What do I think is the proper role and responsibility of lawyers and the legal system?
- What kind of clients do I want to work with and serve?
- How do I feel about law enforcement officers, district attorneys, opposing counsel, the prison system, and the prospects of rehabilitation?
- How prepared am I to handle the complex problems that now confront the legal profession and the practice of law?
- What are my beliefs about how people should work together with associates and partners in an office, on a case?
- How committed am I to fostering and supporting an inclusive culture?
- How confident am I of my own conviction about my firm's stated vision and values? How confident am I about the conviction and commitment of my colleagues?
- How solid are my relationships with constituents, such as clients, colleagues, and judicial officers? Are they built on a firm foundation of trust and good judgment?
- What are my strengths and weaknesses?
- What do I need to do to improve my abilities?
- Am I the right one to be taking the lead at this very moment?

You have probably already wrested with many of these questions. For example, in law school classes, new associate on-boarding, and various informal and formal conversations within the firm.

By extension, being in touch with who you are also means striving to improve how well you understand others near and far from you. While scholars may disagree on the origins of leadership, there is a strong consensus that leaders must be interpersonally competent. Explained one noted legal scholar, "Attempting to train leaders without focusing more effectively on interpersonal skills is, to borrow a colleague's metaphor, like trying to teach geology without the rocks."[27] You must be willing and able to listen and take advice, as well as sometimes lose arguments and follow others. Unless you can develop the trust and respect of others, you will be unable to mobilize people's energies toward higher purposes and motivate them to go with you to places they have never been before. In other words, you will be unable to lead.

Too Much of a Good Thing

However, some fundamental contradictions in leadership are revealed as you struggle to develop yourself as a leader.

First, you will realize that any leadership practice can become destructive if taken to extremes. Challenging the status quo to promote innovation and progressive change, taken to extremes, can create needless turmoil, confusion, and paranoia. The singular focus on one vision of the future can blind you and others to alternatives and the realities of the present.

Exploiting your powers of inspiration can cause others to surrender their will. Overreliance on collaboration may indicate an unwillingness to make critical or unpopular decisions. An obsession with being seen as a role model can push you into isolation for fear of losing your privacy or cause you to be more concerned with style than substance. Constantly worrying about who should be recognized and when you should celebrate can turn you into a gregarious minstrel.[28]

However, the treachery of hubris is far more insidious for leaders than all of these. It is exciting to be a leader, gratifying to have influence, and exhilarating to have scores of people hanging on to your every word. It is empowering to hand out directions and have people fired up to march at your command. In far more subtle ways than anyone would like to admit, you can be seduced by your own power and importance. History reveals that every *evil* leader has been infected with the disease of hubris: they were rulers, not leaders. They became bloated with an exaggerated sense of self and used their leadership gifts to pursue their sinister ends.

These contradictions in leadership highlight that leadership practices are amoral, but the people who use the practices are moral or immoral. This leadership discussion has an ethical dimension that neither leaders nor their followers should take lightly or ignore.

The conflicts and contradictions of leadership can only be resolved if you establish an ethical set of standards on which to base all your actions. You can avoid excessive pride only if you recognize that you are human and need the help of others. All your individual complexities are held together by a fundamental set of values and beliefs, and developing yourself as a leader begins with those fundamental convictions. Clarifying your values and visions is highly personal; no one else can do it for you. To exhibit to others authentic leadership—where words and deeds are consonant—you must be in tune internally. When you clarify the principles governing your life and the ends you seek, you give meaning to your daily decisions and actions.

From Self to Selfless

The late John Gardner—former cabinet secretary of Health, Education, and Welfare; advisor to four U.S. presidents; founder of both Common Cause and Independent Sector; and recipient of the Presidential Medal of Freedom—wrote about the four *moral* goals of leadership: (1) releasing human potential, (2) balancing the needs of the individual and the community, (3) defending the fundamental values of the community, and (4) instilling in individuals a sense of initiative and responsibility.[29]

Attending to these goals will always lift you to higher purposes, and leadership development through self-development is the way to attend to these goals. As you work to become all you can be, you can let go of petty self-interests. Similarly, as you reflect on these aspirations, remember the ABA Model Rules—that lawyers should seek "to attain the highest level of skills, to improve the law and the legal profession, and to exemplify the legal profession's ideals of public service."[30] As in the biblical imperative "To whom much has been given, much will be required,"[31] as you serve the values of justice, freedom, equality, and dignity, you will constantly renew the foundations of democracy.

CHAPTER HIGHLIGHTS

- The legal landscape is complex and constantly changing regarding what society and clients require from their lawyers. To navigate these headwinds, you must have a plan for developing yourself personally and professionally, including leadership development.
- Maintaining a healthy outlook on professional work is particularly important for lawyers because the legal profession is high-stress with high-pressure schedules, deadlines, and work hours where unhealthy reactions (e.g., excessive substance use) are fairly common. Leadership development can help lawyers deal with these stresses.
- The legal profession's future requires lawyers to take greater individual responsibility for leadership development.
- Leadership encompasses many different styles, and exemplary leaders use a combination of these as situationally appropriate.
- Self-development is the key to leadership development, as the leader embodies the self. Controlling baser instincts and cultivating selflessness are means of achieving success on both a personal and a professional level.

Endnotes

Introduction

1. See, e.g., Donald J. Polden and Barry Z. Posner, *Leading in Law: Leadership Development for Law Students* (Durham, NC: Carolina Academic Press, 2020); Deborah L. Rhode and Amanda K. Packel, *Leadership: Law, Policy, and Management* (New York: Wolters Kluwer Law & Business, 2011); Deborah L. Rhode, *Lawyers as Leaders* (New York: Oxford University Press, 2013); Leah W. Teague, Elizabeth M. Fraley, and Stephen Rispoli, *Fundamentals of Lawyer Leadership* (Boston: Aspen, 2021).

Chapter 1: Foundations of Educating Lawyers for Leadership: Why Leadership Development Is Essential for Lawyers

1. American Bar Association, *ABA Profile of the Legal Profession 2022* (Chicago: ABA, 2023), https://www.americanbar.org/news/reporter_resources/profile-of-profession/.
2. Joe Patrice, "The Most Lawyers in the World," *Above the Law* (blog), February 12, 2018, https://abovethelaw.com/2018/02/the-most-lawyers-in-the-world/.
3. Ben W. Heineman Jr., "Law and Leadership," *Journal of Legal Education* 56, no. 4 (2006): 596–614.
4. Donald J. Polden, "Leadership Matters: Lawyers' Leadership Skills and Competencies," *Santa Clara Law Review* 52 (2012): 899–920, at 901.
5. Bloomberg Law, *2021 Law School Preparedness*, p. 4 (2021) (report on survey of law students and faculty regarding preparedness to enter and succeed in law school).
6. According to Worldometers (using United Nations population data), in 2021 the United States had a population of 332,685,557. According to the American Bar Association's *ABA Profile of the Legal Profession 2020* report (Chicago: American Bar Association, 2021), there were 1.3 million active lawyers in the United States. By these figures, there is one active lawyer in the United States for every 255 people; lawyers constitute 0.0039% of the U.S. population. See worldometers.info/world-population/us-population/#:~:text=The%20current%20population%20of%20the,the%20latest%20United%20Nations%20data.
7. U.S. Library of Congress, Congressional Research Service, "Membership of the 118th Congress: A Profile," R46705, October 4, 2023, https://crsreports.congress.gov/product/pdf/R/R47470.

8. Ballotpedia, "Governors and State Executives by Higher Education Background," *Ballotpedia,* updated February 2021, https://ballotpedia.org/Governors_and_state_executives_by_higher_education_background.
9. "Legislators Occupations 2015," National Conference of State Legislatures, 2015, https://www.ncsl.org/about-state-legislatures/state-legislator-demographics.
10. Alexis de Tocqueville, *Democracy in America,* trans. Henry Reeve (University Park: Penn State University Press, 2002), 307, and on lawyers generally, 302–9, http://seas3.elte.hu/coursematerial/LojkoMiklos?Alexis-de-Tocqueville-Democrary-in-America.pdf; see also Phil Neal, "De Tocqueville and the Role of the Lawyer in Society," *Marquette Law Review* 50 (1967): 607–17, at 609.
11. Leah Witcher Jackson Teague, "Training Lawyers for Leadership: Vitally Important Mission for the Future Success (and Maybe Survival) of the Legal Profession and Our Democracy," *Santa Clara Law Review* 58 (2018): 633–72, at 636, 643.
12. Ana Swanson, "How the Most Disliked—and Elected—Profession Is Disappearing from Politics," *Washington Post,* January 16, 2016, https://www.washingtonpost.com/news/wonk/wp/2016/01/19/how-the-most-disliked-and-elected-profession-is-disappearing-from-politics/.
13. Teague, "Training Lawyers for Leadership," 655.
14. Ellen Van Velsor and Joel Wright, *Expanding the Leadership Equation: Developing Next-Generation Leaders* (Greensboro, NC: Center for Creative Leadership, 2012).
15. Leo J. Shapiro and Associates, *Public Perceptions of Lawyers: Consumer Research Findings* (Chicago: American Bar Association, 2002), https://www.americanbar.org/content/dam/aba/administrative/market_research/public_perception_of_lawyers_2002.pdf.
16. Susan T. Fiske and Cydney Dupree, "Gaining Trust as Well as Respect in Communicating to Motivated Audiences about Science Topics," *Proceedings of the National Academy of Sciences* 111, no. 4 (September 16, 2014): 13593–97, https://www.pnas.org/content/111/Supplement_4/13593.full.
17. Michael Asimow, Steve Greenfield, Stefan Machura, Guy Osborn, Peter Robson, Robert Sockloskie, Cassandra Sharp, and Guillermo Jorge, "Perceptions of Lawyers—A Transnational Study of Student Views on the Image of Law and Lawyers," *International Journal of the Legal Profession* 12, no. 3 (2005): 407–36.
18. For example, see Scott A. Milner, Jennifer Mott Williams, and William Childers, "INSIGHT: Tomorrow's Lawyers Must Embrace Innovation, Technology," *Bloomberg Law,* April 8, 2020, https://news.bloomberglaw.com/privacy-and-data-security/insight-tomorrows-lawyer-must-embrace-innovation-technology; see also Kristen Holmquist, "Challenging Carnegie," *Journal of Legal Education* 61 (2012): 353–78.
19. Roland Smith and Paul Morrow, "The Changing Nature of Leadership in Law Firms," *New York State Bar Association Journal* 80 (2008): 33–38, at 34–35.
20. See Donald J. Polden, "Lawyer Leadership in the Practice of Law," *Tennessee Journal of Law and Policy* 14 (2020): 441–65.

21. For example, see Heineman, "Law and Leadership."
22. Melissa Berry, Kendra Brodin, Laura Friedman, Jerry Organ, and Debbie Shapiro, "What Firms Want: The Use of Competency Models in Associate PD," *NALP Bulletin,* May 2021, https://www.nalp.org/uploads/_bulletin_article_uploads/NALPBulletinPDQMay2021AssociateCompetenciesReport.pdf.

Chapter 2: Leadership: What It Means and Why It's Important to Lawyers

1. *Cambridge Dictionary* (2024), s.v. "leader," https://dictionary.cambridge.org/us/dictionary/english/leader.
2. Deborah L. Rhode, "Developing Leadership," *Santa Clara Law Review* 52 (2012): 689–724, at 690n.4.
3. James M. Kouzes and Barry Z. Posner, *The Leadership Challenge: How to Keep Getting Extraordinary Things Done in Organizations,* 7th ed. (Hoboken, NJ: Wiley, 2023), 18.
4. Donald J. Polden, "Leadership Matters: Lawyers' Leadership Skills and Competencies," *Santa Clara Law Review* 52 (2012): 899–920, at 903.
5. Robert H. Jerry II, "Leadership and Followership," *University of Toledo Law Review* 44 (2013): 345–54, at 353.
6. R. T. Collins, C. Algaze-Yojay, and B. Z. Posner, "The Leadership/Management Concept Scale: Differentiating Leadership from Management," *Leadership & Organization Development Journal* 44, no. 5 (2023): 657–77.
7. Kouzes and Posner, *The Leadership Challenge,* loc. cit.
8. Dina Eisenberg, "What Clients Really Want from You," *Law Practice Today,* June 14, 2019, https://www.lawpracticetoday.org/article/what-clients-want/.
9. Melissa Berry, Kendra Brodin, Laura Friedman, Jerry Organ, and Debbie Shapiro, "What Firms Want: The Use of Competency Models in Associate PD," *NALP Bulletin,* May 2021, https://www.nalp.org/uploads/_bulletin_article_uploads/NALPBulletinPDQMay2021AssociateCompetenciesReport.pdf.
10. Id., 19.
11. American Bar Association, Rule 1.2, in *Model Rules of Professional Conduct* (Chicago: American Bar Association, 2021), https://www.americanbar.org/groups/professional_responsibility/publications/model_rules_of_professional_conduct/rule_1_2_scope_of_representation_allocation_of_authority_between_client_lawyer/.
12. Id., Rule 1.4.
13. Id., Rule 1.1, which provides, "A lawyer shall provide competent representation to a client. Competent representation requires the legal knowledge, skill, thoroughness and preparation reasonably necessary for the representation."
14. Id., Rule 2.1.
15. Frigaliment Importing Co. v. B.N.S. International Sales, Corp., 190 F. Supp. 116 (S.D.N.Y. 1960).

16. Leslie A. Gordon, "Most Lawyers Are Introverted, and That's Not Necessarily a Bad Thing," *ABA Journal*, January 1, 2016, https://www.abajournal.com/magazine/article/most_lawyers_are_introverted_and_thats_not_necessarily_a_bad_thing; Ronda Muir, "The Unique Psychological World of Lawyers," *Law People Management* (blog), March 2006, https://www.lawpeopleblog.com/wp-includes/ms-files.php?file=2016/05/LPM-Unique-Psychological-World-of-Lawyers.final_.pdf; Larry Richard, *Leadership in Law Firms: An Expert Guide*, ed. Laura Slater (London, UK: Ark Group), https://www.lawyerbrain.com/wp-content/uploads/2023/04/leadership_in_law_firms_by_lrr_ark_group.pdf; Larry Richard, "The Lawyer Personality: Why Lawyers Are Skeptical," *LexBlog* (blog), February 11, 2013, https://www.lexblog.com/2013/02/11/the-lawyer-personality-why-lawyers-are-skeptical/.
17. Larry Richard, "The Lawyer Types," *American Bar Association Journal*, July 1993, https://www.lawyerbrain.com/wp-content/uploads/2023/04/the_lawyer_types_mbti.pdf. For a recent evaluation of Richard's work in the context of corporate counsel, see "All in the Mind: What Makes Executives Tick," The Legal 500 GC (2020), https://www.legal500.com/gc-magazine/feature/all-in-the-mind/.
18. James M. Kouzes and Barry Z. Posner, *Credibility: How Leaders Gain and Lose It, Why People Demand It*, 2nd ed. (Hoboken, NJ: Wiley, 2011); Barry Z. Posner, "The Influence of Demographic Factors on What People Want from Their Leaders," *Journal of Leadership Studies* 12, no. 2 (2018): 7–16.
19. Kouzes and Posner, *The Leadership Challenge*, 6th ed., 20.
20. Posner, "The Influence of Demographic Factors."
21. For example, see Lauren Morgan Roberts, Anthony J. Mayo, and David A. Thomas, eds., *Race, Work and Leadership: New Perspectives on the Black Experience* (Boston, MA: Harvard Business Review Press, 2019); Virginia Valian, *Why So Slow? The Advancement of Women* (Cambridge, MA: The MIT Press, 1999); Gabriella Gutierrez y Muhs, Yolanda Flores Nieman, Carmen G. Gonzalez, and Angela P. Harris, *Presumed Incompetence: The Intersections of Race and Class for Women in Academia* (Boulder: University Press of Colorado, 2012).
22. Carl I. Hovland, Irving L. Janis, and Harold H. Kelley, *Communication and Persuasion* (New Haven, CT: Yale University Press, 1953). See also James C. McCroskey, "Scales for the Measurement of Ethos," *Speech Monographs* 33 (1966): 65–72; David K. Berlo, James B. Lemert, and Robert J. Mertz, "Dimensions for Evaluating the Acceptability of Message Sources," *Public Opinion Quarterly* 3 (1969): 563–76; and, Robert Cialdini, *Influence: The Psychology of Persuasion* (New York: Collins, 2007).
23. Kouzes and Posner, *The Leadership Challenge*, 7th ed.; James M. Kouzes and Barry Z. Posner, *Everyday People, Extraordinary Leadership: How to Make a Difference Regardless of Your Title, Role, or Authority* (Hoboken, NJ: Wiley, 2020).
24. Barry Z. Posner, "Bringing the Rigor of Research to the Art of Leadership: Evidence behind The Five Practices of Exemplary Leadership® and the

LIP®: Leadership Practices Inventory®, http://www.leadershipchallenge.com/LeadershipChallenge/media/SiteFiles/research/our-research/tlc-our-research-bringing-the-rigor-of-research-to-the-art-of-leadership.pdf. Abstracts of more than eight hundred studies can be accessed at http://www.leadershipchallenge.com/research/others-research.aspx.
25. Kouzes and Posner, *The Leadership Challenge.*
26. Kouzes and Posner, *Everyday People, Extraordinary Leadership.*
27. Frederick F. Reichheld, *The Ultimate Question 2.0* (Boston, MA: Harvard Business Review Press, 2011).
28. Kouzes and Posner, *Everyday People, Extraordinary Leadership.*

Chapter 3: Lawyer-Leaders Model the Way

1. J. M. Kouzes and B. Z. Posner, *The Leadership Challenge: How to Make Extraordinary Things Happen in Organizations*, 7th ed. (Hoboken, NJ: Wiley, 2023).
2. Barry Z. Posner, "Another Look at the Impact of Personal and Organizational Values Congruency," *Journal of Business Ethics* 97, no. 4 (2010): 535–41; James M. Kouzes and Barry Z. Posner, "Finding Your Voice," in *Servant Leadership in Action*, ed. Ken Blanchard and Renee Broadwell (Oakland, CA: Berrett-Koehler, 2018), 109–14.
3. Deborah L. Rhode, "The Professional Responsibilities of Professional Schools: Pervasive Ethics in Perspective," in *Teaching and Learning Professionalism: Symposium Proceedings*, October 2–4, 1996 (Chicago: American Bar Association, 1997), 25.
4. Id., 36.
5. Ronda Muir, "The Unique Psychological World of Lawyers," *Law People* (blog), March 2006, https://www.lawpeopleblog.com/wp-includes/ms-files.php?file=2016/05/LPM-Unique-Psychological-World-of-Lawyers.final_.pdf.
6. Courtney Ward-Reichard, "Rewarding Leaders," *Law Practice* (Nov. 1, 2022), https://www.americanbar.org/groups/law_practice/resources/law-practice-magazine/2022-november-december/rewarding-leaders/?login.
7. Diane Curtis, "Loren Miller Winner Sid Wolinsky Sees No End to His Long Public Interest Career," *California Bar Journal*, September 2011, https://www.calbarjournal.com/September2011/TopHeadlines/TH5.aspx.
8. 2011—Todd L. Belcore," The Chicago Bar Foundation, updated 2021 https://chicagobarfoundation.org/anderson-fellowship-recipients/. (Belcore was awarded an Anderson Fellowship award by the Chicago Bar Foundation for his outstanding work by a young lawyer.)
9. Debra Cassens Weiss, "The Cost of WilmerHale's Gitmo Victory: $17M Worth of Pro Bono Hours," *American Bar Association Journal*, June 25, 2008, https://www.abajournal.com/news/article/the_cost_of_wilmer_hales_gitmo_victory_17m_worth_of_pro_bono_hours.
10. Paul Szoldra, "7 Incredible Stories of Heroism on 9/11," *Business Insider*, September 11, 2017, https://www.businessinsider.com/7-incredible-stories-of-heroism-on-911-2015-9.

11. Dan Schawbel, "How to Use Storytelling as a Leadership Tool," *Forbes,* April 13, 2012, http://www.forbes.com/sites/danschawbel/2012/08/13/how-to-use-storytelling-as-a-leadership-tool/#3fdcf5277ac9. For more on how to write, tell, and use stories to convey important organizational lessons, see Paul Smith, *Lead with a Story: A Guide to Crafting Business Narratives That Captivate, Convince, and Inspire* (New York: AMACOM, 2012).
12. Jennifer Bluestein, "Lawyer Leaders of Today and Tomorrow: How Do We Build Them?," *Law Practice* (November 1, 2022), https://www.americanbar.org/groups/law_practice/resources/law-practice-magazine/2022-november-december/lawyer-leaders-today-tomorrow-how-do-we-build-them/?login.
13. Steve Denning, *The Secret Language of Leadership: How Leaders Inspire Action through Narrative* (San Francisco: Jossey-Bass, 2007); Harrison Monarth, "The Irresistible Power of Storytelling as a Strategic Business Tool," *Harvard Business Review,* March 11, 2014, https://hbr.org/2014/03/the-irresistible-power-of-storytelling-as-a-strategic-business-tool; Paul J. Zak, "Why Your Brain Loves Good Storytelling," *Harvard Business Review,* October 28, 2014, https://hbr.org/2014/10/why-your-brain-loves-good-storytelling; Sean R. Martin, "Stories about Values and Valuable Stories: A Field Experiment of the Power of Narratives to Shape Newcomers' Actions," *Academy of Management Journal* 59, no. 5 (2015): 1707–24.
14. Neha Sampat, "A Call to Deal with Impostor Syndrome," *American Bar Association Journal,* November 20, 2018, https://www.abajournal.com/voice/article/a_call_to_deal_with_impostor_syndrome_a_hidden_source_of_attorney_distress.
15. Brent D. Rosso, Kathryn H. Dekas, and Amy Wrzesniewski, "On the Meaning of Work: A Theoretical Integration and Review," *Research in Organizational Behavior* 30 (2010): 91–127.
16. Alison W. Brooks and Leslie K. John, "The Surprising Power of Questions," *Harvard Business Review,* May/June 2018, 60–67.
17. Douglas Stone and Sheila Heen, *Thanks for the Feedback: The Science and Art of Receiving Feedback Well* (New York: Penguin Random House, 2015).
18. Deborah Tanner, *Talking from 9 to 5: Women and Men at Work* (New York: HarperCollins, 1994).
19. Id.
20. Francesca Gino, "Research: We Drop People Who Give Us Critical Feedback," *Harvard Business Review,* September 16, 2016, https://hbr.org/2016/09/research-we-drop-people-who-give-us-critical-feedback; see also Hayley Blunden, Jennifer M. Logg, Alison Wood Brooks, Leslie K. John, and Francesca Gino, "Seeker Beware: The Interpersonal Costs of Ignoring Advice," *Organizational Behavior and Human Decision Processes* 150 (2019): 83–100.
21. Jack Zenger, "There Is No Feedback Fallacy: Understanding the Value of Feedback," *Forbes,* May 13, 2019, https://www.forbes.com/sites/jackzenger/2019/05/13/there-is-no-feedback-fallacy-understanding-the-value-of-feedback/#3da55df15368.

Chapter 4: Lawyer-Leaders Inspire a Shared Vision

1. J. M. Kouzes and B. Z. Posner, *The Leadership Challenge: How to Make Extraordinary Things Happen in Organizations*, 7th ed. (Hoboken, NJ: Wiley, 2023).
2. Catherine Bailey and Adrian Madden, "What Makes Work Meaningful—or Meaningless," *MIT Sloan Management Review* 67, no. 1 (2016): 52–61.
3. Mark Beese and Ian Paterson, "Why Visionary Leadership Is Critical in Times of Uncertainty," *Law Practice* (Nov. 1, 2022), https://www.americanbar.org/groups/law_practice/resources/law-practice-magazine/2022-november-december/why-visionary-leadership-critical-times-uncertainty/.
4. Jennifer Bluestein, "Lawyer Leaders of Today and Tomorrow: How Do We Build Them?," *Law Practice* (November 1, 2022), https://www.americanbar.org/groups/law_practice/resources/law-practice-magazine/2022-november-december/lawyer-leaders-today-tomorrow-how-do-we-build-them/?login.
5. Association of American Law Schools, *Before the JD: Undergraduate Views on Law School*, 2018, https://www.aals.org/wp-content/uploads/2018/09/BJDReportsHghlights.pdf.
6. Ronit Dinovitzer, Bryant G. Garth, Robert Nelson, Gabriele Plickert, Rebecca Sandefur, Joyce Sterling, and David Wilkins, *After the JD III: Third Results from a National Study of Legal Careers* (Washington, DC: American Bar Foundation and NALP Foundation for Law Career Research and Education, 2014), http://www.americanbarfoundation.org/uploads/cms/documents/ajd3report_final_for_distribution.pdf.
7. Association of American Law Schools, *Before the JD*; Hank Stout, "5 Reasons Why Law School Is Wrong for You (and 5 Reasons Why It Is Right)," American Bar Association *Student Lawyer* (blog), June 28, 2017, https://abaforlawstudents.com/2017/06/28/5-reasons-law-school-wrong-5-reasons-right/.
8. Kouzes and Posner, *The Leadership Challenge.*
9. Beese and Paterson, *Why Visionary Leadership Is Critical.*
10. Id.
11. Aaron Hurst, Adam Pearce, Cammie Erickson, Scott Parish, Lauren Vesty, Allison Schnidman, Meg Garlinghouse, and Andrea Pavela, "Purpose at Work: The Largest Global Study on the Role of Purpose in the Workforce," *Purpose at Work: 2016 Global Report*, LinkedIn and Imperative, 2016, https://cdn.imperative.com/media/public/Global_Purpose_Index_2016.pdf.
12. Jesse Newton and Josh Davis, "Three Secrets of Organizational Success," *Strategy+Business* 76 (Autumn 2014), https://www.strategy-business.com/article/00271?gko=38cde; see also Simon Sinek, *Start with Why: How Great Leaders Inspire Everyone to Take Action* (New York: Portfolio, 2010).
13. Jamie Spannhake, "What Motivates Millennials? Ways Law Firms Are Retaining Young Lawyers," *Attorney at Work*, July 15, 2019, https://www.attorneyatwork.com/what-motivates-millennials-retaining-young-lawyers/.

14. John Beyer, "Startups and Millennials: The Perfect Fit," *Built In*, April 19, 2019, https://builtin.com/company-culture/startups-and-millennials-perfect-fit.
15. Kouzes and Posner, *The Leadership Challenge*.
16. Daniel Goleman, *Social Intelligence: The New Science of Human Relationships* (New York: Bantam, 2006).
17. Barbara L. Fredrickson, *Positivity: Groundbreaking Research Reveals How to Embrace the Hidden Strengths of Positive Emotions, Overcome Negativity, and Thrive* (New York: Crown, 2009).
18. Bernard M. Bass, *Leadership and Performance beyond Expectations* (New York: Free Press, 1985).
19. Fredrickson, *Positivity*.
20. Vanessa Van Edwards, "5 Secrets of a Successful TED Talk," *HuffPost*, December 6, 2017, https://www.huffpost.com/entry/5-secrets-of-a-successful_b_6887472.
21. Markus Koppensteiner, Pia Stephan, and Johannes Paul Michael Jäschke, "From Body Motion to Cheers: Speakers' Body Movements as Predictors of Applause," *Personality and Individual Differences* 74 (2015): 182–85.
22. Anayat Durrani, "Improving Your Nonverbal Performance in Front of a Jury," *Plaintiff*, October 2012, https://www.plaintiffmagazine.com/recent-issues/item/improving-your-nonverbal-performance-in-front-of-a-jury#:~:text=Lawyers%20should%20try%20to%20stay,any%20of%20those%20negative%20gestures.

Chapter 5: Lawyer-Leaders Challenge the Process

1. Anthony C. Johnson, "Tech Disruption, Litigation Finance and ABS Frameworks: The Future of the Legal Industry," *Forbes* (May 3, 2023), https://www.forbes.com/sites/theyec/2023/05/03/tech-disruption-litigation-finance-and-abs-frameworks-the-future-of-the-legal-industry/?sh=4bd0c4db161d.
2. James M. Kouzes and Barry Z. Posner, *The Leadership Challenge: How to Make Extraordinary Things Happen in Organizations*, 7th ed. (Hoboken, NJ: Wiley, 2023).
3. For a survey of the aftermath of the 2007–08 recession in the legal field, see Thomas S. Clay and Eric A. Seeger, "Law Firms in Transition: An Altman Weil Flash Survey," Altman Weil, Inc., 2018, https://www.altmanweil.com/law-firms-in-transition-2018-an-altman-weil-flash-survey/.
4. Matthias Spitzmuller, Hock-Peng Sin, Michael Howe, and Shereen Fatimah, "Investigating the Uniqueness and Usefulness of Proactive Personality in Organizational Research: A Meta-Analytic Review," *Human Performance* 28, no. 4 (2015): 351–79.
5. Davide Nicolini, Maja Korica, and Keith Ruddle, "Staying in the Know," *Sloan Management Review* 56, no. 4 (2015): 57–65.
6. Thomas S. Bateman and J. Michael Crant, "The Proactive Component of Organizational Behavior: Measures and Correlates," *Journal of Organizational*

Behavior 14 (1993): 103–18; J. Michael Crant, "Proactive Behavior in Organizations," *Journal of Management* 26, no. 3 (2000): 435–63; J. Michael Crant and Thomas S. Bateman, "Charismatic Leadership Viewed from Above: The Impact of Proactive Personality," *Journal of Organizational Behavior* 21, no. 1 (2000): 63–75.

7. Daniel H. Pink, *Drive: The Surprising Truth about What Motivates Us* (New York: Riverhead Books, 2011).
8. Ronit Dinovitzer, Bryant G. Garth, Robert Nelson, Gabriele Plickert, Rebecca Sandefur, Joyce Sterling, and David Wilkins, *After the JD III: Third Results from a National Study of Legal Careers* (Washington, DC: American Bar Foundation and NALP Foundation for Law Career Research and Education, 2014), http://www.americanbarfoundation.org/uploads/cms/documents/ajd3report_final_for_distribution.pdf, who identifies sources of job satisfaction for young lawyers.
9. Mihaly Csikszentmihalyi, *Flow: The Psychology of Optimal Experience* (New York: Harper & Row, 1990).
10. Mihaly Csikszentmihalyi, *Beyond Boredom and Anxiety: The Experience of Play in Work and Games* (San Francisco: Jossey-Bass, 1975), 30.
11. Gregory Berns, *Iconoclast: A Neuroscientist Reveals How to Think Differently* (Cambridge, MA: Harvard Business School Press, 2008).
12. Jeffrey H. Dyer, Hal Gregersen, and Clayton M. Christensen, "The Innovator's DNA," *Harvard Business Review* 87, no. 2 (2009): 60–67.
13. Donald J. Polden, "Lawyers, Leadership, and Innovation," *Santa Clara Law Review* 58 (2018): 427–52, at 451n.102 (citing Ian Lopez, "Innovate to Eliminate Bad Ideas? Holland & Knight Leader on Changing the Business Model," *Legaltech News,* February 21, 2018).
14. Jeffrey Rosen, *Conversations with RBG: Ruth Bader Ginsburg on Life, Love, Liberty, and Law* (New York: Henry Holt &. Co., 2019).
15. Douglas Brinkley, "The Man Who Kept King's Secrets," *Vanity Fair,* April 2006, https://archive.vanityfair.com/article/2006/4/the-man-who-kept-kings-secrets.
16. Peter Sims, *Little Bets: How Breakthrough Ideas Emerge from Small Discoveries* (New York: Free Press, 2011).
17. See, for example, Richard H. Thaler and Cass R. Sunstein, *Nudge: Improving Decisions about Health, Wealth, and Happiness* (New York: Penguin Books, 2009); B. J. Fogg, *Tiny Habits: The Small Changes That Change Everything* (New York: Houghton Mifflin Harcourt, 2020).
18. Karl E. Weick, "Small Wins: Redefining the Scale of Social Problems," *American Psychologist* 39, no. 1 (1984): 40–49.
19. Teresa A. Amabile and Steven J. Kramer, *The Progress Principle: Using Small Wins to Ignite Joy, Engagement, and Creativity at Work* (Boston, MA: Harvard Business Review Press, 2011).
20. Amy C. Edmondson, *The Fearless Organization: Creating Psychological Safety in the Workplace for Learning, Innovation, and Growth* (Hoboken, NJ: Wiley, 2019).
21. David Rock, "Managing with the Brain in Mind," *Strategy+Business,* August 27, 2009, https://www.strategy-business.com/article/09306?gko=5df7f.

22. Daniel Kahnerman, *Thinking, Fast and Slow* (New York: Farrar, Straus and Giroux, 2011).
23. Edmondson, *The Fearless Organization.*
24. Charles Duhigg, "What Google Learned from Its Quest to Build the Perfect Team," *The New York Times Magazine*, February 25, 2016, https://www.nytimes.com/2016/02/28/magazine/what-google-learned-from-its-quest-to-build-the-perfect-team.html.
25. O. C. Tanner Institute, *2021 Global Culture Report*, 2021, https://www.octanner.com/search?query=global+culture+report+2021.
26. Heidi K. Brown, "Fear and Lawyering: Create a Work Culture of 'Psychological Safety' That Encourages Taking Intellectual and Creative Risks," *American Bar Association Journal*, May 1, 2019, https://www.abajournal.com/magazine/article/fear-lawyering-psychological-safety.
27. Edgar H. Schein, *Humble Inquiry: The Gentle Art of Asking instead of Telling* (Oakland, CA: Berrett- Koehler, 2013).
28. Edmondson, *The Fearless Organization*, 200.
29. Kouzes and Posner, *The Leadership Challenge.*
30. Paul J. H. Schoemaker and Robert E. Gunther, "The Wisdom of Deliberate Mistakes," *Harvard Business Review* 84, no. 6 (2006): 108–15.
31. Carol S. Dweck, *Mindset: The New Psychology of Success* (New York: Random House, 2006).
32. Albert Bandura and Robert E. Wood, "Effects of Perceived Controllability and Performance Standards on Self-Regulation of Complex Decision Making," *Journal of Personality and Social Psychology* 56 (1989): 805–14; see also Dweck, *Mindset.*
33. Tae Kyung Kouzes and Barry Z. Posner, "Influence of Managers' Mindset on Leadership Behavior," *Leadership & Organization Development Journal* 40, no. 8 (2019): 829–44.
34. See Salvatore R. Maddi, "The Story of Hardiness: Twenty Years of Theorizing, Research, and Practice," *Consulting Psychology Journal: Practices and Research* 54, no. 3 (2002): 175–85; see also Salvatore R. Maddi and Suzanne C. Kobasa, *The Hardy Executive: Health under Stress* (Chicago: Dorsey Press, 1984); Salvatore R. Maddi and Deborah M. Khoshaba, *Resilience at Work: How to Succeed No Matter What Life Throws at You* (New York: AMACOM, 2005).
35. For example, see Paul T. Bartone, Robert R. Roland, James J. Picano, and Thomas J. Williams, "Psychological Hardiness Predicts Success in US Army Special Forces Candidates," *International Journal of Selection and Assessment* 16, no. 1 (2008): 78–81; Reginald A. Bruce and Robert F. Sinclair, "Exploring the Psychological Hardiness of Entrepreneurs," *Frontiers of Entrepreneurship Research* 29, no. 6 (2009): 78–81; Paul T. Bartone, "Social and Organizational Influences on Psychological Hardiness: How Leaders Can Increase Stress Resilience," *Security Informatics* 1 (2012): 1–10; Banafshe Hasanvand, Mohamad Khaledian, and Ali Reza Merati, "The Relationship between Psychological

Hardiness and Attachment Styles with the University Student's Creativity," *European Journal of Experimental Biology* 3, no. 3 (2013): 656–60; Asle M. Sandvik, Anita L. Hansen, Sigurd William Hystad, Bjørn Helge Johnsen, and Paul T. Bartone, "Psychopathy, Anxiety, and Resiliency—Psychological Hardiness as a Mediator of the Psychopathy–Anxiety Relationship in a Prison Setting," *Personality and Individual Differences* 72 (2015): 30–34.

36. See Susan Daicoff, "Lawyer, Know Thyself: A Review of Empirical Research on Attorney Attributes Bearing on Professionalism," *American University Law Review* 46 (1997): 1337–1427, at 1346–48.
37. Emily Esfahani Smith, "On Coronavirus Lockdown? Look for Meaning, Not Happiness," *New York Times*, April 7, 2020, https://www.nytimes.com/2020/04/07/opinion/coronavirus-mental-health.html.

Chapter 6: Lawyer-Leaders Enable Others to Act

1. "Lessons from Practicing Lawyers: Why Attorneys Work Together," *The Practice* 1, no.6 (Sept./Oct.2015), https://clp.law.harvard.edu/knowledge-hub/magazine/issues/teamwork-and-collaboration/lessons-from-practicing-lawyers/.
2. James M. Kouzes and Barry Z. Posner, *The Leadership Challenge: How to Make Extraordinary Things Happen in Organizations*, 7th ed. (Hoboken, NJ: Wiley, 2023).
3. Michael B. Gurtman, "Trust, Distrust, and Interpersonal Problems: A Circumplex Analysis," *Journal of Personality and Social Psychology* 62 (1992): 989–1002; Glenn D. Grace and Thomas Schill, "Social Support and Coping Style Differences in Subjects High and Low in Interpersonal Trust," *Psychological Reports* 59 (1986): 584–86.
4. James A. Driscoll, "Trust and Participation in Organizational Decision Making as Predictors of Satisfaction," *Academy of Management Journal* 21 (1978): 44–56.
5. Larry Richard, "The Lawyer Personality: Why Lawyers Are Skeptical," *What Makes Lawyers Tick?* (blog), February 11, 2013, https://www.lawyerbrainblog.com/2013/02/the-lawyer-personality-why-lawyers-are-skeptical/.
6. Pamela S. Shockley-Zalabak, Sherwyn Morreale, and Michael Hackman, *Building the High-Trust Organization: Strategies for Supporting Five Key Dimensions of Trust* (San Francisco: Jossey-Bass, 2010).
7. James M. Kouzes and Barry Z. Posner, *Everyday People, Extraordinary Leadership: How to Make a Difference Regardless of Your Title, Role, or Authority* (Hoboken, NJ: Wiley, 2020).
8. David B. Sarnoff and Natalie W. Loeb, "The Case for Active Listening," *PLI Chronicle: Insights and Perspectives for the Legal Community*, April 2021, https://plus.pli.edu/Details/Details?rows=10&fq=title_id~3A2822~325651~2229202B~id~3A282B22~325651-ATL4~2229~&facet=true&qt=legal_boolean&mode=Group_By_Series.

9. Jack Zenger and Joseph Folkman, "What Great Listeners Actually Do," *Harvard Business Review*, July 14, 2016, https://hbr.org/2016/07/what-great-listeners-actually-do.
10. Id.
11. Lindsey P. Gustafson, Aric Short, and Neil W. Hamilton, "Teaching and Assessing Active Listening as a Foundational Skill for Lawyers as Leaders, Counselors, Negotiators, and Advocates," *Santa Clara Law Review*, 62 (2022).
12. American Bar Association, "ABA Profile of the Legal Profession 2020," July 2020, https://www.americanbar.org/content/dam/aba/administrative/news/2020/07/potlp2020.pdf; Ronit Dinovitzer, Bryant G. Garth, Robert Nelson, Gabriele Plickert, Rebecca Sandefur, Joyce Sterling, and David Wilkins, *After the JD III: Third Results from a National Study of Legal Careers* (Washington, DC: American Bar Foundation and NALP Foundation for Law Career Research and Education, 2014), http://www.americanbarfoundation.org/uploads/cms/documents/ajd3report_final_for_distribution.pdf.
13. Dinovitzer et al., *After the JD III.*
14. Adam Grant, *Give and Take: Why Helping Others Drives Our Success* (New York: Penguin Group, 2013).
15. Id.
16. Robert Axelrod, *The Evolution of Cooperation*, rev. ed. (New York: Basic Books, 2006).
17. William Poundstone, *Prisoner's Dilemma: John Von Neumann, Game Theory, and the Puzzle of the Bomb* (New York: Doubleday, 1992).
18. Francis J. Flynn, "How Much Should I Give and How Often? The Effects of Generosity and Frequency of Favor Exchange on Social Status and Productivity," *Academy of Management Journal* 46, no. 5 (2003): 539–53.
19. John Thackray, "Feedback for Real," *Gallup Management Journal* 1, no. 1 (2001): 12–17; Marcus Buckingham and Curt Coffman, *First, Break All the Rules* (New York: Simon & Schuster, 1999); Gallup, *State of the Global Workplace* (New York: Gallup Press, 2017); Susan Rebstock Williams and Rick L. Wilson, "Group Support Systems, Power, and Influence in an Organization: A Field Study," *Decision Sciences* 28, no. 4 (1997): 911–37; Patty Azzarello, "Why Sharing Power at Work Is the Very Best Way to Build It," *Fast Company*, January 18, 2013, https://www.fastcompany.com/3004867/why-sharing-power-work-very-best-way-build-it; Edward L. Deci, Anja H. Olafsen, and Richard M. Ryan, "Self-Determination Theory in Work Organizations: The State of a Science," *Annual Review of Organizational Psychology and Organization Behavior* 4 (2017): 19–43.
20. Mauricio R. Delgado, "Reward-Related Responses in the Human Striatum," *Annals of the New York Academy of Science* 1104 (2007): 70–88; Dominic S. Fareri, Laura N. Martin, and Mauricio R. Delgado, "Reward-Related Processing in the Human Brain: Developmental Considerations," *Development & Psychopathology* 20, no. 4 (2008): 1191–1211; Mauricio R. Delgado, M. Meredith Gillis, and Elizabeth Phelps, "Regulating the Expectation of Reward," *Nature Neuroscience* 11, no. 8 (2008): 880–81; Mauricio R. Delgado and James G. Dilmore, "Social and Emotional Influences on Decision-Making and the Brain," *Minnesota Journal of Law, Science & Technology* 9, no. 2 (2008): 899–912; Bernard W. Balleine,

Mauricio R. Delgado, and Okihide Hikosaka, "The Role of Dorsal Striatum in Reward and Decision-Making," *Journal of Neuroscience* 27 (2007): 8159–60.
21. Debra Cassens Weiss, "These Common Mistakes Can Lead to Lawyer Ethics Complaints," *American Bar Association Journal*, February 10, 2016, https://www.abajournal.com/news/article/these_common_mistakes_can_lead_to_lawyer_ethics_complaints.
22. See Dan Pinnington and Ian Hu, "2017 Practice Management," American Bar Association, *TechReport*, December 1, 2017, https://www.americanbar.org/groups/law_practice/publications/techreport/2017/practice_management/.
23. See, for example, Albert Bandura, *Self-Efficacy: The Exercise of Control* (New York: Freeman, 1997); James E. Maddux, "Self-Efficacy: The Power of Believing You Can," in *The Oxford Handbook of Positive Psychology*, ed. Shane J. Lopez and C. R. Snyder, 2nd ed. (New York: Oxford University Press, 2011), 335–44; Eric Chester, *On Fire at Work: How Great Companies Ignite Passion in Their People without Burning Them Out* (Shippensburg, PA: Sounds Wisdom, 2015).
24. Robert Wood and Albert Bandura, "Impact of Conceptions of Ability on Self-Regulatory Mechanisms and Complex Decision Making," *Journal of Personality and Social Psychology* 56 (1989): 407–15.
25. James M. Kouzes and Barry Z. Posner, *Learning Leadership: The Five Fundamentals of Becoming an Exemplary Leader* (Hoboken, NJ: Wiley, 2016).
26. Paul Leone, "Take Your ROI to Level 6," *Training Industry Quarterly* 1, no. 1 (2008): 14–18, http://www.nxtbook.com/nxtbooks/trainingindustry/tiq_2008spring/.
27. "The Frontline Leader Project: Exploring the Most Critical Segment of Leaders," Development Dimensions International, https://www.ddiworld.com/reports/frontlineleaderproject.
28. Robert J. Derocher, "Mentoring Helps New and Experienced Lawyers Make the Connection," *Bar Leader* 30, no. 6 (2006), https://www.americanbar.org/groups/bar_services/publications/bar_leader/2005_06/3006/mentoring/; David B. Sarnoff, Natalie Loeb, and David Robert, "Attorney Mentoring in the 21st Century," *PLI Chronicle: Insights and Perspectives for the Legal Community*, June 2021, https://plus.pli.edu/Details/Details?fq=id:(330315-ATL6).
29. Cynthia Pladziewicz, "Coaching and Career Development," in *The Art and Science of Strategic Talent Management in Law Firms*, ed. Terri Mottershead (St. Paul, MN: Thomson Reuters, 2010), 187, 190–91.

Chapter 7: Lawyer-Leaders Encourage the Heart

1. Alison E. Smith, Lee Jussim, Jacquelynne Eccles, Michelle VanNoy, Stephanie Madon, and Polly Palumbo, "Self-Fulfilling Prophecies, Perceptual Biases, and Accuracy at the Individual and Group Levels," *Journal of Experimental Social Psychology* 34, no. 6 (1998): 530–61; Dov Eden, "Leadership and Expectations: Pygmalion Effects and Other Self-Fulfilling Prophecies in Organizations," *The Leadership Quarterly* 3, no. 4 (1992): 271–305.

2. R. J. Blitzer, C. Petersen, and L. Rogers, "How to Build Self-Esteem," *Training and Development Journal* 47, no. 2 (1993): 59.
3. David L. Cooperrider, "Positive Image, Positive Action: The Affirmative Basis of Organizing," in *Appreciative Management and Leadership: The Power of Positive Thought and Action in Organizations*, ed. Suresh Srivastva and David L. Cooperrider, and Associates (San Francisco: Jossey-Bass, 1990), 1–14.
4. David Scott Yeager, Valerie Purdie-Vaughns, Julio Garcia, Nancy Apfel, Patti Brzustoski, Allison Master, William T. Hessert, Matthew E. Williams, and Geoffrey L. Cohen, "Breaking the Cycle of Mistrust: Wide Interventions to Provide Critical Feedback across the Racial Divide," *Journal of Experimental Psychology* 143, no 2. (2014): 804–24.
5. Sari Fried-Fiori, "Competency-Based Development Programs," in *The Art and Science of Strategic Talent Management*, ed. Terri Mottershead (Eagan, MN: Thomson/West, 2011), 119–22.
6. Susan Manch, "Competencies and Competency Models: An Overview," in Mottershead, *The Art and Science of Strategic Talent Management*, 77–83.
7. See Adrian Gostick and Chester Elton, *Managing with Carrots: Using Recognition to Attract and Retain the Best People* (Layton, UT: Gibbs Smith, 2001); S. J. Ashford and K. E. M. DeStobbeleir, "Feedback, Goal Setting, and Task Performance Revisited," in *New Developments in Goal Setting and Task Performance*, ed. E. A. Locke and G. P. Latham (New York: Routledge, 2013), 51–64.
8. See Gerry Riskin, "Leadership: Agility in the Face of Fragility," *Law Practice Magazine*, November 1, 2020, https://www.americanbar.org/groups/law_practice/publications/law_practice_magazine/2020/nd20200/nd20riskin/.
9. Paulette A. McCarty, "Effects of Feedback on the Self-Confidence of Men and Women," *Academy of Management Journal* 29, no. 4 (1986): 840–47.
10. Elad N. Sherf, Ravi S. Gajendran, and Barry Z. Posner, "Seeking and Finding Justice: Why and When Managers' Feedback Seeking Enhances Justice Enactment," *Journal of Organizational Behavior* 42, no. 6 (2021): 741–66.
11. Terrence E. Deal and M. K. Key, *Corporate Celebrations: Play, Purpose, and Profit at Work* (San Francisco: Berrett-Koehler, 1998).
12. Tom Rath, *Vital Friends: The People You Can't Afford to Live Without* (New York: Gallup Press, 2006); Tom Rath and Jim Harter, *Well Being: The Five Essential Elements* (New York: Gallup Press, 2010).
13. Bob Nelson, *1001 Ways to Reward Employees*, 2nd ed. (New York: Workman, 2005).
14. Kerry Roberts Gibson, Kate O'Leary, and Joseph R. Weintraub, "The Little Things That Make Employees Feel Appreciated," *Harvard Business Review*, January 23, 2020, https://hbr.org/2020/01/the-little-things-that-make-employees-feel-appreciated.
15. Robert A. Emmons, *Thanks! How Practicing Gratitude Makes You Happier* (New York: Houghton Mifflin, 2008).
16. David Brooks, *The Social Animal: The Hidden Sources of Love, Character, and Achievement* (New York: Random House, 2011).

17. Wayne E. Baker, *Achieving Success through Social Capital: Tapping the Hidden Resources in Your Personal and Business Networks* (San Francisco: Jossey-Bass, 2000).
18. Shawn Achor, *Happiness Advantage: The Seven Principles That Fuel Success and Performance at Work* (New York: Crown Business, 2010).
19. Susan Pinker, *The Village Effect: How Face-to-Face Contact Can Make Us Healthier and Happier* (New York: Penguin Random House, 2015).
20. Marcial Losada and Emily Heaphy, "The Role of Positivity and Connectivity in the Performance of Business Teams: A Nonlinear Dynamics Model," *American Behavioral Scientist* 47, no. 6 (2004): 740–65.
21. Leonard L. Berry, A. Parasuraman, and Valerie A. Zeithaml, "Improving Service Quality in America: Lessons Learned," *Academy of Management Executive* 8, no. 2 (1994): 32–45.
22. Olga Stavrova and Daniel Ehlebracht, "Cynical Beliefs about Human Nature and Income: Longitudinal and Cross-Cultural Analyses," *Journal of Personality and Social Psychology* 110, no. 1 (2016): 116–32.
23. Julianne Holt-Lunstad, Timothy B. Smith, Mark Baker, Tyler Harris, and David Stephenson, "Loneliness and Social Isolation as Risk Factors for Mortality: A Meta-Analytic Review," *Perspectives on Psychological Science* 10, no. 2 (2015): 227–37.
24. Robert C. Ford, Frank S. McLaughlin, and John W. Newstrom, "Questions and Answers about Fun at Work," *Human Resource Planning*, 26 no. 4 (2003): 18–33, at 22.
25. Tiffany McDowell, Sheba Ehteshami, and Kyle Sandell, "Are You Having Fun Yet?" *Deloitte Review* 24 (2019): 133–44.
26. Robert Provine, *Laughter: A Scientific Investigation* (New York: Penguin, 2001). See also Alan W. Gray, Brian Parkineons, and Robin I. Dunbar, "Laughter's Influence on the Intimacy of Self-Disclosure," Motivation and Emotion 31, no. 1 (2007): 28-43.
27. Young Gin Choi, Junehee Kwon, and Wansoo Kim, "Effects of Attitudes vs. Experience of Workplace Fun on Employee Behaviors," *International Journal of Contemporary Hospitality Management* 25, no. 1 (2013): 410–27; Katerina Georganta and Anthony J. Montgomery, "Exploring Fun as a Job Resource: The Enhancing and Protecting Role of a Key Modern Workplace Factor," *International Journal of Applied Positive Psychology* 1 (2016): 107–31.
28. See, for example, Daniel Sgroi, "Happiness and Productivity: Understanding the Happy-Productive Worker," Social Market Foundation, October 2015, https://www.smf.co.uk/wp-content/uploads/2015/10/Social-Market-Foundation-Publication-Briefing-CAGE-4-Are-happy-workers-more-productive-281015.pdf; Barry Chignell, "Six Reasons Why Fun in the Office is the Future of Work," CIPHR, May 22, 2018, https://www.ciphr.com/advice/fun-in-the-office/; Greg Winteregg, *Fun at Work: More Time, Freedom, Profit and More of What You Love to Do* (Clearwater, FL: Matterhorn Business Development, 2019).
29. O. C. Tanner Learning Group, "Performance Accelerated: A New Benchmark for Initiative Employee Engagement, Retention, and Results," 2024, https://edubirdie.com/wp-content/uploads/2024/02/White-Paper-Performance-Accelerated.pdf.

30. Gary Klein, *The Sources of Power: How People Make Decisions* (Cambridge, MA: The MIT Press, 1998); Gary Klein, *The Power of Intuition: How to Use Your Gut Feelings to Make Better Decisions at Work* (New York: Crown Business, 2004).
31. See, for example, Gary Spence, *How to Win an Argument Every Time* (New York: St. Martin's Press, 1995); and, Nick Westergaard, "5 Types of Stories Leaders Need to Tell," *Harvard Business Review*, September 22, 2023, https://hbr.org/2023/09/5-types-of-stories-leaders-need-to-tell.

Chapter 8: Personal Values and Professional Ethics as Lawyer-Leaders

1. The Law School Admission Council, which administers the LSAT entrance examination and manages a large part of all approved law schools' admission processing, has created a program that rolls out the importance of professional identity formation to prelaw applicants. See LSAC Professional Identity Formation Program, https://www.lsac.org/professional-identity-formation-program. Recent amendments to the ABA's Standards for Approval of Law Schools, Standard 303 (b) (2023-24) provides that law schools "shall provide substantial opportunity to students for . . . (3) the development of a professional identity."
2. "How Our Test Contributes to Comprehensive and Fair Law School Admissions," LSAC, June 19, 2019, https://www.lsac.org/blog/how-our-test-contributes-comprehensive-and-fair-law-school-admissions#:~:text=The%20results%20are%20consistently%20clear,%2Dpoint%20average%20(GPA).
3. Neil Hamilton, "The Major Transitions in Professional Formation and Development from Being a Student to Being a Lawyer Present Opportunities to Benefit the Students and the Law School," *Baylor Law Review* 72 (Winter 2021): 139–69, https://law.baylor.edu/sites/g/files/ecbvkj1546/files/2023-11/11%20Hamilton.pdf.
4. Neil W. Hamilton and Louis Bilionis, *Law Student Professional Development and Formation: Bridging Law School, Student, and Employer Goals* (New York: Cambridge University Press, 2022).
5. Marjorie Shultz and Sheldon Zedeck, "Predicting Lawyer Effectiveness: Broadening the Basis for Law School Admissions Decisions," *Law and Social Inquiry, Journal of the American Bar Foundation* 36, no. 3 (2011): 620–61, at 661.
6. Hamilton and Bilionis, *Law Student Professional Development and Formation.*
7. Jennifer Bluestein, "Lawyer Leaders of Today and Tomorrow: How Do We Build Them?," *Law Practice* (November 1, 2022), https://www.americanbar.org/groups/law_practice/resources/law-practice-magazine/2022-november-december/lawyer-leaders-today-tomorrow-how-do-we-build-them/?login.
8. William M. Sullivan, Anne Colby, Judith Welch Wegner, Lloyd Bond, and Lee S. Shulman, *Educating Lawyers: Preparation for the Profession of Law* (San Francisco: Jossey-Bass/Wiley, 2007).

9. Id.
10. See Susan Manch, "Competency-Based Performance Management: Evaluations, Advance and Compensation," in *The Art and Science of Strategic Talent Management in Law Firms,* ed. Terri Mottershead (Eagan, MN: Thomson/West, 2010), 154; Sari Fried-Fiori, "Competency-Based Development Programs," in Mottershead, *The Art and Science of Strategic Talent Management,* 119 (describing the critical role of mentoring and coaching of law firm associates as a key element of their becoming proficient practitioners and as a tool for evaluation and retention).
11. Barry Z. Posner, "When Learning How to Lead, An Exploratory Look at Role Models," *Leadership & Organizational Development Journal* 42, no. 5 (2021): 802–18.
12. Major, Lindsey and Africa, "Gen-Z Attorneys Increasingly Aspire to Career Paths Beyond BigLaw, New Survey from MLA Finds" (May 10, 2023), https://www.mlaglobal.com/en/about-us/press-releases/gen-z-attorneys-increasingly-aspire-to-career-paths-beyond-biglaw-new-survey-from-mla-finds#:~:text=Additionally%2C%20a%20combined%2053%25%20of,partner%20at%20a%20law%20firm.
13. See G. Andrew, H. Benjamin, Alfred Kaszniak, Bruce Sales, and Stephen B. Shanfield, "The Role of Legal Education in Producing Psychological Distress among Law Students and Lawyers," *American Bar Foundation Research Journal* 11, no. 2 (1986): 225–52; Patrick Schiltz, "On Being a Happy, Healthy, and Ethical Member of an Unhappy, Unhealthy, Unethical Profession," *Vanderbilt Law Review* 52 (1999): 871–951.
14. Susan Daicoff, *Lawyer, Know Thyself: A Psychological Analysis of Personality Strengths and Weaknesses* (Washington, DC: American Psychological Association, 2004), 146–48.
15. John Bliss, "The Professional Identity of Lawyers," *The Practice* 2, no. 3 (2016), https://thepractice.law.harvard.edu/article/the-professional-identity-formation-of-lawyers/.
16. John Grisham, *The Rainmaker* (New York: Dell, 2011).
17. Id.
18. Donald G. McNeil Jr., "Fauci on What Working for Trump Was Really Like," *New York Times,* February 13, 2021 (updated), https://www.nytimes.com/2021/01/24/health/fauci-trump-covid.html.
19. Major, Lindsey & Africa, "2019 Millennial Attorney Survey: New Expectations, Evolving Beliefs and Shifting Career Goals," Above the Law, https://cdn2.hubspot.net/hubfs/209075/MLA_MillenialSurvey_040519_forWeb-1.pdf.
20. Lori Berman, Heather Bock, and Juliet Aiken, *Accelerating Lawyer Success: How to Make Partner, Stay Healthy, and Flourish in a Law Firm* (Chicago: American Bar Association, 2016), 46–58.
21. Deborah L. Rhode and Amanda K. Packel, *Leadership: Law Policy, and Management* (New York: Wolters Kluwer Law and Business, 2011), 163 (citing Arie de Geus, "Beware: Innovation Kills!" in *Leading for Innovation,* ed.

Francis Hesselbein, Iain Somerville, and Marshall Goldsmith [San Francisco: Jossey-Bass, 2002], 225–38, at 226).

22. James M. Kouzes and Barry Z. Posner, *Everyday People, Extraordinary Leadership: How to Make a Difference regardless of Your Title, Role, or Authority* (Hoboken, NJ: Wiley, 2020).
23. Steve Armstrong and Tim Leishman, "Developing Partners: An End to Sink or Swim," in Mottershead, *The Art and Science of Strategic Talent Management*, 305. See also Courtney Ward-Reichard, "Rewarding Leaders," *Law Practice* (Nov. 1, 2022).
24. See Bill George, Peter Sims, Andrew N. McLean, and Diana Mayer, "Discovering Your Authentic Leadership," *Harvard Business Review*, February 2007, https://hbr.org/2007/02/discovering-your-authentic-leadership.
25. Daniel Goleman, *Emotional Intelligence: Why It Can Matter More Than IQ* (New York: Random House, 2005).

Chapter 9: Making Decisions, Leading Innovation

1. Stephen Embry, "Perspectives: You Know Good Leadership When You See It," *Law Practice* (Nov. 1, 2022).
2. Brian Tait, "Traditional Leadership vs. Servant Leadership," *Forbes*, March 11, 2020, https://www.forbes.com/sites/forbescoachescouncil/2020/03/11/traditional-leadership-vs-servant-leadership/?sh=52741e4d451e.
3. Noel M. Tichy and Warren G. Bennis, *Judgment: How Winning Leaders Make Great Calls* (New York: Portfolio, 2007), 9–10.
4. Peter Drucker, "The Effective Decision," *Harvard Business Review*, January 1967, https://hbr.org/1967/01/the-effective-decision.
5. Stephen Embry, "Perspectives."
6. Ram Charan, "Conquering a Culture of Indecision," *Harvard Business Review*, January 2006, https://hbr.org/2006/01/conquering-a-culture-of-indecision.
7. Peter J. Boyer, "A Different War," *New Yorker*, July 1, 2002, https://www.newyorker.com/magazine/2002/07/01/a-different-war.
8. John P. Kotter, *Leading Change*, rev. ed. (Boston, MA: Harvard Business Review Press, 2012); John P. Kotter and Dan S. Cohen, *Heart of Change: Real-Life Stories of How People Change Their Organizations* (Boston, MA: Harvard Business Review Press, 2012).
9. Donald J. Polden, "Lawyers, Leadership, and Innovation," *Santa Clara Law Review* 58 (2018): 427–52, at 442–43 (citing Thomas S. Clay and Eric A. Seeger, *2018 Law Firms in Transition: An Altman Weil Flash Survey* [Willow Grove, PA: Altman Weil, Inc., 2018], iii).
10. Polden, "Lawyers, Leadership, and Innovation," 443.
11. Ibid.
12. Deborah L. Rhode and Amanda K. Packel, *Leadership: Law, Policy, and Management* (New York, Wolters Kluwer Law and Business, 2011), 163.

13. See Polden, "Lawyers, Leaders and Innovation" (describing the failure of several national law firms unable to address the challenges of the new, post-recession legal world).
14. "Marketplace of Ideas: What Innovation Is—and Isn't," *The Practice* 5 (Jan./Feb. 2019), https://clp.law.harvard.edu/knowledge-hub/magazine/issues/adaptive-innovation/marketplace-of-ideas/.
15. David Horth and Dan Buchner, "Innovative Leadership: How to Use Innovation to Lead Effectively, Work Collaboratively, and Drive Results," white paper (Greensboro, NC: Center for Creative Leadership, 2014), 6–7, https://www.ccl.org/wp-content/uploads/2015/04/InnovationLeadership.pdf.
16. Polden, "Lawyers, Leadership, and Innovation."
17. Greg Satell, "The 4 Types of Innovation and the Problems They Solve," *Harvard Business Review*, June 2, 2017, https://hbr.org/2017/06/the-4-types-of-innovation-and-the-problems-they-solve.
18. Horth and Buchner, *Innovative Leadership.*
19. Glenn Llopis, "5 Ways Leaders Enable Innovation," *Forbes*, April 7, 2014, https://www.forbes.com/sites/glennllopis/2014/04/07/5-ways-leaders-enable-innovation-in-their-teams/#52e5ea948c4c.
20. Polden, "Lawyers, Leadership, and Innovation."
21. Theresa Amabile and Steven Kramer, *The Progress Principle: Using Small Wins to Ignite Joy, Engagement, and Creativity at Work* (Boston, MA: Harvard Business School Press, 2011).
22. Kristi Hedges, "How to Drive Innovation in Five Steps," *Forbes*, April 10, 2014, https://www.forbes.com/sites/work-in-progress/2014/04/10/how-to-drive-innovation-in-five-steps/#7fbf68a53d4b.
23. Horth and Buchner, *Innovative Leadership*, 13.

Chapter 10: Becoming a Team Leader

1. Jon R. Katzenbach and Douglas K. Smith, "The Discipline of Teams," *Harvard Business Review*, July/August 2005, https://hbr.org/1993/03/the-discipline-of-teams-2.
2. Heidi K. Gardner, "Collaboration in Law Firms," *The Practice* 1, no. 6 (Sept./Oct. 2015), https://thepractice.law.harvard.edu/article/collaboration-in-law-firms/.
3. Ben W. Heineman Jr., "Law and Leadership," *Journal of Legal Education* 56 (2006): 596–614, at 607.
4. Gardner, "Collaboration in Law Firms"; see also Heidi K. Gardner, *Smart Collaboration: How Professionals and Their Firms Succeed by Breaking Down Silos* (Boston, MA: Harvard Business Review Press, 2017).
5. Andre Martin, "What's Next?: The 2007 Changing Nature of Leadership Survey," white paper (Greensboro, NC: Center for Creative Leadership, 2015), http://cclinnovation.org/wp-content/uploads/2020/03/whats-next-the-2007-changing-nature-of-leadership-survey_2015.pdf.

6. Mike Myatt, "10 Communication Secrets of Great Leaders," *Forbes*, April 4, 2012, https://www.forbes.com/sites/mikemyatt/2012/04/04/10-communication-secrets-of-great-leaders/?sh=7643b5ba22fe.
7. Deborah J. Barrett, "Leadership Communications: A Communication Approach for Senior-Level Managers," in *Handbook of Business Strategy* (Emerald Group Publishing, 2006), 385–90, https://scholarship.rice.edu/bitstream/handle/1911/27037/Leadership+Communication++A+Communicatin+Approach+for+SeniorLeel+Managers++Barrett.pdf?sequence=2.
8. Neil Hamilton, "Fostering and Assessing Law Student Teamwork and Team Leadership Skills," *Hofstra Law Review* 48 (2019): 619–57; Lynda Gratton and Tamara J. Erickson, "Eight Ways to Build Collaborative Teams," *Harvard Business Review*, November 2007, https://hbr.org/2007/11/eight-ways-to-build-collaborative-teams; Martine Haas and Mark Mortensen, "The Secrets of Great Teamwork," *Harvard Business Review*, June 2016, https://hbr.org/2016/06/the-secrets-of-great-teamwork.
9. Amy C. Edmondson, *The Fearless Organization: Creating Psychological Safety in the Workplace for Learning, Innovation and Growth* (Boston, MA: Harvard Business Review Press, 2018); Amy Edmondson, "Teamwork on the Fly," *Harvard Business Review*, April 2012, https://hbr.org/2012/04/teamwork-on-the-fly-2.
10. Haas and Mortensen, "The Secrets of Great Teamwork."
11. Edmondson, "Teamwork on the Fly."
12. Edmondson, *The Fearless Organization.*
13. Bryan L. Bonner and Alexander R. Bolinger, "Bring Out the Best in Your Team," *Harvard Business Review*, September 2014, https://hbr.org/2014/09/bring-out-the-best-in-your-team.
14. Cass R. Sunstein and Reid Hastie, "Making Dumb Groups Smarter: The New Science of Group Decision Making," *Harvard Business Review*, December 2014, 90–92, https://hbr.org/2014/12/making-dumb-groups-smarter.
15. David Rock and Heidi Grant, "Why Diverse Teams Are Smarter," *Harvard Business Review*, November 4, 2016, https://hbr.org/2016/11/why-diverse-teams-are-smarter.
16. Benham Tabrizi, "75% of Cross-Functional Teams Are Dysfunctional," *Harvard Business Review*, June 2015, https://hbr.org/2015/06/75-of-cross-functional-teams-are-dysfunctional.

Chapter 11: Developing Emotional Intelligence and Handling Adversity

1. Keld Jenson, "Intellect Is Overrated: What You Really Need to Succeed," *Forbes*, April 12, 2012.
2. James M. Kouzes and Barry Z. Posner, *The Leadership Challenge: How to Make Extraordinary Things Happen in Organizations*, 7th ed. (Hoboken, NJ: Wiley, 2023); Ronda Muir, *Beyond Smart: Lawyering with Emotional Intelligence* (Chicago: American Bar Association, 2017).

3. Roland B. Smith and Paul Marrow, "The Changing Nature of Leadership in Law Firms," *New York State Bar Journal* 80, no. 7 (Sept. 2008): 33–38, at 33.
4. Daniel Goleman, "Leadership That Gets Results," *Harvard Business Review*, March/April 2000, https://hbr.org/2000/03/leadership-that-gets-results.
5. Natalie Loeb and David B. Sarnoff, "EQ versus IQ: What Smart Lawyers and Law Firms Need to Know about Emotional Intelligence," *PLI Current: The Journal of PLI Press* 4, no. 1 (2020), https://static1.squarespace.com/static/5c26b8695b409b7ffc6ca248/t/5e710003d98ddb7a3c013c12/1584463875317/Loeb+PLI+Article+EQ+v+IQ+_Vol.4_No.1_2020.pdf.
6. "How Emotional Intelligence Makes You a Better Lawyer," American Bar Association, October 2017, https://www.americanbar.org/news/abanews/publications/youraba/2017/october-2017/how-successful-lawyers-use-emotional-intelligence-to-their-advan/.
7. Heidi Gardner, *Smart Collaboration: How Professionals and Their Firms Succeed by Breaking Down Silos* (Boston, MA: Harvard Business Review Press, 2016).
8. Harvey Deutschendorf, "Why Emotionally Intelligent People Are More Successful," *Fast Company*, June 22, 2015, https://www.linkedin.com/posts/harvey-deutschendorf-6371904_why-emotionally-intelligent-people-are-more-activity-7017646252888637440-vHC5/. See also Jessica Thiefels, "The Ultimate Guide to Emotional Intelligence in the Workplace and Beyond," *Fast Company*, October 30, 2023, https://www.fastcompany.com/3047455/why-emotionally-intelligent-people-are-more-successful.
9. Muir, *Beyond Smart*.
10. Daniel Goleman, *Emotional Intelligence: Why It Matters More Than IQ* (New York: Random House, 1995).
11. Roland B. Smith, "The Struggles of Lawyer-Leaders and What They Need to Know," *New York State Bar Journal* (March/April 2009): 38–40.
12. Goleman, *Emotional Intelligence*.
13. Amy Zipkin, "MANAGEMENT: The Wisdom of Thoughtfulness," *New York Times*, May 31, 2000, https://www.nytimes.com/2000/05/31/business/management-the-wisdom-of-thoughtfulness.html.
14. Cary Cherniss and Daniel Goleman, eds., *The Emotionally Intelligent Workplace: How to Select For, Measure, and Improve Emotional Intelligence in Individuals, Groups, and Organizations* (San Francisco: Jossey-Bass, 2001).
15. Daniel Goleman, Richard E. Boyatzis, and Annie McKee, "Primal Leadership: The Hidden Driver of Great Performance," *Harvard Business Review*, November/December 2001, https://hbr.org/2001/12/primal-leadership-the-hidden-driver-of-great-performance.
16. Id.
17. Our thanks to Professor Neil Hamilton for sharing his research on the skill of self-reflection and his "Assessment of a Student's Skill of Reflection Based on a Number of Experiences Where the Students Did Individual Reflection Writing Assignments."
18. Jordon Furlong, "How to Lead Your Team through a Global Crisis," *Law Practice* (Nov. 1, 2020), https://www.americanbar.org/groups/bar-leadership/

publications/bar_leader/2020_21/january-february/how-to-lead-your-team-through-a-global-crisis/.
19. Mark A. Cohen, "The Golden Age of the Legal Entrepreneur—Why Now and Why It Matters," *Forbes*, June 1, 2018, https://www.forbes.com/sites/markcohen1/2018/06/01/the-golden-age-of-the-legal-entrepreneur-why-now-and-why-it-matters/?sh=55924f3d7803; Jonathan Marciano, "10 Lawyers-Turned-Entrepreneurs Creating a Revolution in Law," *Entrepreneur*, June 14, 2017, https://www.entrepreneur.com/article/295194.
20. Jared S. Allen, Regan M. Stevenson, Ernest H. O'Boyle, and Scott Seibert, "What Matters More for Entrepreneurship Success? A Meta-Analysis Comparing General Mental Ability and Emotional Intelligence in Entrepreneurial Setting," *Strategic Entrepreneurship Journal* (Nov. 2020), https://onlinelibrary.wiley.com/doi/full/10.1002/sej.1377.
21. Howard H. Stevenson and David E. Gumpert, "The Heart of Entrepreneurship," *Harvard Business Review*, March 1985, https://hbr.org/1985/03/the-heart-of-entrepreneurship. See also, Thomas R. Eisenmann, "Entrepreneurship: A Working Definition," *Harvard Business Review*, January 10, 2013, https://hbr.org/2013/01/what-is-entrepreneurship.
22. Stevenson and Gumpert, "The Heart of Entrepreneurship."
23. Robert Kiyosaki, *Rich Dad, Poor Dad: What the Rich Teach Their Kids about Money That the Poor and Middle Class Do Not*, 2nd ed. (Plata Publishing, 2017).
24. James M. Kouzes and Barry Z. Posner, *Turning Adversity into Opportunity* (San Francisco: Jossey-Bass, 2014).
25. Bill J. Bonnstetter, "New Research: The Skills That Make an Entrepreneur," *Harvard Business Review*, December 7, 2012, https://hbr.org/2012/12/new-research-the-skills-that-m.; Thomas J. Law, "Entrepreneurial Mindset: 20 Ways to Think Like an Entrepreneur," *Oberlo*, December 11, 2020, https://www.oberlo.com/blog/entrepreneurial-mindset.
26. Thomas S. Clay and Eric A. Seeger, *2018 Law Firms in Transition: An Altman Weil Flash Survey* (Willow Grove, PA: Altman Weil, Inc., 2018), iii.
27. Donald J. Polden, "Lawyers, Leadership, and Innovation," *Santa Clara Law Review* 58 (2018): 427–52; Clay and Seeger, *2018 Law Firms in Transition.*
28. Joshua D. Margolis and Paul Stoltz, "How to Bounce Back from Adversity," *Harvard Business Review*, January/February 2010, https://hbr.org/2010/01/how-to-bounce-back-from-adversity.
29. Salvatore, R. Maddi, "The Story of Hardiness: Twenty Years of Theorizing, Research, and Practice," *Consulting Psychology Journal: Practices and Research* 54, no. 3 (2002): 175–85.
30. Margolis and Stotz, "How to Bounce Back."
31. Mark Beese and Ian Paterson, "Why Visionary Leadership Is Critical in Times of Uncertainty," *Law Practice* (Nov. 1, 2022), https://www.americanbar.org/groups/law_practice/resources/law-practice-magazine/2022-november-december/why-visionary-leadership-critical-times-uncertainty/.

32. Kouzes and Posner, *Turning Adversity into Opportunity*; Barry Z. Posner, "Leadership Strategies for the Next Normal," *IEEE Engineering Management Review* 48, no. 3 (2020): 19–23; Chris Nichols, Shoma Chatterjee Hayden, and Chris Trendler, "4 Behaviors That Help Leaders Manage a Crisis," *Harvard Business Review,* April 2, 2020, https://hbr.org/2020/04/4-behaviors-that-help-leaders-manage-a-crisis.
33. Nichols, Hayden, and Trendler, "4 Behaviors That Help Leaders Manage a Crisis."
34. Donald Robertson, *Build Your Resistance: How to Survive and Thrive in Any Situation* (London: John Murray Press, 2012).
35. Rob Cross, Karen Dillon, and Danna Greenberg, "The Secret to Building Resilience," *Harvard Business Review,* January 29, 2021, https://hbr.org/2021/01/the-secret-to-building-resilience. See also, Margolis and Stoltz, "Bounce Back from Adversity."
36. Angela Duckworth, *Grit: The Power of Passion and Perseverance* (New York: Scribner, 2018).
37. Arran Caza and Barry Z. Posner, "How and When Does Grit Influence Leaders' Behavior?," *Leadership & Organizational Development Journal* 40, no. 1 (2019): 124–34; Arran Caza and Barry Z. Posner, "Mixed Associations Between Grit and Transformational Leadership Behavior," *Journal of Leadership Studies,* 15, no. 3 (2021): 6–20.
38. Cross, Dillon, and Greenberg, "The Secret to Building Resilience."
39. "21 Day Grit and Growth Mindset Challenge: Days 1–10," American Bar Association, https://www.americanbar.org/groups/diversity/women/initiatives_awards/grit-project/21-day-grit-challenge/#:~:text=The%20ABA%20Commission%20on%20Women,women%20lawyers%20have%20in%20common.%E2%80%9D&text=Do%20them%20on%20your%20own,the%20challenges%20and%201 earnings%20together.
40. Clay and Seeger, *2018 Law Firms in Transition.*
41. Polden, "Lawyers, Leadership, and Innovation," 442–43.

Chapter 12: Leading the Charge for Diversity, Equity, and Inclusion

1. See, e.g., "Your 'One-Stop Shop' for Enacting Diversity, Equity, and Inclusion," American Bar Association, https://www.americanbar.org/groups/diversity/resources/about_us/; see also Eric Chung et al., "A Portrait of Asian Americans in the Law," *The Practice* 5, no. 1 (2018), https://thepractice.law.harvard.edu/article/a-portrait-of-asian-americans-in-the-law/.
2. "Diversity & Inclusion 360 Commission: Executive Summary," American Bar Association, August 2016, https://www.americanbar.org/content/dam/aba/administrative/diversity-inclusion-center/di-360-commission-executive-summary.pdf.

3. Jill Switzer, "Can Lawyers of Color and Women Get Ahead Now?" *Above the Law*, June 17, 2021, https://abovethelaw.com/2021/06/can-lawyers-of-color-and-women-get-ahead-now/.
4. "5-Year US Applicants and Applications Trends," Law School Admission Council, 2022, https://report.lsac.org/VolumeSummary.aspx.
5. Id.
6. American Bar Association, "ABA Profile of the Legal Profession 2023," https://www.abalegalprofile.com/demographics.html.
7. "ABA Profile 2023"; Chung et al., "Portrait of Asian Americans."
8. "ABA Profile 2023."
9. "Your 'One-Stop Shop.' "
10. American Bar Association, "ABA Profile of the Legal Profession 2022."
11. "Women's History Month," United States Courts, https://www.uscourts.gov/about-federal-courts/educational-resources/annual-observances/womens-history-month.
12. Alicia Bannon and Janna Adelstein, "State Supreme Court Diversity—February 2020 Update," Brennan Center for Justice, February 20, 2020, https://www.brennancenter.org/our-work/research-reports/state-supreme-court-diversity-february-2020-update; Nia-Malika Henderson, "White Men Are 31 Percent of American Population. They Hold 65 Percent of All Elected Offices," *Washington Post*, October 8, 2014, https://www.washingtonpost.com/news/the-fix/wp/2014/10/08/65-percent-of-all-american-elected-officials-are-white-men/.
13. Deborah L. Rhode, "From Platitudes to Priorities: Diversity and Gender Equity in Law Firms," *Georgetown Journal of Legal Ethics* 24 (2011): 1041–77, at 1049.
14. Sam Skolnik, "White Men Land Firm Partnerships at Fastest Rates, ABA Finds," Bloomberg Law (May 24, 2022) (report on 2019 data from 287 American law firms and more than 100,000 lawyers). https://www.bloomberglaw.com/bloomberglawnews/business-and-practice/XDMPKU3G000000?bna_news_filter=business-and-practice#jcite.
15. Id.
16. Nicole E. Negowetti, "Implicit Bias and the Legal Profession's 'Diversity Crisis': A Call for Self-Reflection," *Nevada Law Journal* 15 (2015): 930–58, at 935–36.
17. Dolly Chugh, *The Person YOU Mean to Be: How Good People Fight Bias* (New York: Harper Collins, 2018).
18. See Luis J. Diaz and Patrick C. Dunican Jr., "Ending the Revolving Door Syndrome in Law," *Seton Hall Law Review* 41 (2011): 947–1003, at 977.
19. Negowetti, "Implicit Bias," 942–49.
20. Justin Nix, Bradley A. Campbell, Edward H. Byers, and Geoffrey P. Alpert, "A Bird's Eye View of Civilians Killed by Police in 2015," *Criminology and Public Policy* 16, no. 1 (2017): 309–40, at 310 (emphasis in original).
21. Id., 311, 315.
22. Rhode, "From Platitudes to Priorities."
23. See Leah Jackson Teague and Donald J. Polden, "More Diversity Requires More Inclusive Leaders Leading by Example in Law Organizations," *Hofstra*

Law Review 48 (2020): 681–703, at 699–702; Donald J. Polden and Jenna M. Anderson, "Leadership to Address Implicit Bias in the Legal Profession," *Santa Clara Law Review* 62; 63 (2021).

24. One example is the National Association of Women Lawyers' annual survey on the status of women in the profession (https://www.nawl.org/p/cm/ld/fid=2019), and another is the National Association of Law Placement and their "2020 Report on Diversity in U.S. Law Firms" (https://www.nalp.org/uploads/2020_NALP_Diversity_Report.pdf).
25. Negowetti, "Implicit Bias," 930; Rhode, "From Platitudes to Priorities."
26. Joan C. Williams, *Fair Measure: Toward Effective Attorney Evaluations*, 2nd ed. (Chicago: American Bar Association, 2008).
27. For a review of recent literature, see Teague and Polden, "More Diversity."
28. Thomas Kochan, Katerina Bezrukova, Robin Ely, Susan E. Jackson, Aparna Joshi, K. E. Jehn, D. Leonard, David Levine, and D. Thomas, "The Effects of Diversity on Business Performance: Report of the Diversity Research Network," *Human Resource Management* 42, no. 1 (2003): 3–21, at 5.
29. Ella Washington and Camille Patrick, "3 Requirements for a Diverse and Inclusive Culture," Gallup, September 17, 2018, https://www.gallup.com/workplace/242138/requirements-diverse-inclusive-culture.aspx; Molly Werhan, "3 Reasons Why Your Law Firm Needs to Care about Diversity +Inclusion," *Columbus Business First*, November 19, 2019, https://www.bizjournals.com/columbus/news/2019/11/19/3-reasons-why-your-law-firm-needs-to-care-about.html.
30. Rocío Lorenzo, Nicole Voigt, Miki Tsusaka, and Katie Abouzahr, "How Diverse Leadership Teams Boost Innovation," Boston Consulting Group, January 23, 2018, https://www.bcg.com/publications/2018/how-diverse-leadership-teams-boost-innovation.
31. David Rock and Heidi Grant, "Why Diverse Teams Are Smarter," *Harvard Business Review*, November 4, 2016, https://hbr.org/2016/11/why-diverse-teams-are-smarter.
32. Teague and Polden, "More Diversity."
33. Id.
34. Rob Bogosiand and Charlene Rosseau, "How and Why Millennials are Shaking up Organizational Cultures, *Rutgers Business Review 2*, no. 3 (Fall 2017), 386–394.
35. "The 2016 Deloitte Millennial Survey: Winning Over the Next Generation of Leaders," Deloitte, 2016, https://www2.deloitte.com/content/dam/Deloitte/global/Documents/About-Deloitte/gx-millenial-survey-2016-exec-summary.pdf.
36. "Better Quality of Work Life Is Worth a $7,600 Pay Cut for Millennials," Businesswire, April 7, 2016, https://www.businesswire.com/news/home/20160407005736/en/Quality-Work-Life-Worth-7600-Pay-Cut.
37. Werhan, "3 Reasons Why."
38. American Bar Association, Rule 8.4(g), *Model Rules of Professional Conduct* (Chicago: American Bar Association, 2020).

39. "Visible Invisibility: Women of Color in Law Firms," ABA Commission on Women in the Profession, 2006, https://www.americanbar.org/content/dam/aba/administrative/women/visibleinvisibility-execsummary.pdf.
40. Ibram X. Kendi, *How to Be an Antiracist* (New York, Random House, 2019).
41. Nika White, "What Does It Really Mean to Be an Ally?," *Nika White Consulting* (blog), July 16, 2021, https://www.nikawhite.com/2019/07/16/what-does-it-really-mean-to-be-an-ally/; "What It Means to Be an 'Ally' and 8 Ways to Do It," Ben and Jerry's, https://www.benjerry.com/whats-new/2016/be-an-ally#:~:text=We%20need%20to%20listen%20(not,The%20spotlight%20is%20not%20ours.
42. Project Implicit, https://implicit.harvard.edu/implicit/takeatest.html.
43. Adam Bryant and Kevin Sharer, "Are You Really Listening?" *Harvard Business Review*, March/April 2021, https://hbr.org/2021/03/are-you-really-listening.
44. Janet Foutty, Terri Cooper, and Shelley Zalis, "Shift/Forward: Redefining Leadership: The Inclusion Imperative," Deloitte, June 2018, https://www2.deloitte.com/content/dam/Deloitte/us/Documents/about-deloitte/us-shift-forward-redefining-leadership.pdf.
45. Cory Edwards, "Business Processes: Why Your Desk Is a Dangerous Place to Watch the World," *Forbes*, November 29, 2011, https://www.forbes.com/sites/dell/2011/11/29/business-processes-why-your-desk-is-a-dangerous-place-to-watch-the-world/?sh=d4e22a3105e6.
46. Lori Berman, Heather Bock, and Juliet Aiken, *Accelerating Lawyer Success: How to Make Partner, Stay Healthy, and Flourish in a Law Firm* (Chicago: American Bar Association, 2016), 65–66, 78–80.
47. Teague and Polden, "More Diversity."
48. Jennifer Miller, "Why Some Companies Are Saying 'Diversity and Belonging' Instead of 'Diversity and Inclusion,'" *New York Times*, May 13, 2023, https://www.nytimes.com/2023/05/13/business/diversity-equity-inclusion-belonging.html.
49. Marianne Coleman, "Leadership and Diversity," *Education Management Administration and Leadership* 40, no. 5 (2012): 592–609.
50. Roland B. Smith and Paul Bennett Marrow, "The Changing Nature of Leadership in Law Firms," *New York State Bar Association Journal* 80, no. 7 (Sept. 2008): 36.

Afterword: Looking to the Future: Leadership Development to Produce Better Lawyers

1. Roland B. Smith, "The Struggles of Lawyer-Leaders and What They Need to Know," *New York State Bar Association Journal* 81, no. 3 (March/April 2009): 40.
2. Id.
3. Nick Petrie, "Future Trends in Leadership Development," white paper (Greensboro, NC: Center for Creative Leadership, 2011), https://law.scu.edu/wp-content/uploads/leadership/Future-Trends-in-Leadership-Development.pdf.

4. Donald J. Polden, "Leading Law Firms in the 'New Normal': Recovering from Crises through Leadership Development," *Santa Clara Law Review* 223 (2023): 63.
5. Donald J. Polden, "Lawyers, Leadership, and Innovation," *Santa Clara Law Review* 58 (2018): 427–52, at 442–43.
6. Jordon Furlong, "How to Lead Your Team through a Global Crisis," *Law Practice* (Nov. 1, 2020), https://www.americanbar.org/groups/bar-leadership/publications/bar_leader/2020_21/january-february/how-to-lead-your-team-through-a-global-crisis/.
7. Petrie, "Future Trends."
8. Smith, "The Struggles of Lawyer-Leaders."
9. "Directory of Lawyer Assistance Programs," American Bar Association, https://www.americanbar.org/groups/lawyer_assistance/resources/lap_programs_by_state/; see also Priscilla Henson, "Drug & Alcohol Addiction Treatment for Lawyers," American Addiction Centers, last updated January 11, 2021, https://americanaddictioncenters.org/rehab-guide/workforce/white-collar/lawyers/treatment-options; "Drug Use Disorders," American Bar Association, May 8, 2018, https://www.americanbar.org/groups/lawyer_assistance/resources/drug_abuse_dependence/.
10. Patrick Krill, Ryan Johnson, and Linda Albert, "The Prevalence of Substance Use and Other Mental Health Concerns among American Attorneys," *Journal of Addiction Medicine* 10, no. 1 (2015): 46–52, https://journals.lww.com/journaladdictionmedicine/Fulltext/2016/02000/The_Prevalence_of_Substanc e_Use_and_Other_Mental.8.aspx.
11. Mark A. Cohen, "Why Are Lawyers So Unpopular and Stressed?" *Bloomberg Law*, September 30, 2015, https://news.bloomberglaw.com/business-and-practice/why-are-lawyers-so-unpopular-and-stressed/.
12. Henson, "Substance Abuse Treatment."
13. Lawrence S. Krieger, "Institutional Denial about the Dark Side of Law School, and Fresh Empirical Guidance for Constructively Breaking the Silence," *Journal of Legal Education* 52, nos. 1 and 2 (2002): 112–29.
14. Rachel Casper, "The Full Weight of Law School: Stress on Law Students Is Different," *Lawyers Concerned for Lawyers*, January 18, 2019, https://www.lclma.org/2019/01/18/the-full-weight-of-law-school-stress-on-law-students-is-different/.
15. Krieger, "Institutional Denial."
16. Susan Swaim Daicoff, "Expanding the Lawyer's Toolkit of Skills and Competencies: Synthesizing Leadership, Professionalism, Emotional Intelligence, Conflict Resolution, and Comprehensive Law," *Santa Clara Law Review* 52 (2012): 795–874, at 837–38.
17. Id.
18. Petrie, "Future Trends."
19. Roland Smith and Paul Morrow, "The Changing Nature of Leadership in Law Firms," *New York State Bar Association Journal* 80 (2008): 33–38, at 34–35; Donald J. Polden, "Leading Institutional Change: Law Schools and Legal Education in a Time of Crisis," *Tennessee Journal of Law and Public Policy* 83 (2015/16): 949–81.

20. Robert Kegan and Lisa Lahey, *Immunity to Change: How to Overcome It and Unlock Potential in Yourself and Your Organization* (Cambridge, MA: Harvard Business Press, 2009).
21. Petrie, "Future Trends."
22. Barry Z. Posner, "It's How Leaders Behave That Matters, Not Where They Are From," *Leadership & Organizational Development Journal* 34, no. 6 (2013): 573–87.
23. Arran Caza, Brianna Caza, and Barry Z. Posner, "Transformational Leadership across Cultures: Follower Perception and Satisfaction," *Administrative Sciences* 11, no. 32 (2021), https://doi.org/10.3390/admsci11010032.
24. Daniel Goleman, "Leadership That Gets Results," *Harvard Business Review*, March/April 2000, https://hbr.org/2000/03/leadership-that-gets-results; Bruna Martinuzzi, "Exploring 7 Common Leadership Styles: Find Your Own," American Express, October 16, 2019, https://www.americanexpress.com/en-us/business/trends-and-insights/articles/the-7-most-common-leadership-styles-and-how-to-find-your-own/.
25. Susan Snyder and Sara Littauer, "Leadership Flexibility: How Outstanding Partners Gets Results," *Strategies: The Journal of Legal Marketing* 7, no. 3 (2005): 4–8.
26. James M. Kouzes and Barry Z. Posner, *The Leadership Challenge: How to Make Extraordinary Things Happen in Organizations*, 7th ed. (Hoboken, NJ: Wiley, 2023).
27. Deborah L. Rhode, "Lawyers as Leaders," *Michigan State Law Review*, 2010 (2010): 413–22.
28. Kouzes and Posner, *The Leadership Challenge.*
29. John W. Gardner, *On Leadership* (New York: Free Press, 1993).
30. American Bar Association, Preamble para. 7, *Model Rules of Professional Conduct* (Chicago: American Bar Association, 2020).
31. Luke 12:48.

Acknowledgments

It gives us great pleasure, and a sincere sense of appreciation, to acknowledge the many people who contributed to this book and our efforts to develop generations of lawyer-leaders. Of course, with deep humility, any errors or omissions remain with the authors!

First, to a group of colleagues and friends who reviewed either our earlier book (*Leading in Law: Leadership Development for Law Students*) or the draft of this book, contributing their insights and suggestions for improvement and practical application. We know that this book is better because of their thoughtfulness, and we hope the final product is one to which they are proud to say they made their important contribution: Lori Berman (Hogan Lovells US LLP), Doug Blaze (University of Tennessee), Ausra Deluard (Dentons US LLP), Neil Hamilton (St. Thomas University), Mark Michels (Meta and Santa Clara University), John Mitchell (KM Advisors), Paula Monopoli (University of Maryland), Joe Reeder (Greenberg Traurig), and David Sarnoff (Loeb Leadership).

About the Authors

Donald J. Polden is dean emeritus and professor of law at Santa Clara University, where he served as dean of the School of Law for ten years. He is a well-recognized authority on leadership education and development for lawyers and law students. He drew national attention to the need for more formal and research-based scholarship and curriculum development in legal education through the early creation of a law school course on lawyers as leaders. Professor Deborah Rhode of Stanford, another early pioneer of lawyer leadership education, referred to Don as "truly a founding father of the field of lawyers and leadership."

Don also is a demonstrated leader, serving as dean of two major law schools from 1993 to 2013 and promoting legal education within the American Bar Association and the Association of American Law Schools. His list of significant leadership roles includes chair of the ABA committee that established accreditation standards for more than two hundred law schools, leading dozens of law school accreditation teams, and serving as president of the Memphis Bar Association, to name a few. While at Santa Clara University, Don has served as director of the law school's Center for Global Law and Policy, responsible for ten international legal education programs, several of which he taught in while also lecturing on comparative law at universities in China and Hungary. Don is frequently called upon to serve as a mediator, arbitrator, and judicial officer in many Santa Clara campus disciplinary proceedings.

Following service as Santa Clara's dean, Don has been actively engaged in teaching and scholarship, especially in the areas of leadership development, professional identity formation of law students and new lawyers, and lawyering skills and competencies. He also continues to teach corporate, sports, and antitrust law, and cofounded and led Santa Clara's nationally prominent Institute for Sports Law and Ethics. Don consults with law firms on leadership development of their lawyers, such as intellectual property and corporate law powerhouse Haynes Boone, and lectures at the U.S. Army's Judge Advocate General graduate program on leadership development of U.S. Army lawyer officers, the University of Calgary law school, and others.

Don created and leads Santa Clara's Institute for Lawyer Leadership Education, which has conducted several national conferences and workshops on educating lawyers and students in leadership in the legal profession, including five leadership workshops for legal education hosted by Santa Clara from 2005 to 2013. He was instrumental in the 2018 launch of a new Section on Leadership for the Association of American Law Schools. This section includes more than six hundred members, representing nearly one hundred law schools' courses and programs. The section meets annually to promote leadership education in law schools, advance legal scholarship concerning law and leadership, and arrange programming. In 2020–21, Don served as chair of the section.

Don received an undergraduate degree in business economics from The George Washington University and his JD from Indiana University School of Law. During law school, he wrote for the *Indiana Law Review* and following graduation served as a judicial law clerk on both state appellate and federal trial courts. He practiced antitrust law, including participating in five federal jury trials, and he argued several cases in the U.S. Courts of Appeal and the U.S. Supreme Court. Don is licensed to practice law in the state of Iowa and federal courts.

Don has been teaching leadership for lawyers' classes for more than a decade and is a frequent speaker at national conferences, other law schools' classes, and within law firms on leadership and the legal profession. He is the author of numerous law review articles on lawyer leadership, which have been published in the *Baylor Law Review, Santa Clara Law Review,* the *Hofstra Law Review,* the *Tennessee Law Review,* and the *Tennessee Journal of Law and Policy.* His antitrust scholarship has been published in the *Harvard Journal on Legislation,* and his work has been cited by the U.S. Supreme Court. Don coauthored *Sports, Ethics and Leadership* and *Leading in Law: Leadership Development for Law Students* (with Barry Posner), and he has authored several book chapters on lawyer leadership, employment law, and government regulation law. Don received the Edwin Owens Lawyer of the Year award given by the Santa Clara University Law School.

Barry Z. Posner is the Michael J. Accolti, S. J. Professor of Leadership at Santa Clara University and chair of the Management and Entrepreneurship Department in the Leavey School of Business, where he previously served for twelve years as dean, six years as associate dean for graduate programs, and six years as associate dean for executive education. Barry has received the Association for Talent Development's highest award for *Distinguished Contribution to Workplace Learning and Performance.* He has been recognized as one of the top fifty leadership coaches in America, ranked among the most influential HR thinkers in the world by *HR* magazine, and *Inc.* magazine included him among the world's top seventy-five leadership and management experts.

Barry is the coauthor (with Jim Kouzes) of the award-winning and best-selling leadership book *The Leadership Challenge.* Now in its seventh edition, with more than three million copies in print, the book continues to be a groundbreaking research study, combining keen insights with practical applications, and has been translated into twenty-two foreign languages. It is listed among *The 100 Best Business Books of All Time,* receiving book-of-the-year honors by the American Council of Health Care Executives and *Fast Company,* and the Critics' Choice Award from the nation's book review editors. Kouzes and Posner's *Leadership Practices Inventory (LPI)* has been called "the most reliable, up-to-date leadership instrument available today." The 360-degree online version has been completed by more than four million people.

Barry has coauthored other award-winning, inspiring, and practical books on leadership: *Everyday People, Extraordinary Leadership: How to Make a Difference Regardless of Your Title, Role, or Authority*; *Leading in Law: Leadership Development for Law Students*; *Leadership in Higher Education: Practices that Make a Difference*; *Stop Selling & Start Leading*; *Learning Leadership: The Five Fundamentals for Becoming an Exemplary Leader*; *Turning Adversity into Opportunity*; *Finding the Courage to Lead*; *Great Leadership Creates Great Workplaces*; *Credibility: How Leaders Gain and Lose It, Why People Demand It*; *The Truth about Leadership: The No-Fads, Heart-of-the-Matter Facts You Need to Know*; *Encouraging the Heart: A Leader's Guide to Rewarding and Recognizing Others*; *A Leader's Legacy*; *Extraordinary Leadership in Australia and New Zealand*; *Making Extraordinary Things Happen in Asia*; and *The Student Leadership Challenge.*

Barry is an internationally renowned scholar who has published more than one hundred research and practitioner-oriented articles in such publications as the *Harvard Business Review, Academy of Management Journal, Journal of Applied Psychology, Human Relations, Personnel Psychology, Journal of Selling,* and *IEEE Transactions on Engineering Management.* He has served on a number of public and nonprofit boards, such as the American Institute of Architects, Berkeley Food Network, Center for Excellence in Nonprofits, Global Women's Leadership Network, Sigma Phi Epsilon Fraternity, SVCreates, and Uplift Family Services.

He received an undergraduate degree in political science from the University of California–Santa Barbara, a master's degree from The Ohio State University in public administration, and his PhD in organizational behavior and administrative theory from the University of Massachusetts, Amherst. At Santa Clara, he has received several outstanding teaching and leadership honors, including the President's Distinguished Faculty Award and the School's Extraordinary Faculty Award. Barry has been a visiting professor at the University of Western Australia, Hong Kong University of Science and Technology, Sabanci University (Istanbul), the University of Auckland (New Zealand), and Seattle University. He has made presentations and conducted leadership development programs for corporations across the globe and has been involved with leadership development efforts at more than seventy-five college campuses.

Index